A. R. Ammons
and the Poetics of Widening Scope

A. R. Ammons. (Courtesy of Cornell University Photography. Photo by Peter Morenus.)

A. R. Ammons and the Poetics of Widening Scope

Steven P. Schneider

Rutherford • Madison • Teaneck
Fairleigh Dickinson University Press
London and Toronto: Associated University Presses

Associated University Presses
440 Forsgate Drive
Cranbury, NJ 08512

Associated University Presses
25 Sicilian Avenue
London WC1A 2QH, England

Associated University Presses
P.O. Box 338, Port Credit
Mississauga, Ontario
Canada L5G 4L8

The paper used in this publication meets the requirements of the American National Standard for Permanence of Paper for Printed Library Materials Z39.48-1984.

Library of Congress Cataloging-in-Publication Data

Schneider, Steven P.
    A. R. Ammons and the poetics of widening scope / Steven P. Schneider.
        p.   cm.
    Includes bibliographical references and index.
    ISBN 0-8386-3507-5 (alk. paper)
    1. Ammons, A. R., 1926–   —Criticism and interpretation.
2. Poetics.   I. Title.
PS3501.M6Z85   1994
811'.54—dc20   92-55122
                                                              CIP

PRINTED IN THE UNITED STATES OF AMERICA

To my wife, Rivca,
whose encouragement and vision
contributed so much to my work.

Contents

Abbreviations

Quotations from A. R. Ammons's works are cited in the text using the following abbreviations. When lines are sufficiently located by sections of longer poems, no citation appears.

CI   *Corsons Inlet: A Book of Poems.* Ithaca: Cornell University Press, 1965.

T   *Tape for the Turn of the Year.* Ithaca: Cornell University Press, 1965.

CP   *Collected Poems 1951–1971.* New York: W. W. Norton, 1972.

S   *Sphere: The Form of a Motion.* New York: W. W. Norton, 1974.

D   *Diversifications: Poems.* New York: W. W. Norton, 1975.

SP   *The Snow Poems.* New York: W. W. Norton, 1977.

CT   *A Coast of Trees.* New York: W. W. Norton, 1981.

WH   *Worldly Hopes.* New York: W. W. Norton, 1982.

LEC   *Lake Effect Country.* New York: W. W. Norton, 1983.

SV   *Sumerian Vistas.* New York: W. W. Norton, 1987.

RSP   *The Really Short Poems of A. R. Ammons,* New York: W. W. Norton, 1990.

Preface

This is a study of A. R. Ammons's vision and how it shapes his poetic processes, forms, and subjects. My own interest in Ammons stems in part from his strong attraction to modern science. As I began to examine the impact of astronomy, biology, and other sciences on his work, I discovered that Ammons is committed to the concept of "widening scope."[1] Scope, for Ammons, refers to both his own mental and visual range, and to that of his readers.

Walt Whitman, in his 1855 Preface to *Leaves of Grass*, asked: "Who knows the curious mystery of the eyesight?" Over a century later A. R. Ammons, in his most well-known poem, "Corsons Inlet," declares that "there is no finality of vision." Ammons's poetry testifies to the mystery and the transformative power of sight that Whitman alludes to in his Preface. Ammons extends the American visionary tradition into the late twentieth century, as he explores the expansive possibilities of sight and science.

Recent breakthroughs in astronomy, biology, lasers, and satellite technology have all led to new and important discoveries. The *New York Times* reported in March 1992 that "a lost city buried in the sands of Arabia, perhaps the fabled Ubar, was found in November [1991] by archaeologists following ancient caravan routes detected by radar imaging on a space shuttle."[2] Evidence in support of the Big Bang theory of creation comes from recent detection of electromagnetic radiation, called microwaves, left over from the initial explosion. New studies show that the use of lasers may help to correct nearsightedness, an affliction of the computer age.

A. R. Ammons, who has written a poem entitled "Laser," who alludes to the Big Bang in his great long poems, and who explores the poetic implications of archaeology, would see in these recent discoveries confirmation of the poetic possibilities of widening scope. Astronomy, for example, enables him to widen scope, cognitively, through its newly discovered facts, and visually, through its ever-developing optical technologies: the impulse of astronomy is to extend the range of the senses. Ammons

incorporates astronomical data and imagery in his work with
the purpose of broadening our vision, and he incorporates biological and cellular imagery in order to intensify our vision: his
concerns become both telescopic and microscopic.

Ammons's intention to widen scope, however, is not shaped
solely by his knowledge of science. He is also in the tradition of
the poet-naturalist, observing keenly the natural world without
the benefit of the magnifying lenses of the astronomer or cell
biologist. His poetry of widening scope encompasses a broad
range of perceptions. This study is intended to trace how Ammons and his poems evoke the possibilities and mysteries of
sight, as his vision moves both outward into the world and inward ("in-sight") into the reflective self. This outward and inward movement of observation in Ammons's work helps to
explain why critics have identified him both as a poet of the
mind and as a poet of nature.

My introduction examines the critical response to Ammons,
with a focus on how he has been discussed as a poet of science.
Until now, much of this discussion has been truncated. This
initial chapter develops how Ammons's emphasis on scope and
observation (vision) places him within a tradition of poetry
and science.

Ammons's American Romantic forebears, Emerson, Whitman,
and Thoreau, were all keenly aware of visual perception, and
like Ammons they formulated different ways to react to and make
use of science. His connection to these writers is essential, as he
and his critics have attested. The second chapter considers some
of the ways Ammons both employs the strategies of his American
Romantic forebears and diverges from them.

Chapter 3 is an analysis of Ammons's "visual calisthenics."
Many of his poems result from visual encounters with the landscape, and in that chapter those encounters are examined in detail to show how they function to widen scope. By encouraging
his readers to exercise distance vision and peripheral vision,
Ammons hopes to break down rigid forms of perception and
thought. His ever-attentive eye tracks the flow of natural "events,"
which are then recorded in his poems.

While the third chapter focuses on the natural eye, the fourth
chapter is a study of Ammons's telescopic and microscopic vision. As his long poems Sphere and "Essay on Poetics" demonstrate, astronomy and biology provide him with a rich source of
inspiration, metaphor, and language. They also help to signifi-

cantly shape his vision, much as a walk around an inlet helps to shape his perceptions in the earlier "Corsons Inlet."

Chapters 5 and 6 examine the vast body of work produced by Ammons since the publication of *Sphere* (1974), still considered his most successful and most important long poem. These chapters assess his more recent poetic accomplishments, including *Sumerian Vistas* (1987) and *The Really Short Poems of A. R. Ammons* (1990), with an eye toward how they reflect and modify his ongoing concerns with widening scope.

I was fortunate to receive from A. R. Ammons an advance copy of his long poem *Garbage* just as this book was being completed. The Epilogue examines the new poem in the context of my critical approach to his work.

Acknowledgments

I am fortunate to have benefited from the insights and assistance of many helpful individuals along the way. I am especially indebted to Ed Folsom, who first encouraged me in my study and who provided thorough and thoughtful criticism on the manuscript in progress. He also served as an important friend throughout the process.

Thanks to Adalaide Morris, whose comments during the initial writing stages were extremely helpful. Robert Rabinoff's knowledge of recent discoveries in physics, astronomy, and biology was invaluable to me. Particular thanks to Shelby Stephenson, who provided me with sound editorial criticism on a completed draft of the manuscript and useful information about the life of A. R. Ammons. Thanks also to my colleagues Jeanne Heuving and Patrick Morris for their encouragement and helpful suggestions during the publication process. A note of appreciation to Jane Decker, who helped me to find the time and resources to complete this project. For helpful conversations at the beginning and end, I wish to express my gratitude to Tom Centolella and Jim Karpen.

Thanks to Chuck Bigham, director of the Computer Lab at the University of Washington, Bothell, for assisting me in the preparation of the manuscript. A grant from the Graduate School Fund of the University of Washington enabled me to quote generously from the work of A. R. Ammons and several other poets. My appreciation to Debra E. Soled, Jan Beran, Sally Anderson, and Dick Magnuson for their attentiveness to detail.

A special note of thanks to Archie Ammons, who shared with me the entire text of his poem *Garbage* long before its scheduled publication.

And finally, I wish to warmly thank my wife, Rivca, who had the patience and vision to support me in so many ways while I was working on this project.

*   *   *

Permission to reprint from the following sources is hereby acknowledged:

16   ACKNOWLEDGMENTS

The Really Short Poems of A. R. Ammons, by permission of the author and W. W. Norton & Company, Inc. Copyright (c) 1990 by A. R. Ammons.

Tape for the Turn of the Year, by A. R. Ammons, by permission of the author and W. W. Norton & Company, Inc. Copyright (c) 1965 by Cornell University.

Collected Poems 1951–1971, by A. R. Ammons, by permission of the author and W. W. Norton & Company, Inc. Copyright (c) 1972 by A. R. Ammons.

Diversifications, poems by A. R. Ammons, by permission of the author and W. W. Norton & Company, Inc. Copyright (c) 1975 by A. R. Ammons.

Sphere: The Form of a Motion, by A. R. Ammons, by permission of the author and W. W. Norton & Company, Inc. Copyright (c) 1974 by A. R. Ammons.

Worldly Hopes, poems by A. R. Ammons, by permission of the author and W. W. Norton & Company, Inc. Copyright (c) 1982 by A. R. Ammons.

Lake Effect Country, poems by A. R. Ammons, by permission of the author and W. W. Norton & Company, Inc. Copyright (c) 1983 by A. R. Ammons.

The Snow Poems, by A. R. Ammons, by permission of the author and W. W. Norton & Company, Inc. Copyright (c) 1977 by A. R. Ammons.

Sumerian Vistas, poems by A. R. Ammons, by permission of the author and W. W. Norton & Company, Inc. Copyright (c) 1987 by A. R. Ammons.

The Poetry of Robert Frost, edited by Edward Connery Lathem. Copyright 1923, © 1969 by Holt, Rinehart and Winston. Copyright© 1923, 1951 by Robert Frost. Reprinted by permission of Henry Holt and Company, Inc.

Selected Poetry of Robinson Jeffers, by Robinson Jeffers. Copyright© 1933 and renewed 1961 by Robinson Jeffers. Reprinted by permission of Random House, Inc.

A. R. Ammons
and the Poetics of Widening Scope

1

Introduction: The Poet and the Scientist

Walt Whitman: Hurrah for positive science! long live exact demonstration!

. . . .

Gentlemen, to you the first honors always!
Your facts are useful, and yet they are not my dwelling,
I but enter by them to an area of my dwelling.
                              —Section 23, "Song of Myself"

A. R. Ammons: "Much of what is impersonally, flatly new to us arises from scientific insight and technological innovation. It is part of the result of a poem to personalize and familiarize, to ingest and acquaint—to bring feelings and things into manageable relationships."
                              —*Chelsea*

In 1975 A. R. Ammons's poetic career reached its pinnacle. He received the Bollingen Prize for his book-length volume *Sphere: The Form of a Motion* and two years before, Ammons's *Collected Poems 1951–1971* had earned him the National Book Award for poetry. The poet who stood in awe of mountains had himself, in the words of one critic, become a "mountain."[1] His meteoric rise was astonishing given his inconspicuous and in many ways unpromising beginnings. His first volume, *Ommateum*, went unnoticed and sold very few copies. Ammons did not publish his second volume until close to ten years later. Although *Expressions of Sea Level* drew some positive responses from critics, notably Wendell Berry in the *Nation*, Ammons's poetic career seemed far less than dazzling at the time of its publication in 1964.[2]

As Ammons's reputation has grown, so too has the number of critical responses to his work. Before *Collected Poems 1951–1971* was published in 1972, only a handful of critics concerned themselves with Ammons. In the winter of 1973, how-

ever, *Diacritics* devoted an entire issue to his work, with articles
by a number of prestigious critics, including Harold Bloom, Jose-
phine Miles, and Jerome Mazzaro.[3] Both Bloom and Miles were
early supporters of the poet, and Bloom has done more than any
other single critic to advance Ammons's reputation. In 1986,
Shelby Stephenson, editor of *Pembroke Magazine*, devoted an
entire issue of that journal to Ammons and his work on the
occasion of the poet's sixtieth birthday.[4] In the same year Harold
Bloom edited a collection of critical essays on Ammons, many
of which were written in the 1970s, Ammons's decade of poetic
honors and recognition.[5] More recently, James S. Hans and
Willard Spiegelman have written important chapters on Ammons in their books on modern and contemporary American
poetry.[6]

Different critics naturally read Ammons in different ways.
Bloom, for example, emphasizes the poet's Emersonian heritage,
linking him to Whitman, and accenting Ammons's own particular version of and aversion to the Sublime. Bloom's readings of
Ammons thus rarely focus on the many poems of the natural
order that run through the geography of the poet's work. Wendell
Berry, on the other hand, reads Ammons primarily as a "nature
poet." Berry—poet, critic, and farmer—is most interested in Ammons's concern for natural cycles and processes. John Elder, in
his essay on Ammons entitled "Poetry and the Mind's Terrain,"
printed in *Imagining the Earth: Poetry and the Vision of Nature*,
tries to reconcile these two opposing views.[7]

Elder sees Wordsworth as an important "ancestor" of Ammons: both poets are great walkers, both great lovers of nature,
and both keenly self-conscious. Elder looks for the meeting of
objective and subjective in Ammons's work: "Ammons is indeed
a poet of mind, and of human loneliness within the natural
world. But a reading of Ammons also makes apparent that the
mind's swerve is persistently determined by the 'literalness' of
natural fact: nature's order, which is above all an intricate process, brings the redemption of continual disorder and deflection
to the mind's otherwise self-centered round."[8] The extent to
which natural "events" correct the mind's tendency to dwell on
itself is part of the focus of my third chapter. Elder's important
essay outlines how mind and nature mesh in the poetry: "the
intensity with which the poet notices and appreciates the details
of the natural world fuses mind and nature."[9]

Ammons has also attracted critical attention because of his
ability to unite science with poetry. The poet's own interest in

science dates as far back as his college days at Wake Forest, where his majors were "from time to time pre-med, biology, chemistry, general science."[10] Ammons's training in science, unlike that of his American forefather Walt Whitman, was both formal and academic. After receiving his Bachelor of Science degree, he continued to read *Scientific American* and admits to being "pretty much aware of what was taking place as of late in science."[11] Ammons also had ample opportunity to apply his knowledge of chemistry and biology while working twelve years in New Jersey for a firm that manufactured glass for laboratory equipment.

It is important to note that Ammons denies consciously setting out to introduce scientific terminology into poetry. Rather, if we are to believe him, the process was a "natural" one. He says of his scientific influence in a 1986 interview: "It was perfectly natural for me to speak that way and to write that way." He goes on to explain "because what I knew and understood, and the things that I thought I could see into with some clarity, were deeply informed by the reading I had done and the experiences I had had which you might call scientific."[12]

From the outset (the title of his first volume, *Ommateum*, is a zoological term meaning "compound eye"), Ammons's poems have drawn extensively on the language and discoveries of science. An Ammons poem often involves the reader in a twofold process. On the one hand, the poems introduce readers to and actively engage them in scientific material they might otherwise remain indifferent to, e.g., the light cone in astronomy. Simultaneously, many of the poems require the reader to know or consult outside materials, texts on biology, physics, and astronomy, in order to fully comprehend the poetry. Unless one knows, for example, what a "white dwarf" is, or how the eye converts radiant to electrical energy, one will remain partly mystified by Ammons's references to such terms and processes. In a sense, his poems help us to know science; in another sense, they require us to know it. Like other modern and post-modern poets, Ammons requires readers to re-make their minds in order to read his poetry. It is not unusual, for example, to have to consult a text on astronomy in order to understand Ammons's complex allusions to the evolution of galaxies. Or one might need to do background reading in biology in order to understand other poetic passages. In this regard, he places great demands upon a reader.

By incorporating scientific materials in his poems, Ammons is helping to bridge the gap between poets and scientists. Nothing thrills him more than an astronaut who writes poetry, as he declares in section 125 of *Sphere*—"(I see in one of the monthlies an astronaut / is writing poems—that's what I mean, guys)"—for he is a prime example of integration, synthesizing observation with poetic expression, perhaps even integrating the two hemispheres of the brain. It is important to note from the start that Ammons's understanding of scientific materials is not superficial—that his borrowings from science are not elementary. He is not writing from primers on biology and astronomy, nor is he writing new primers for the reader. Instead he imaginatively makes use of concepts and discoveries that are both complex and current.

There have been various critical attempts to clarify the relations between science and Ammons's poetry. Most of these have focused on language. Berry and Richard Howard, both early advocates of Ammons's work, call attention to the "large proportion of scientific language" in Ammons's poetry.[13] Other critics have written on how the scientific terminology in his poetry is balanced by common, more colloquial speech. But the impact of science on Ammons's poetry goes far beyond his selection of words. Scientific discoveries open Ammons's mind to an expansive world beyond the narrow boundaries of self. His contemplation of recent astronomical data, for example, or his fascination with cellular activity, enables Ammons to widen the scope of his visual perception and his knowledge of the physical universe. He is transformed by his encounters, and in the process becomes himself a transformer, turning scientific discovery into poetry.

This expansive influence of science on Ammons's poetry has been commented on in passing by only a few critics. Alan Holder, in his book *A. R. Ammons*, notes that "science does not function primarily as a source of metaphors for Ammons, but as a supplier of knowledge and concepts whose contemplation gives him pleasure."[14] Philip Fried, in his dissertation on Ammons, "Three Essays on the Poetry of A. R. Ammons," draws attention to the impact of evolutionary and ecological sciences on Ammons.[15] Miriam Marty Clark, in her article "The Gene, the Computer, and Information Processing in A. R. Ammons," discusses the gene and the computer as important information processors in Ammons's longer poems.[16] Willard Spiegelman, in a chapter of *The Didactic Muse*, sees Ammons as a didactic poet who "shares Auden's and Nemerov's interest in scientific discovery and James Merrill's impulse to present 'poems of science.'"[17] John Elder, in his study, links Ammons with Gary Snyder, another contemporary poet who has immersed himself in scientific materials. Elder writes:

> Expansive subject matter serves a similar function in the poetry of Snyder and Ammons; though their voices remain personally self-conscious, revelations of nature's intricacy burst continuously through the frameworks of their understanding, as well as through conventional Western attitudes. Rather than domesticating nature, the poets are themselves assimilated into its ever-emerging and overwhelming particularity. The richness of natural process shatters human expectations, recentering mental circles and broadening their necessary circumference. Poetry's landscape is an ecotone where human and natural orders meet.[18]

In his long ecological poem "Extremes and Moderations," Ammons urges his readers to break through the confining boundaries of city life "into the lofty assimilations" (CP, 335). He means for his readers to enter the vast currents of nature so that they assimilate ("become one with") invigorating energies. He aims, at least in that poem, to reconnect readers with the earth and to redefine their relationship to the world and to themselves. The rich diversity of the natural world is Ammons's subject—and his ever-attentive eye records it in all its particularity. The poems are the log of a late-twentieth-century walker, a man steeped in biology, ecology, and astronomy, whose natural encounters burst in upon his own awareness and—through his poems—his readers' awareness.

A. R. Ammons takes facts from botany and biology to discover correspondences between plant life and human life. He makes use of his astronomical observations and readings to discover a ray of connection between what is out there and what is interior to himself. At times he fails. Instead of being reunited, Ammons on occasion feels intensely lonely, terrified, and his records of these moments are poignant reminders of the failure of vision to achieve a harmonizing relationship with the world.

My subject then is Ammons's poetics of widening scope. Many of his poems result from visual encounters with the flux of "events" in the natural world. Several years ago I co-authored a book, The Athletic Eye, with a behavioral optometrist who had great success in modifying his patients' visual skills through training exercises. That book explains how athletes can improve sports performance by enhancing their processing of visual stimuli. We show what the key visual skills are for different sports, and how they can be further developed through exercise.[19] My work in behavioral optometry has encouraged me to think of vision as a dynamic process, and my readings of Ammons's poems build on this understanding.

The development of lenses has revolutionized humanity's vision of the world, and in recent times the electron microscope and the space telescope have dramatically widened the scope of our understanding. Ammons puts to good use the latest findings in astronomy and biology, and throughout this study I trace his poetic treatment of these discoveries.

That Ammons draws on the materials of science for the language and the conceptual framework for many of his poems is not without precedent. In America, both Walt Whitman and Robinson Jeffers drew from their scientific studies a rich vocabulary for their poems and ideas that shaped the way they saw humanity and the universe. The results of their encounters, however, are entirely different. Whereas Whitman finds in science corroboration of his own expansive vision of self and the world, Jeffers describes science as "inhuman." Typically, Jeffers accentuates the cold and indifferent ("inhuman") qualities of the vision science presents of the world.[20] Whereas the nineteenth-century Romantic celebrates the vastness and splendor of astronomy, Jeffers refers to the "useless intelligence of far stars."[21] In his article "Science and the Poetry of Robinson Jeffers," Hyatt Waggoner remarks that in Jeffers "time and again we find astronomical images used to give point to the brooding on human insignificance."[22] In Whitman, just the opposite is true. In "On the Beach at Night Alone," Whitman looks up at the stars, only to discover "a vast similitude interlocks all."[23] Ammons writes in the Whitmanian scientific tradition, celebrating the expanded scope gained through astronomical and biological observation.

Unlike earlier twentieth-century American poets, including Jeffers, Frost, and Eliot, Ammons is not alienated by what he learns from science. Instead, like Whitman, he often expresses wonder—in large measure derived from what science teaches him about the cosmos. In *Tape for the Turn of the Year*, his book-length diary poem, there are many instances where the poet records the scientist's awe before the workings of natural law. Ammons imagines how the biochemist must feel on seeing two discrete molecules link with each other to form a compound.

> the biochemist, first
> seeing how
> two molecules select each

other & interlink
   must think he
   beholds
   a face of God:

                        (T, 54–55)

That hydrogen and oxygen, for example, *select* each other and pair to form water is indicative of a guiding intelligence—"a face of God"—manifest in the physical universe and observed most precisely by the trained scientist. In this instance, Ammons mutes his own reverence for the phenomenon by adding a distancing notion of perspective in the three words "must think he." The communion (between hydrogen and oxygen) is a holy event in the scientist's eyes, not necessarily in Ammons's. While it is true that as a contemporary poet Ammons is more self-conscious and therefore perhaps more cautious than Whitman about expressing *his own* exuberance and spiritual appreciation for scientific phenomena, he nonetheless will often *directly* express a "religious" attitude toward nature's mechanisms. He has said, "I feel deeply religious but in a naturalistic way."[24] Ammons is "religious" in the same sense as defined by Albert Einstein in a famous statement:

The most beautiful experience we can have is the mysterious. It is the fundamental emotion which stands at the cradle of true art and true science. Whoever does not know it and can no longer wonder, no longer marvel, is as good as dead, and his eyes are dimmed. It was the experience of mystery—even if mixed with fear—that engendered religion. A knowledge of the existence of something we cannot penetrate, our perceptions of the profoundest reason and the most radiant beauty, which only in their most primitive forms are accessible to our minds—it is this knowledge and this emotion that constitute true religiosity; in this sense, and in this alone, I am a deeply religious man.[25]

In the above section of *Tape*, Ammons refers to the human body as "a miraculous / residence— / temple / we should try to keep / the right spirit in" (T, 54). The source for his praise is found in the detailed anatomical and biological description of the body, which emphasizes the specialization of its parts and their working together to facilitate processes like digestion. He writes:

```
        we are
        "held together":
        minerals—such  as
                    calcium—
           selected, refined
           & deposited to high
           purities
                 give support:
        specialized tissues
        bind us to the bones: an
        outer cage
        protects softer organs:
                    lovely
              loose mesenteries—
                 permitting digestion's
                 roil & change—
        hold intestines in place:
           so
           the exchanges can go
           on, the trades in
                 blood, lymph,
           food, waste, water:
           traffic through
        barriers, each selective,
        responsive:
        if you have condemned the
        body, you have
        condemned a miraculous
              residence—
              temple
              we should try to keep
        the right spirit in:
```

(T, 53–54)

This biological, chemical, and anatomical analysis yields a picture of a smoothly functioning system ("mechanism"). Moreover, Ammons's biological description evokes the purposefulness inherent in the many primal substances that constitute the physical body. Specific tissues cushion us even as they link us with skeletal frames. Substances mesh and interlock; the architecture is both intricate and efficient. Mesenteries support intestines so that digestive exchanges can occur; the internal map is designed for materials to "traffic through" without chaos. Indeed, Ammons does construct a "residence" of the body—and yet this is no mere house, but rather a "temple." The body's wholeness suggests "holiness," warranting reverence rather than abuse. The encounter with matter yields spirit, and this is not atypical in Ammons's work.

The poet's response to anatomical functioning is emotional and aesthetic. He assimilates the facts of science into the testimony of his poetry, and in this way is an exponent of what Elder calls "the science of the heart."[26] In his essay on science and poetry, "Structures of Evolving Consciousness," Elder explains in some detail that the great modern philosopher of science, Alfred North Whitehead, advocated "subjectivity and emotions in the pursuit of knowledge."[27] Whitehead felt "the rise of philosophical dualism and . . . scientific materialism were simultaneous . . . and led to a neglect of nature and the human heart."[28] The split between mind and heart, science and poetry, that Whitehead objects to was also criticized by several Romantic poets, especially Emerson and Wordsworth. Ammons, who is a poetic descendant of these writers, and who acknowledges Whitehead as an influence, strives to overcome the schism that has led to, in Whitehead's words, "the divorce of science from the affirmations of our aesthetic and ethical experiences."[29]

According to Whitehead, what forms the novelty of the age of science, an age that has progressed and endured for four centuries now, is a particular tinge or cast of thought. He explains in "The Origins of Modern Science" (*Science and the Modern World*) that "this new tinge to modern minds is a vehement and passionate interest in the relation of general principles to irreducible and stubborn facts."[30] He adds that science "requires an active interest in the simple occurrences of life for their own sake."[31] This "active interest" was pursued by both scientists and artists increasingly attentive to natural phenomena. Whitehead views Galileo as a pivotal figure in the development of modern science, citing Galileo's commitment to the truth of his observations, despite persecution.

In his controversial work *Siderus Nuncius*, or "The Starry Messenger," Galileo described what were then revolutionary astronomical observations. The moon's surface was rough, rather than smooth; the fixed stars were not perfectly round but "have rather the aspect of blazes whose rays vibrate around them and scintillate a great deal."[32] He also discovered four "new" planets, previously unobserved, that swiftly revolved about Jupiter. These observations upset philosophers' and churchmen's belief in a sky where all known bodies were supposed to be already accounted for, and where heavenly bodies were thought to be smooth and perfectly round. His statement written to the Grand

Duchess Christina defending these and other observations has proved far more enduring than any made by his detractors. He writes "that in discussions of physical problems we ought to begin not from the authority of scriptural passages, but from sense-experiences and necessary demonstrations.[33] The primary organ of perception for Galileo was the eye, and he helped to establish attentive observation as a method of inquiry.

Long before the controversy that engulfed Galileo, Whitehead recalls, St. Benedict, founder of the Benedictine monasteries in sixth-century Italy, had developed "an eye for the importance of ordinary things." According to Whitehead, "we owe it to St. Benedict that the monasteries were the homes of practical agriculturalists, as well as of saints and of artists and men of learning. The alliance of science with technology, by which learning is kept in contact with irreducible and stubborn facts, owes much to the practical bent of the early Benedictines."[34]

Just as attentive observation was the catalyst for much modern science, so too did this sharpening of vision nourish the arts. Whitehead writes that "the whole atmosphere of every art exhibited a direct joy in the apprehension of the things which lie around us. The craftsmen who executed the late medieval decorative sculpture, Giotto, Chaucer, Wordsworth, Walt Whitman, and, at the present day, the New England poet Robert Frost, are all akin to each other in this respect. The simple immediate facts are the topics of interest, and these reappear in the thought of science as the 'irreducible stubborn facts.'"[35] Herein lies the fundamental bond that links poet-scientists as chronologically distant as Lucretius and Ammons, and as temperamentally different as Ammons and Jeffers—their fascination with the "simple immediate facts." How they mold the facts of nature in the context of their works, how they choose to present them and what ultimately they see in them, is cause for great differences, yet in their attentiveness to the physical universe they link themselves to the great tradition of modern science.

When Whitehead published his book *Science and the Modern World* (1925), the twentieth-century revolution in physics had only just begun. In 1915, Einstein proposed his general theory of relativity. Quantum theory, or the new physics, was just being developed. In his book *The Tao of Physics*, Fritjof Capra gives an overview of the experiments and ideas with which classical physics has been superseded. Capra notes that at the turn of the century "Rutherford's experiments had shown that atoms, instead of being hard and indestructible, consisted of vast regions of space in which extremely small particles moved, and now quantum theory had made it clear that even these particles were nothing like the solid objects of classical physics."[36] Max Planck discovered that light has both a particle and a wave nature. As physicists probed deeper and deeper into the fundamental constituents of matter, they discovered that it was not solid and predictable, but composed of "wave-like patterns of probabilities."[37] The "irreducible, stubborn facts" Whitehead alludes to become, in quantum physics, elusive probabilities, contingent on human perspective and human sensory apparatus.

The experiments of Bohr and Heisenberg in the late 1920s demonstrated the difficulty in measuring the interplay of subatomic particles. Capra cites Henry Stapp on this subject: "The basic problem with observation in atomic physics is that . . . 'the observed system is required to be isolated in order to be defined, yet interacting in order to be observed.'"[38] Bohr, Heisenberg, and other pioneers of the new physics devised elaborate methods of measuring the newly discovered subatomic particles. In the process they discovered that the scientist influences the properties of the objects observed.

The new physics widened the scope of our understanding the universe, and at the same time showed that the human observer of the universe cannot be detached, but participates in and influences his or her observations. Ammons, cognizant of the new physics, participates in all that he sees. He rarely stands apart as a detached observer. His unifying vision, though threatened periodically by moments of doubt and terror, nevertheless is consonant with quantum theory, which "forces us to see the universe not as a collection of physical objects, but rather as a complicated web of relations between the various parts of a unified whole."[39] This is the discovery of Ammons's great long poems "Essay on Poetics," "Extremes and Moderations," and Sphere: The Form of a Motion.

2

"Curious" Science: Ammons and His Forebears

"In the enormous range of his work, from the briefest confrontations with the visual to long powerful visionary poems . . . he has extended into our present and our future the great American tradition of which Emerson and Whitman were the founders."
—Citation for the 1973 National Book Award in Poetry

Of the three great American Transcendental writers—Emerson, Whitman, and Thoreau—Emerson has attracted Ammons's attention the most. Ammons's reflections on Emerson seem contradictory, perhaps intentionally so, in order to keep us slightly off balance. This seems plausible given Ammons's preference for "confusion to over-simplified clarity."[1] On the one hand, Ammons seems unequivocal in acknowledging Emerson as a literary forefather, as a man who in Ammons's terms is "speaking my central concerns more beautifully than I could say them myself."[2] On the other hand, however, Ammons seems to distance himself as much as possible from the author of *Nature*. In the 1972 *Diacritics* interview he says "it is nearly impossible for me to identify closely with Emerson because he comes from Concord, and I from a rural and defeated South. You know, there are just too many wave lengths that we don't share." Yet in the very same interview, when asked to acknowledge his literary forefathers, Ammons responds: "In American literature, it's Whitman and Emerson." He goes on to confess that "Emerson led me to the same sources that he discovered himself—to Indian and Chinese philosophy which, when I was younger, I read a good deal."[3]

Although his testimony is contradictory, Ammons on balance seems to favor his Emersonian connection. When asked whether reviewers have made too much of him as an Emersonian, he replied: "I don't think so." But Ammons is careful to avoid appearing too consciously Emersonian, that is, simply as one who puts into poetry the ideas of the great essayist. Ammons states, almost in the same breath with the previous statement, that "I didn't read Emerson that much or that well before Harold Bloom started speaking of him."[4] Bloom did not publish his first article on Ammons until 1971. By that date Ammons had already published seven volumes of his work.[5]

Ammons's commitment to and his hedging away from Emerson seems instructive in at least two ways. First, it demonstrates Ammons's resistance to what he calls in "Corsons Inlet" a "bind of thought," a too narrow perception that might hem him in. His poetry reflects this disposition, often taking as its subject the distinctions between the provisional in nature and what he calls rigid and fixed forms of thought. Second, I think one could do well to learn from Ammons's own preference for openness; that is, one can find suggestions in Ammons of Emerson, but one would be wise not to limit oneself by tying him too closely to Emerson.

Despite Ammons's hedging about Emerson's influence, critics have insisted on Ammons's Emersonianism. Hyatt Waggoner, in a 1973 *Salmagundi* article, writes that "Ammons is a visionary poet in the Neoplatonic tradition introduced and best represented in our (American) poetry by Emerson. I would guess that he has read a good deal of Emerson and pondered much on what he has read."[6] Bloom, in one of his early articles on Ammons, writes that "Ammons is the direct and rightful heir, since Robinson and Frost, of Emerson's central line that commenced with Thoreau and Whitman." He adds that "Ammons, though a Southerner and a man obsessed with Minute Particulars, is the most Emersonian poet we have had since Whitman's petering out after 1860."[7] Yet for all the comparisons that have been made between Emerson and Ammons, very little has been said about the way Ammons both shares and modifies Emerson's approach to science.

Bloom, in his many articles on Ammons, makes only one fleeting allusion to Ammons's "curious" use of science, which seems to resemble what Emerson called "true science."[8] In his earlier essay from *Ringers in the Tower*, Bloom laments the scientific strain in Ammons, which he calls "ecological and almost geological." His emphasis on Ammons as a poet of the mind and of the Sublime causes Bloom to disregard Ammons as a poet of science.[9] Patricia Parker, in her essay on Ammons in *Diacritics*, suggests that Ammons "is the twentieth-century equivalent to what Emerson described in "The Poet.'"[10] Parker, however, does not explore in much detail Ammons's willingness to incorporate, just as Emerson had called for, seemingly unpoetic ("scientific") material in his poems. Janet De Rosa, in her doctoral dissertation on Ammons, argues that "the use of science and its terminology is part of Ammons' Romantic Transcendental heritage."[11] Yet she fails to explore just how Ammons's use of science is part of this heritage. While the critical discussion has focused on Emerson and Ammons, we need also to explore Ammons's "curious science" in relation to Whitman and Thoreau, both of whom incorporated scientific discoveries extensively into their writings.

Emerson's attitudes about science were curiously ambivalent, on the one hand deriding the science of his day, on the other hand making use of it to better understand the self. Ultimately, Emerson reserved his contempt for *detached observation* through what he called in his journal "cold, arithmetical eyes." He spent a good deal of time writing and lecturing about how best to bridge the gap between the seer and the world of nature. Because the eye was the primary organ connecting the interior world of the self with the external world of nature, he naturally had a good deal to say about visual perception.

The problem with the science of his day, Emerson complained, was that it remained unimaginative, too coldly detached, too superficial. In "The Poet" he complains that "our science is sensual, and therefore superficial. The earth and the heavenly bodies, physics and chemistry, we sensually treat, as if they were self-existent; but these are the retinue of that Being we have."[12]

Elsewhere he writes, "External Nature is only a half. The geology, the astronomy, the anatomy, are all good, but t'is all a half."[13] Reason, that faculty of mind that intuitively found connections between the facts and their observer, was required to make them whole. Emerson feared the empiricists' emphasis on analysis would blind man to the deeper meaning of Nature. Excessive calculation also would deprive the observer of the sense of wonder Emerson prized.

In contrast to seeing through "cold, arithmetical eyes," Emerson proposed what I have come to think of as "relational" seeing: perception that starts with the premise that relationship can be discovered between the facts of science and the self. All knowledge, including the scientific, should lead to a greater enlightenment of the self. This is what Sherman Paul in his book on

Emerson's Angle of Vision, has called "humanized science."[14]
To a great extent Ammons also engages science in this way, employing what Bloom calls "curious" science. In Ammons, however, I do not detect the constant undercurrent of disdain that
Emerson has for what we might think of as hard science. Moreover, Ammons does not seem as driven to discover correspondences between the facts of science and the human mind.

To overcome the schism between poetic vision and analytical
seeing, Emerson developed his own definition of science. Believing that "science is nothing but the finding of analogy, identity, in the most remote parts," he encouraged the discovery of
the symbolic value of scientific fact. "The poet alone knows astronomy, chemistry, vegetation and animation, for he does not
stop at these facts, but employs them as signs."[15] In contrast to
this, he ridicules the detached and literal use of facts characteristic of eighteenth-century science, which, Paul writes, "searched
piecemeal into a nature no longer spiritually intimate with
man."[16] Emerson's statement in *Nature* epitomized the distaste
he had for such an approach: "All the facts in natural history
taken by themselves have no value, but are barren, like a single
sex." One who takes facts *only* by themselves, or literally, fails
to see their relation to each other or to the human mind. "But
marry it to human history and it is full of life." By connecting
a fact of natural history to human history, we make that fact
lively and relevant. Emerson went on to explain why:

> Whole floras, all Linnaeus' and Buffon's volumes, are dry catalogues
> of facts; but the most trivial of these facts, the habit of a plant, the
> organs, or work, or noise of an insect, applied to the illustration of
> a fact in intellectual philosophy, or in any way associated to human
> nature, affects us in the most lively and agreeable manner.[17]

By referring all objective knowledge back to the self, Emerson felt
that the facts would be redeemed and vivified. His distinction
between the symbolic and the literal use of facts mirrored his
distinction between the two faculties of mind. Reason, in its
imaginative, intuitive capacity, perceives relationships in Nature
and discovers analogies between the facts of science and the
human mind. However, "the Understanding is a willed, empiri-
cal, practical mode of consciousness."[18]

Emerson ridicules naturalists who "freeze their subject under
the wintry light of the Understanding." In contrast, the better
student of Nature perceives relationships between his percep-

tions and himself: "The instincts of the ant are very important, considered as the ant's; but the moment a ray of relation is seen to extend from it to man . . . then all its habits . . . become sublime."[19] Here we think of Whitman's spider in the poem "A Noiseless Patient Spider," "launching forth filament, filament, filament, out of itself." Whitman links the activity of the spider with that of his own soul, thereby perceiving relationship between the external phenomenon and an internal state. Thoreau also engages in "relational" seeing when he describes the ant battle in *Walden*, drawing a parallel between the ferocity of the ants' fighting and the human propensity for such behavior. The Puritan poets, of course, also discovered "signs" in nature. Ammons too, as we shall discover, engages in analogic perception. In his poem "The Yucca Moth" he likens himself and the rest of us to a moth, which "hangs out" in the leaves of the plant to rest from its night journeys. The implication is that we too can find solace in nature from our "darker flights." In all these examples the discovery of relationship begins with the act of looking, literally *seeing*. What Emerson called for, and what we find in these examples, is the discovery of metaphor during the act of perception.

Emerson urged others to discover the reciprocity he himself found between Nature and Spirit. Explaining this reciprocity as boldly as he ever would, in "The American Scholar," he writes:

> . . . nature is the opposite of the soul, answering to it part for part. One is seal, and one is print. Its beauty is the beauty of his own mind. Its laws are the laws of his own mind. Nature then becomes to him the measure of his attainments. So much of nature as he is ignorant of, so much of his own mind does he not yet possess.[20]

According to this logic, our knowledge of Nature is a measure of our self-knowledge. The poet, who possessed keen powers of perception, could ultimately see the universal in a single fact. Of Thoreau, Emerson says in his "Biographical Sketch" that "the depth of his perception found likeness of law throughout Nature, and I know not any genius who so swiftly inferred universal law from the single fact."[21] Emerson also admired Thoreau's ability to describe external phenomena in relation to internal ones. This method of description usually begins with literal observations of Nature that are figuratively transformed in the process of contemplation. We will examine this process both in Thoreau and in Ammons.

Emerson's traditional Romantic objection to science is perhaps best typified in a September 1839 Journal entry, where he reflected on an aurora:

> Here came the other night an Aurora so wonderful, a curtain of red and blue and silver glory, that in any other age or nation it would have moved the awe and words of men and mingled with the profoundest sentiments of religion and love, and we all saw it with cold, arithmetical eyes, we knew how many colors shone, how many degrees it extended, how many hours it lasted, and of this heavenly flower we beheld nothing more.[22]

This is a particularly good point to explore the conjunction of Ammons's attitudes toward science with those of Emerson. In some ways Ammons fulfills the Emersonian approach to science, which is metaphysical ("The axioms of physics translate the laws of ethics"), and yet in other ways, he seems to derive great pleasure in the very kind of measuring and calculating Emerson ridicules. Gauging "how many" is one characteristic way Ammons reacts to and interprets phenomena. In "Cascadilla Falls," Ammons picks up a stone and calculates the measure of the cosmic forces that are at work upon it:

> I went down by Cascadilla
> Falls this
> evening, the
> stream below the falls,
> and picked up a
> handsized stone
> kidney-shaped, testicular, and
>
> thought all its motions into it,
> the 800 mph earth spin,
> the 190-million-mile yearly
> displacement around the sun,
> the overriding
> grand
> haul
>
> of the galaxy with the 30,000
> mph of where
> the sun's going:
> thought all the interweaving
> motions
> into myself: dropped

                    the stone to dead rest:
                    the stream from other motions
                    broke
                    rushing over it:
                    shelterless,
                    I turned

                    to the sky and stood still:
                    Oh
                    I do
                    not know where I am going
                    that I can live my life
                    by this single creek.

                                                            (CP, 206–7)

This poem begins, as so many of Ammons's poems do, with
the poet taking a walk, leading to a series of perceptions. As
Ammons explains, this is "exactly the mode I try to jump into
. . . you get to that ordinary level of things and, in a normal,
almost journalistic way, you go into action, things happen, and
then they end. Meanwhile they describe a curvature of some sort
that's either narrative, or myth or structure or whatever, but it *is*,
it *exists*."[23] As a "reporter" on the beat of "Cascadilla Falls,"
Ammons picks up a "kidney-shaped, testicular" stone, cast out,
worked over, and shaped by water. He shares with the reporter
a willingness to circulate, to walk about, to remain open to the
events around him, albeit the nature of these events usually transcends the concerns of the daily newspaper.

    In "Cascadilla Falls" Ammons is particularly fascinated by the
"motions" this "testicular" stone is subject to—the "800 mph
earth spin," the long annual journey it takes around the sun, the
position it occupies in the vast swirl of the galaxy. In considering
the object from the point of view of a geologist or an astronomer,
Ammons records in precise terms the measure of these various
motions. His willingness to calculate, to measure phenomena in
this way, distinguishes him from Emerson. Ammons, as Alan
Holder has written, "exhibits a distinctly scientific turn of mind
in his own direct encounters with nature."[24] Ammons, of course,
is not purely a scientist, nor does his record here ultimately serve
a "scientific" purpose, although we as readers are treated to some
interesting scientific facts. The effect of these facts is to startle
the poet and his reader into an awareness of the speed and power
of the cosmic forces that work upon a seemingly stationary object. We are treated to increments of increasing expansion and

speed, as we contemplate first the 800-mph spin of the earth, then the even larger figure of the 190 million-mile displacement around the sun, and finally the "grand / haul / of the galaxy"—all of which seem vaster and faster when compared to the "inert" stone. In "Cascadilla Falls," a simple stone becomes a vehicle for suggesting the vastness of the cosmos and its activity.

Ammons, in what is an Emersonian gesture, thinks "all the interweaving / motions / into myself . . ."—that is, he takes them into himself, becoming cognizant that indeed he is subject to the same cosmic motions as the stone. Also, the stone is described in organic terms, like fossilized pieces of himself—"testicular, kidney-shaped." Ammons thus discovers the "ray of relation" Emerson sought in all his encounters with scientific fact.

The final "curvature" of this recorded event is surprising, for the poet initially leads us to believe that he may be isolated, in a sense atomized, in the face of these huge forces: "shelterless / I turned / to the sky and stood still." Here Ammons feels released from the experience of so much motion by realizing that it makes stillness possible. The next three lines sustain a curve of feeling, with the poet stating his lack of direction—"Oh / I do / not know where I am going." This tension is diffused by the final two lines of the poem, where the poet states his willingness to live out his life by the creek where the stone now rests, the motion of the spring pouring over it. This resolution is in fact consistent with Ammons's repeated turnings to nature as the source for his poetry and vision. Although initially he may feel ambivalence, even confusion, about existing indefinitely by the stream, his discoveries provide him with the solace to sustain his "journeyings."

Ammons is content to live out his existence by the stream, which in its constant motion is a reminder of the greater motions at work in the universe. Holder, in another reading of the poem, finds in the poet's statement, "I do / not know where I am going," reference to a lack of psychological direction and an attempt by Ammons to distinguish himself from the stone, whose motions he shares.[25] I find that the ending of the poem, rather than expressing lack of direction, expresses an affirmation of direction, a desire on the part of the poet to remain there, "still" with the stone and stream, to observe them in the vast play of the galaxy. Ammons distinguishes himself from the stone, however, by the self-reflective nature of his own consciousness.

Ammons's appreciation for statistics is not unique to "Cascadilla Falls." Throughout his work we see him fascinated by measure, by the mathematical record of movement—whether it be

waves of light or storm patterns or rockets lifting off. In section
39 of *Sphere* he exhibits an almost boyish joy in the account of
a rocket liftoff:

> Apollo 16 just blasted
> off: it's 1400 miles downrange at 16,000 mph, orbit
> established: a stirring bit of expenditure there in the
>
> blastoff into freefall's silent, floating speed: hurry back,
> boys: look out your window at North America: I'm right
> under that big cloud: it hasn't budged in six months:
>
> (S, 28)

Here again, the poet enjoys recording the measure of vast forces,
albeit man-made ones. Ammons uses the facts and figures to
evoke his wonder before the emblem of space-age power. In these
lines he also fulfills Emerson's challenge to include technology
within the context of our poetry—the railroad has simply been
replaced by the rocket. There is also a genuine fascination in the
technology itself, in the engineering that has enabled this craft
to register a speed of 16,000 mph.

The most striking example of Ammons's fascination with scientific measure occurs in his long poem "Essay on Poetics." In
what turns out to be a series of double-edged gestures, the poet
sets out to determine the longitude and latitude of an elm tree,
the diameter of one of its branches, and then the weight gain
experienced by elmworms as they eat the tree's leaves. On the
one hand, the resulting descriptions exemplify the poet-scientist's own analytical bent. On the other hand, these passages tend
to parody the very impulse to measure in the first place, for as
Ammons realizes, eventually "it's necessary to be quiet in the
hands of the marvelous" (CP, 304). The elm tree is susceptible
to too many variables, like drifts and shifts in the ground, to be
exactly recorded. Listen to him as he proceeds to calculate the
interaction of elmworms and the tree's leaves:

> I think now of growth at the edges of the leaves as the
> reverse of the elmworm's forage:
>
> the elmworm, I haven't seen any this year—one spring
> there were millions—is as to weight an interesting
> speculation:
> as he eats the leaf lessens but of course the weight is
> added to himself, so on a quick scale the

transformation is one to one:
but the worm makes waste, the efficiency of his mechanisms
average and wasteful: in the long range, then,
worms lighten trees and let in light: but that's
another problem: could it be maintained that
the worm lets in light enough
to increase growth equal to his destruction:
　　it's a good point, a true variable, but surely
any sudden defoliation by a plague of worms
would be harmful: a re-entry of winter (though possibly
with all of winter's possibility): time and number figure
mysteriously here

(CP, 305)

Whoever would have thought to include the dynamics of elm-worms in a poem about poetics? Yet Ammons discovers in the metamorphosis of worm and tree one truth of nature: that inter-actions are complex and sometimes destructive. Ammons also registers a genuine fascination for the behavior of elmworms, without feeling compelled to liken their behavior to his own. He even takes pleasure, despite the worms' destructive capabilities, "in the possibilities the event presents to mind." The problem he tackles is one of distribution ("the worm makes waste"), and as Ammons muses over the relative effects of elmworm blight, the reader cannot help but appreciate the subtlety of his consid-erations.

The final lines are telling, as they attempt to summarize the complexity of the phenomenon: "time and number figure / mys-teriously here." The mystery of time and number, as reflected in these passages, fascinates Ammons and further distinguishes him from Emerson. The nineteenth-century transcendentalist earnestly tried to find in the facts of science corroboration for some moral law or internal state, always keeping in mind that the facts were secondary to the parallel he could discover in them. Ammons, on the other hand, is willing to entertain the sheer facts themselves—how time and number figure—both in the sense of the configuration they form and how they add up. Yet even as we trace Ammons's interest in measure, we cannot escape his penchant for using calculation as a springboard to personal discovery. The thinking of motions into the kidney-shaped stone in "Cascadilla Falls" is a scientific gesture, but the thinking of those motions back into himself seems Emersonian.

In addition to engaging science on its own terms, Ammons further separates himself from Emerson by incorporating both a playful and humorous tone in some of his poems that draw on scientific materials. In discussing science, Emerson was for the most part deadly serious. In his sermon "Astronomy," he argued in earnest that Copernican astronomy "made the theological *scheme of Redemption* absolutely incredible."[26] His tone in this sermon and in his many journal and essay references to science is always forthright, serious, contemplative. Ammons, by contrast, is capable of a playful and subtle humor in his use of science that never would have occurred to Emerson. In "Spaceship," a poem ignored by critics, Ammons humorously underscores the gap between astronomical fact and visible reality, only to point out why for so long divines and even scientists could believe the earth was stationary.

> It's amazing all
> this motion going
> on and
> water can lie still
> in glasses and the gas
> can in the
> garage doesn't rattle.

(CP, 322)

The motion Ammons alludes to is of course the rotation of the earth on its axis; yet he is certainly aware of the earth's other motions—its revolution around the sun, its movement with the sun around the center of the galaxy, and its still further movement within the galaxy on its journey toward Andromeda. Given all this activity, and given that the earth (our "spaceship") may participate in still other movements, it is indeed "amazing" that things remain stationary at all. It is not because of the great speed of the earth that objects remain stationary, as Holder suggests, but rather because the *regularity* of its motion maintains an equilibrium.[27] If the earth's motion were irregular, then the equilibrium configuration would always be changing. To demonstrate this law of nature, Ammons pursues the commonplace, which takes him into the American garage and kitchen, where, lo and behold, neither glasses filled with water nor cans filled with gas exhibit one shiver. Despite all this cosmic whirl, the objects most likely to wobble seem to remain still. The contrast between scientific fact and visible reality is both amusing and instructive. It is amusing to think what life might in fact be like if the regularity of the earth's motion were disturbed, all those glasses of water sliding around the table. However, Ammons's experiment testi-

fies to the design in creation and teaches us the principle of the
regularity of motion.

The form of the poem, as well as its statement, demonstrates
the co-existence of stability and motion. No single line comes to
a halt, except of course the final one, and Ammons keeps the
words from resting through his own vigorous enjambement. Although his rattling syntax jars us here, the sense of the poem
holds steady, finally.

This little demonstration also aptly and subtly indicates why
for centuries men did in fact believe the earth was stationary—
our daily reality seemed to make this indisputable. Ammons
points out the limitations of a too constrictive understanding of
the universe. More importantly, he is playing two conceptions of
reality against one another. His ability to entertain himself and
the reader in this casual and good-humored way is indicative of
his own willingness to treat scientific fact playfully.

In "Spring Coming," another poem where Ammons treats the
scientific playfully, he derives humor from the collision of precise botanical terms with colloquial speech:

> The caryophyllaceae
> like a scroungy
> frost are
> rising through the lawn:
> many-fingered as leggy
>   copepods:
> a suggestive delicacy,
> lacework, like
> the scent of wild plum
>   thickets:
> also the grackles
> with their incredible
> vertical, horizontal,
> reversible
> tails have arrived:
> such nice machines.
>
> (CP, 226)

Words with very specific botanical and zoological denota-
tions—like "caryophyllaceae" and "copepods"—are jammed next
to graphic, more colorful, common language, like "scroungy" and
"leggy," with a surprising and amusing result. Ammons, in evoking the advent of spring, begins by speaking in the language of the
botanist. However, he refuses to restrict himself to botanical terms

and creates two arresting similes, drawing on colloquial speech. Actually, the second of the two—"many-fingered as leggy / copepods"—combines the colloquial and the zoological in a single phrase—"leggy copepods"—which, after all, is what the "claws" at the end of the long pink petals on a particular kind of corolla are supposed to look like. We are asked to see the plant's emerging "fingers" as both "leggy" and crustacean-like ("copepods"). This is at best a feat requiring one to scurry between dictionaries for both terms and visual pictures. Yet the collision of diction (and dictionaries), if you are not frustrated by it, is both good-humored and educational; through his verbal and visual acrobatics Ammons informs as he entertains us about the nascent signs of one plant's return to appreciable life.

At the end of the poem Ammons shifts focus, from plant to grackles. Here again for humorous effect he contrasts precise terminology with colloquial speech. The words "vertical," "horizontal," and "reversible" (geometrically exact) are sandwiched between "incredible" and "tails," and we are treated to a delightful account of the versatility and mobility of grackles. The final line of the poem—"such nice machines"—understates Ammons's appreciation not only for the engineering of the grackles' versatile tails, but also for mechanism in general. As Holder has correctly pointed out, "the words 'mechanism' and 'machine,' used in conjunction with objects or beings found in nature, are 'honorific terms' for Ammons."[28]

Although Ammons exhibits a broader range of attitudes and feelings in his approach to science than Emerson does, he does not discard the Emersonian penchant for discovering relationship between scientific facts and moral truths. In Tape for the Turn of the Year, when Ammons meditates on the internal processes of human digestion, the conclusion he reaches is that the body should be honored because it is a beautiful "temple." In this instance the facts of science (anatomy) yield a metaphysical (spiritual) truth. The result is to instill wonder in the reader for the orderly functioning of nature, and, as Paul has noted of Emerson, "wonder reborn was the first affirmation of transcendental experience."[29]

Whether exhibiting a fascination with calculation and measure or humorously juxtaposing two different kinds of diction or perceptions of "reality," Ammons broadens the reader's awareness of the universe. Moreover, when Ammons discovers relationships between external and internal phenomena, he causes us to see the world and our relationship to it anew, as he does in one of the

concluding passages of *Sphere*. In this passage Ammons looks
to astronomy for an affirmation of order and to geology for an
affirmation of unity amidst diversity:

> lately, we've left out the high ranges of music,
> the planetary, from our response, though the one sun is here
> as usual and the planets continue to obey holy roads: the
>
> galaxy is here, nearly too much to speak of, sagely and
> tremendously observing its rotation: we do have something to
> tune in with and move toward: not homogeneous pudding but
>
> united differences, surface differences expressing the common,
> underlying hope and fate of each person and people, a gathering
> into one place of multiple dissimilarity, each culture to its
>
> own cloth and style and tongue and gait, each culture, like
> the earth itself with commonlode center and variable surface,
> designed-out to the exact limit of ramification, to discrete
>
> 154
>
> expression into the visible, specific congruence of form and
> matter, energy moving into the clarification of each face, hand,
> ear, mouth, eye, billions: still with the sense of the continuous
>
> running through and staying all the discretions
>
> (S, 78–79)

In these passages Ammons alludes to two scientific facts: the
first concerning the predictability of the planets in their elliptical
paths around the sun, the second concerning the earth's structure. That Ammons uses the adjective "holy" to describe the
circuits of the planets around the sun, that he calls this movement the "high ranges of music," and that he speaks of the galaxy
"sagely . . . observing its rotation" is testimony to the reverence
and awe this poet still feels before the *celestial sphere*. Ammons's
feelings are reminiscent of Emerson, for whom the far was "holy."
In his sermon "Astronomy," Emerson too speaks of the music of
the stars: "the song of the morning stars was really the first hymn
of praise and will be the last; the face of nature . . . the lights of
the skies are to a simple heart the real occasions of devout feeling
more than vestries and sermon hearings."[30] On the brink of aban-
doning his formal religious affiliations, Emerson finds in nature
the real source of reverence. Ammons appeals to this same nature

when he writes, "we do have something to / tune in with and move toward." Like Emerson before him, Ammons admires the design apparent in the celestial sphere. Both Emerson and Ammons appeal to the "sky of law" as a model for inner strength, order, grace.[31]

Emerson, of course, began *Nature* by encouraging a solitary walk beneath the night sky: "If a man would be alone, let him look at the stars. . . . One might think the atmosphere was made transparent with this design, to give man, in the heavenly bodies, the perpetual presence of the sublime."[32] Ammons, at the very conclusion of his book-length poem *Sphere*, also appeals to his reader to look up—at the planets, those huge "stars" still the source of sublime transcendence. Ammons's description of the planets obeying "holy roads" corroborates Emerson's statement in "Astronomy" of some 150 years ago, that "investigations . . . have brought to light the most wonderful proofs of design— beneficent design—operating far and near in atoms and in systems, reaching to such prodigious extent both of time and space . . . that the mind cannot weigh them without ever increasing surprise and delight."[33] The late-twentieth-century poet of science, having lived through a time of unparalleled chaos, knows even more intensely how essential it is that the mind discover proper models of "surprise and delight."

He urges the reader to hear "the high ranges of music" so he or she can approximate the harmony, for Ammons knows that the lack of harmony between peoples and governments can now mean the end of the planet. As it has always been, the problem is too geocentric a point of view—which ultimately leads to a distortion of perspective, a misbelief that we are at the center of things. Emerson found in astronomy a cure for this ailment, for he knew, as the ancient and modern astronomer knew, that "an important result of the study of astronomy has been to . . . humble our view of ourselves."[34] Ammons too appeals to the cosmic awareness astronomy cultivates in the observer. The coexistence of different cultures ultimately depends on each developing an astronomy of statecraft, an appreciation for their interconnectedness.

Ammons converts the earth into a symbol of unity and diversity, "with commonlode center and variable surface." He pursues the analogy vigorously, linking the earth's surface uniqueness with the uniqueness of individual human forms, yet reminding us of a common underlying center. The coexistence of unity and variety, then, in the very structure of the earth should serve as a model to its inhabitants, too often forgetful (with dire consequences) of the unity that does in fact underlie diversity. Ammons has discovered moral truths in the facts of geology and astronomy, using them, as Emerson himself would, to inspire an inward revolution, a rotation of the mind toward greater harmony.

If Ammons shares with Emerson a penchant for looking up, for exercising distance vision, it is with Thoreau that he shares an equal propensity for looking down—for inspecting closely the flora of the earth. Thoreau's writings testify to the truth he stated in his review of the "Natural History of Massachusetts": "Nature will bear the closest inspection; she invites us to lay our eye level with the smallest leaf, and take an insect view of its plain."[35] Ammons has responded to this invitation.

The small and seemingly insignificant became more important to Ammons after he moved from North Carolina—with its open vistas—to Millville, New Jersey, where the landscape did not invite the eye to engage so freely in distance vision. Of this shift in locale Ammons says that, "after readjusting my vision to look for small things, I found very beautiful indeed and became very much attached to the shore and land there."[36] "Kind," one of many fable poems where Ammons engages Nature in dialogue (in this instance in the form of a redwood), teaches the value of searching for the small and humble. The redwood cannot understand the poet, who would rather stoop in the hidden recesses of the woods than look up at the majestic tree.

> I can't understand it
>   said the giant redwood
>   I have attained height and distant view,
>   am easy with time,
>
>   and yet you search the
>   wood's edge
> for weeds
> that find half-dark room in margins
>   of stone
>   and are
> as everybody knows
>   here and gone in a season
>
>   O redwood I said in this matter
> I may not be able to argue from reason

but preference sends me stooping
seeking
   the least,
   as finished as you
   and with a flower

(CP, 188)

Ammons's response reveals the secret of the naturalist-poet, who knows that beauty manifests itself in many ways, often in overlooked places, and that one must be alert to the small as well as the large. Even the most humble weed offers its pleasures. Ammons's willingness to entertain the small, the detailed, even the microscopic, aligns him with Thoreau, who "had an eye to the unfrequented nooks and corners of the farm."[37]

Given Ammons's intense love of the rural, it is surprising that more has not been said of his similarities to Thoreau, who also shares his intense love of the woods and the countryside. When asked in an interview to pick a time in history in which to live, Ammons responded, "It would be about the early nineteenth century in America." He went on to explain why:

> I think of America when it was rural . . . the village rural community without cars or that kind of transportation . . . with horses and streams and a nearly pure environment of streams and sky. It must have been very beautiful.[38]

The rural village Ammons describes sounds like it might be found in a Cooper novel, say *The Pioneers*. By the time of Thoreau, however, that very pure village environment had been disturbed, and Thoreau felt compelled to move beyond the village in search of still greater purity. Ammons too seems compelled to move beyond the restrictions of the town to a more rural vista, although Ammons for the most part does not travel as far into the back country as Thoreau did, often making his discoveries in his own backyard. Ammons's attraction to nature derives in part from his childhood experience, where as a young boy he lived on the family farm in Whiteville, North Carolina. Of his grammar school years, Ammons says:

> It was a time of tremendous economic and spiritual privation, even loneliness. . . . But all this privation was compensated for by a sense of the eternal freshness of land itself. So I substituted for normal human experience, which was unavailable to me much of the time, this sense of identity with the things around me.[39]

This "sense of identity" with the environment is manifested in Ammons's work in many ways, from his talking to mountains and trees to his visual encounters and records of outdoor life. What William Ellery Channing said of Thoreau—"the walk with him was for work"—could also be said of Ammons, whose circulations in and around Ithaca, New York, provide him with the subject matter for many of his poems. Ammons's retreat to nature, like Thoreau's, is also motivated by a desire to escape the meanness of humanity. In "Resort" he emphasizes the "regenerative" nature of Nature in contrast to the "fang & fury" of humanity:

> Beautiful nature,
> say
> the neuter lovers
>
> escaping
> man / woman nature,
> man
>
> fierce competitive,
> woman
> taunting
>
> treacherous:
> regenerative nature,
> they say
>
> fingering the cool
> red-dotted lichen
> on an old
>
> water-holding
> stump:
> sweet neutrality,
>
> a calm love where
> man and woman
> are fang & fury.

(CI, 20)

For A. R. Ammons, as for Henry David Thoreau, nature is a "resort" in the sense that it is a way out of "man / woman nature," competition, all the treachery of the human social sphere. Nature is the last "resort" in that it provides relief not found elsewhere, a place where we re-sort priorities and discover a new relation to the universe. However, it is also a way into a field of pleasure, regeneration, and wisdom—a "resort" one goes to for relaxation and entertainment. It can also be, as it was for Emerson, a source of perpetual youth:

> In the woods is perpetual youth. Within these plantations of God a decorum and sanctity reign, a perennial festival is dressed, and the guest sees not how he should tire of them in a thousand years. . . . Standing on the bare ground—my head bathed by the blithe air, and uplifted into infinite space—all mean egotism vanishes.[40]

The disappearance of egotism and boundaries prompts the "neuter lovers" of Ammons's poem to spend their time "fingering the cool / red-dotted lichen." Although there is a hint of a mocking gesture toward these so-called neuter lovers, the gesture is also playful and self-mocking. After all, A. R. Ammons, like Thoreau before him, spends much of his time as a neuter lover. His poems reach out to an "old / water-holding / stump." They embrace that "calm love and sweet neutrality" which make nature attractive to the poet. In contrast, Ammons portrays humanity— both man and woman—as "fierce" and "taunting." In the final image of the poem, he likens humanity to the vicious and the violent—both "fang" and "fury." Ammons starkly contrasts the world of the naturalist with the world of social interaction, and we are left with the rationale for his own turning to nature. Thoreau, who in his life even more intensely than Ammons turned his back on humanity, also found in society "fang" and "fury." The most striking example of this occurs in his comment on the ant battle described in *Walden*. Closely observing two of the more ferocious combatants, Thoreau writes:

> The smaller red champion had fastened himself like a vise to his adversary's front, and through all the tumblings on that field never for an instant ceased to gnaw at one of his feelers near the root, having already caused the other to go by the board; while the stronger black one dashed him from side to side, and, as I saw on looking nearer, had already divested him of several of his members. They fought with more pertinacity than bulldogs. Neither manifested the least disposition to retreat. It was evident that their battle cry was "Conquer or die."[41]

After continuing to describe in great detail the gruesomeness of the battle, Thoreau ironically comments: "I was myself excited somewhat even as if they had been men. The more you think of it, the less the difference."[42] Although Thoreau finds "fang" and "fury" in nature, more characteristically, like Ammons's neuter lovers, he can be found fingering lichen, recording the discovery of some new plant, or sounding the depths of the pond, all of which provide relief, solace, and enlightenment.

Not surprisingly, both Ammons and Thoreau have been criticized as being too coldly detached from humanity. Even Walt Whitman, whom Thoreau visited on occasion, was reported by Herbert Gilchrist to have said:

> I liked Thoreau, though he was morbid. I do not think it was so much a love of woods, streams, and hills that made him live in the country, as from a morbid dislike of humanity. I remember Thoreau saying once, when walking with him in my favourite Brooklyn—"What is there in the people? Pshaw! what do you (a man who sees as well as anybody) see in all this cheating political corruption?" I did not like my Brooklyn spoken of in this way.[43]

Ammons has had to answer similar charges. In an interview with Ammons, Cynthia Haythe asks him: "How would you reply to those reviewers who accuse you of being a cold poet?" Ammons does not deny the accusation but offers this advice to his readers:

> I would say they're right. There is an aspect of my work that's defensive. I should appear cold to almost anyone on first contact with my work. But it seems to me the more of the work they know, the more it returns to them, the more another nature—welcoming and generous, I think—would begin to emerge.[44]

It is this other "nature," both "welcoming" and "generous," that links Ammons and Thoreau. Both exhibit an intense interest in natural objects and in natural occurrences. And, as we have learned from Whitehead, this interest formed a common bond between the man of science and the poet. Emerson, however, had questioned this alliance, for observation of the "simple, immediate facts," an activity that had characterized eighteenth-century science, too often resulted in fragmentation, in partial knowledge, in what he called only "a half." Both Thoreau and Ammons are aware of the Emersonian critique of overly analytical perception, and to a large extent overcome this problem through seeing correspondences. Yet unlike Emerson, each is willing to surrender to the literal fact. Just as significantly, both Thoreau and Ammons present the readers with *deeper* ways of seeing the natural world—both through what Thoreau called the natural eye and through the lenses of science.

Thoreau, in characterizing his own activity, often accents the visual component. Toward the beginning of *Walden* he informs us: "For many years I was self-appointed inspector of snow-storms, and did my duty faithfully, surveyor, if not of highways, then of forest paths and all across-lot routes." He goes on to remark: "I have had an eye to the unfrequented nooks and corners of the farm."[45] The activity of surveying seems remarkably appropriate in describing the activity of both Ammons and Thoreau. For a good surveyor must have a good eye—must be adept at gauging distance. The sheer number of passages in *Walden* that begin with Thoreau sighting some natural event—("In the morning I *watched* the geese from the door"; "I *observed* a very slight and graceful hawk"; "While I was *surveying*, the ice, which was sixteen inches thick, undulated under a slight wind like water")—is evidence of just how important the visual sense was to him.[46] The keenness of his perception was not lost upon those who observed him. Emerson spoke of his "strong, serious, blue eyes," which "could estimate the measure of a tree very well."[47]

In his biographical sketch, Emerson described a higher kind of seeing, whereby Thoreau "referred every minute fact to cosmical laws."[48] William Ellery Channing echoed Emerson when he said of Thoreau that "he observed nature, yet not for the sake of nature, but of man."[49] Yet Channing and Emerson qualified their view of Thoreau as a symbolist. Channing, in his chapter entitled "Nature," elaborates on Thoreau's obsession with "complete accuracy" and writes that, "the particular and definite were much to Thoreau," implying that the facts themselves may have been sufficient.[50] Emerson too described Thoreau as a naturalist, "who knew the country like a fox or a bird."[51]

These dual tendencies manifest in Thoreau's 1837 journal entries. On December 16, 1837, Thoreau wrote, "how indispensable to a correct study of Nature is a perception of her true meaning. The fact will one day flower out into a truth."[52] The notion that facts would indeed blossom into something more, into the kinds of truths that Emerson thought they should, prompted Thoreau in his review of the "Natural History of Massachusetts" to criticize the volumes as being *merely* a compendium of facts. Yet in the same month Thoreau himself praised Goethe for "giving an exact description of objects as they appear to him," whereby "even the reflections of the author do not interfere with his descriptions."[53]

According to Perry Miller, Thoreau had early in his career "comprehended one of the major problems of the Romantic movement . . . of striking and maintaining the delicate balance between object and reflection, of fact and truth, of minute observation and generalized concept."[54] These two tendencies—to discover in facts moral truths and, at the same time, to record the facts in and for themselves—are closely aligned with two different ways of perceiving the world. In the first instance one looks at objects always with an eye for their relationship to the perceiver. In the second instance one sees the concrete and the specific vividly and sympathetically but does not feel compelled to relate the facts to their observer. These two modes of seeing in turn yield two different modes of discourse—metaphoric and literal, or subjective and objective description.

The writer who constantly perceives analogy in Nature expresses relationship between the self and Nature through metaphor. The writer who abandons the self for the world is no longer primarily concerned with analogy, but is he is more concerned with a faithful, substantive, and literal rendering of the truth. What Emerson objected to, and what Thoreau himself cautioned against in the later journal entries, was an extreme form of the literal mode of seeing and expression. In September 1851, Thoreau writes: "I must walk more with free senses. It is as bad to study stars and clouds as flowers and stones."[55] He is in essence reminding himself not to get locked into too narrow a mode of perception.

In most of his writings Thoreau manages to walk a very thin line between the two different modes of perception and discourse. We are treated to passages that begin with literal seeing and in the process are transformed into discoveries of the most striking interior truth. But Thoreau is also very much a naturalist, and his literal descriptions of the facts are oftentimes as striking as his metaphoric passages.

Perhaps the most memorable example of Thoreau's analogy-perceiving mind at work occurs at the end of *Walden*. He begins the passage with a simile: "The life in us is like the water in the river." Typically, he amplifies the simile, enriching it through explanation: "It may rise this year higher than man has known it, and flood the parched uplands; even this may be the eventful year, which will drown out all our muskrats." Yet this is only the prelude to a greater metamorphosis. Continuing, Thoreau presents the reader with an account of a bug's history, from being deposited as an egg in a tree to being hatched from a leaf of a table in a farmer's kitchen. Then, in a single sentence, Thoreau converts the material fact of the bug's hatching into a spiritual sign, asking: "Who does not feel his faith in a resurrection and immortality strengthened by hearing of this?" He then develops the analogy by describing the process of rebirth as it might unfold in a person's life:

> Who knows what beautiful and winged life, whose egg has been buried for ages under many concentric layers of woodenness in the dead dry life of society, deposited at first in the alburnum of the green and living tree, which has been gradually converted into the semblance of its well-seasoned tomb,—heard perchance gnawing out now for years by the astonished family of man, as they sat round the festive board,—may unexpectedly come forth from amidst society's trivial and handselled furniture, to enjoy its perfect summer life at last![56]

Here then is the mythopoeic nature of Thoreau's mind at work. He not only perceives a ray of relation between the bug's miraculous journey and man's possibilities for a "beautiful and winged life," but he also renders point by point the process for both insect and man. In the first instance, he describes that process literally, drawing on his knowledge of trees and insects. Then, after the pivotal question, he describes the process metaphorically; the concentric layers of the tree become "the dead dry leaf of society."

Walden's conclusion is but one example of Thoreau the analogist at work. Throughout that work he discovers the universal in the particular, as when he asserts that "the phenomena of the year take place in a pond on a smaller scale," or when he discovers "that this one hillside illustrated the principle of all the operations of Nature."[57] Yet Thoreau also operated in a different mode, a mode of perception and rhetoric that did not treat all of Nature as a symbol but rather yielded to the rainbow, or the pickerel, or even the pond, without reflection or contemplation.

In *A Week on the Concord and Merrimack Rivers, Walden, The Maine Woods,* and *Excursions,* we find the writings of a man who spent his life wandering outdoors and who, as a result, vivified that world through language as no other American writer had. Time after time, as in the long descriptions of fish at the beginning of *A Week* or in the surveying passages of *Walden,* Thoreau presents to the reader arresting descriptions of the natural world without circling back to the self. In these passages Thoreau does not strive for the symbolic; rather, he strives to capture through exact and sympathetic description the natural world he observed so patiently and accurately. Because the fineness of his sentences matched the fineness of his perceptions, we are ready to agree with him that "a true account of the actual is the rarest poetry."[58]

Even the common perch takes on a luster in Thoreau's description: "The common perch, *Perca flavescens*, which name describes well the gleaming, golden reflections of its scales as it is drawn out of the water, its red gills standing out in vain in the thin element, is one of the handsomest and most regularly formed of our fishes. . . . "[59] Thoreau, the naturalist, is unafraid of the Latin names of things—the sound of which suggests the image of what it is he describes.

As his essay on "The Succession of Forest Trees" also indicates, Thoreau was comfortable in this descriptive style. His primary concern in that essay is to explain how a "single forest tree or a forest springs up naturally where none of its kind grew before."[60] The clarity of his presentation and the breadth of his knowledge illustrate just how seriously he took his work as a naturalist.

Thoreau worked as a surveyor and studied in his leisure plants, insects, trees, and animals. It was only natural that his practical knowledge should find its way into his books. In "The Pond in Winter" chapter of *Walden*, he explains in a long factual discourse the process of determining the pond's depth.

As I sounded through the ice I could determine the shape of the bottom with greater accuracy than is possible in surveying harbors which do not freeze over, and I was surprised at its general regularity. In the deepest part there are several acres more level than any field which is exposed to the sun, wind, and plow. In one instance, on a line arbitrarily chosen, the depth did not vary more than one foot in thirty rods; and generally, near the middle, I could calculate the variation for each one hundred feet in any direction beforehand within three or four inches.[61]

Who is talking here, surveyor or symbolist nature poet? Or is it both? The information appears to be factual; the voice is impersonal. In one sense we are listening to the record of a man concerned only with facts. Yet at the end of this long passage on measuring the depth of a pond, Thoreau the transcendentalist comments: "What I have observed of the pond is no less true in ethics."[62] The analogist, who rides on facts "as the horses of thought,"[63] develops an elaborate conceit, suggesting that the method for discovering the point of greatest depth in a pond be applied to gauging the depth of a person's character:

> Such a rule of the two diameters not only guides us toward the sun in the system and the heart in man, but draw lines through the length and breadth of the aggregate of a man's particular daily behaviors and waves of life into his coves and inlets, and where they intersect will be the height or depth of his character.[64]

Now the surveyor's method takes on a rich new resonance. Perhaps Thoreau's rhetorical strategy from the outset was to prepare the reader for the conceit that followed the surveyor's description. Nevertheless, one would have to be quite dull not to appreciate the literal accuracy and descriptive beauty of the factual material that preceded the figurative passage.

Thoreau seems to alternate between the mode of the naturalist—seeing with the eye that surrenders itself to detailed observation of phenomena—and the mode of the Emersonian transcendentalist—always looking with an eye for relationships. Sometimes, as in the passages just discussed, the description by the naturalist precedes the description by the transcendentalist. At other times the reverse is true. Often the two modes interact so that within a single passage we get literal description and then sudden metaphoric transformation. It is no wonder that we find both types of perception operative in Thoreau, who, after all, described himself as a "mystic, a transcendentalist, and a natural philosopher to boot."[65]

The same could be said of A. R. Ammons. Like Thoreau, he possesses an uncanny mastery of the names of plants and animals, and a vast array of technical knowledge gleaned from his readings in astronomy, geology, biology, and other sciences. In his poems he often surrenders himself to the objects of his perception, dazzling the reader—sometimes with an account of the actual, at other times with his array of facts. But Ammons, like Thoreau, often stands back to comment on his perceptions, to place in a larger context the interior truth of what it is he is seeing. And like Thoreau, one cannot always be sure whether Ammons is in the literalist mode or the metaphoric, whether he is after the facts or some transcendental truth they point to.

Ammons's short poem "Transducer" is a good example of the thin margin this poet sometimes creates between recording the facts and craftily employing them for some greater truth. On first reading, "Transducer" seems purely a description of solar activity without comment or broader significance other than to call attention to an interesting phenomenon:

>Solar floes
>big as continents
>plunge rasping
>against each other:
>the noise
>flaring into space,
>into thinner & thinner
>material means
>becomes two million
>degrees of heat.

(CP, 240)

Here he presents a description of solar prominences; the collision of these giant arcs of gaseous materials results in "flaring." It is true that Ammons moves beyond the literal in his description of this phenomenon, comparing the prominences to "floes" and likening their size (some of which have been recorded as 205,000 miles high, almost the distance from the earth to the moon) to that of continents. But initially it seems that Ammons does not try to tie the event to some interior truth, nor does there appear to be a transcendental story in the collision that occurs. Instead, we are informed about one kind of solar phenomenon, where energy is transduced, that is, converted from one form to another. On first reading, Ammons's poem rests in its record of the facts and its appeal largely depends on how interesting we find the phenomenon and his record of it.

Upon further reflection, however, the title of the poem and Ammons's poetic engagement with the phenomenon yields some interesting truths. "Transducers" are "various substances or devices, as a piezoelectric crystal or a photoelectric cell, *that convert input energy of one form into output energy of another.*"[66] In the context of the poem, the kinetic energy of the gigantic solar prominences ("transducers") is transformed into heat energy. In another sense, Ammons himself acts as a *transducer*—his record of the event transforms the physical energy of the phenomenon into the verbal energy of the poem. The event in nature reflects the very kind of activity the poet-scientist engages in as he attempts to bring "things and feelings into manageable relationships."[67] As a *transducer,* he transforms his observations of the laws of nature into poems.

Solar prominences are recorded by radio telescopes, which are sensitive enough to detect the radioactivity of these gaseous arcs. The "rasping" Ammons describes and the "noise" he alludes to would be detected only by such a telescope, and either directly (through firsthand experience) or indirectly (through reading about it) he has availed himself of this knowledge, thus extending the range of his own vision and ours through this relatively new technology. In this instance, the radio telescope, of course, does not enable one to literally *see* farther and clearer, as many other kinds of telescopes do. Instead, it enables its listener to learn about the universe through reception of radio waves from outer space. The radio telescope and similar kinds of high technology seem in effect to reduce the visual, turning reality into mathematical patterns of sound and echo data. Ammons, however, takes these data and re-creates the physical phenomena for the reader.

In "Essay on Poetics," Ammons exhibits even more intensely his interest in the factual when he describes tree pollination. His description matches Thoreau's accuracy and concreteness in "The Succession of Forest Trees." After first considering the seeds of an elm seed, Ammons moves on to the shape and spin of a maple tree seed and then on to the simple dandelion:

> there's the maple seed's oar-wing:
> it spins too
> (simply, on an ordinary day)
> but in a gust can glide broadside:
>
> (dandelion seeds in a head are
> noted for their ability to become detached
> though attached:
> with a tiny splint-break
> the wind can have a bluster of them:
> the coming fine of an intimation):

(CP, 307)

In these passages, like those recording his attempt to measure the weight of an elm tree's leaves, Ammons's detailed observation illustrates a firm grasp of botany. But Ammons notes at the end of this section of the poem that his records are merely "facts, one-sided extensions," and "are hampered by being ungreat poetry" (CP, 307). The implication is that the facts themselves do not ultimately interest us enough, do not captivate us, do not plumb the depths of our imaginative capabilities. That may indeed be true. Ammons, like Thoreau, has been criticized for being too much of a literalist, too interested in the scientific fact and not enough in its imaginative potential.[68] But in trying to gauge an elm tree, or in considering how its seeds are carried by the wind, Ammons has proved that "a book may be written on the interpenetrations of / appearance of an elm tree" (CP, 307). Despite Ammons's own reservations about his inexhaustible descriptions of leaves and seeds and branches in "Essay on Poetics," and despite the condemnation of some critics, he has persisted in this mode over the course of his career.

While these examples illustrate Ammons's surrender to the purely factual, which can mean literal scientific fact or, as discussed here, sympathetic observation without constructing analogies, Ammons does readily assume the role of the transcendentalist. We see Ammons again putting facts to metaphysical use at the conclusion of his poem "Essay on Poetics." Here Ammons appeals to biological models of integration, contemplating the similarity of their structure and the structure of poems. The entire thrust of this section is to find significant relationship between scientific fact and poetry, to ultimately provide a rationale for the study of poetry itself. Throughout the poem Ammons has been concerned with the "one:many mechanism"; earlier he declared "the main confluence / is one:many which all this essay is about" (CP, 300).

As the poem builds to its conclusion, Ammons looks to make a final statement about poetics. Surprisingly, he inserts in the poem two prose passages from scientific texts. The first passage, from Robert Miller's book The Sea, describes how worms and other small organisms—"amoebas, flagellates, bacteria, or even filterable viruses"—have developed the ability to reduplicate small parts "permitting increase in size with completely coordinated function."[69] In the context of the "one:many" confluence, the segments (many) of worms result in a highly adaptable organism (the one). Ammons himself might have observed, like the author of the passage he quotes, that "it is hard to develop enthusiasm for worms, but it took nature more than a billion years to develop a good worm—meaning one that has specialized organs for digestion, respiration, circulation of the blood and excretion of wastes."[70] The appreciation for structure and mechanism, the subtle humor derived from contemplating an unlikely hero (the worm), the attentiveness to the small and the detailed, are all characteristic of Ammons's work.

What most appeals to Ammons about worms is their integration of one and many. This integration can be found in other living systems, and Ammons quotes from *The Science of Botany* a passage on the constituents of living matter, worth reproducing in its entirety because of the lucidity with which it describes biological manifestation of the one:many confluence.

> We may sum up. Carbohydrates, fats, proteins, nucleic acids, and their various derivatives, together with water and other inorganic materials, plus numerous additional compounds found specifically in particular types of living matter—these are the molecular bricks out of which matter is made. To be sure, a mere random pile of such bricks does not make a living structure, any more than a mere pile of real bricks makes a house. First and foremost, if the whole is to be living, the molecular components must be organized into a specific variety of larger microscopic bodies; and these in turn, into actual, appropriately structured cells.[71]

Here then is a description of the "building blocks" of creation, noting that a principle of organization is necessary for a whole to emerge from many parts. The biological observation of structure yields a hierarchical picture—in each instance parts come together to form larger wholes that ultimately produce holistic function. Ammons's inclusion of these passages from scientific texts in his long poem about "poetics" is indeed a measure of how deeply he is immersed in his scientific materials. Of interest here is the ray of relation Ammons discovers between these facts and "poetics," the stated subject of his poem. As he explains it, "poems are verbal / symbols for these organizations" (CP, 314). The poem, like the worm, like living matter itself, exhibits a "one:many" confluence:

> they imprint upon the mind
> examples of integration in which the energy flows with maximum

> effect and economy between the high levels of oneness and the
> numerous subordinations and divisions of diversity:
>
> (CP, 314–15)

The component parts of a poem work together in a fashion similar to the component parts of living systems. Ammons knows that "each part can, while insisting on / its own identity, contribute to the whole" (CP, 315). The flow between the whole poem and its individual parts is parallel to the flow of energy between a living system and its individual parts.

This flow, as it turns out, is the flow of life itself, for living matter depends upon the smooth and harmonious interaction between its many parts and the whole system. Blood must be circulated; waste must be eliminated. The "life-blood" of a poem also depends upon the life-giving force of its components—in turn the circulation of energy from the whole poem back to its supporting and discrete entities helps to energize them. In this extended and unusual conceit Ammons moves beyond the merely factual to contemplate some greater truth.

He then goes one step further, to explain in what may seem a very uncontemporary, even banal, gesture why poems should be taught: "they are convenient examples / of the supreme functioning of one and many in an organization of / cooperation and subordination" (CP, 315). Metaphor, simile, assonance, and rhythm all cooperate and yet subordinate themselves to the whole, just as fats, proteins, and nucleic acids cooperate and subordinate themselves to the living system they support. The "young," and we can presume the middle-aged and the elderly, need to be exposed to poems both because they provide a useful model of cooperation and because, when well executed, they produce the experience of pleasure at some deep level of the mind. Ammons has moved beyond the factual accounts of the one:many confluence and taken them deep into the mind, discovering in the poem an archetype of ideal organization ("mechanism") also manifested in nature.

If it still remains true, as Emerson once believed, that "our American character is marked by a more than average delight in accurate perception,"[72] then it would be fair to conclude that both Thoreau and Ammons are distinctly American. Ammons, like Thoreau, looks with the eye of the naturalist, observing and collecting facts throughout the body of his work and producing startling poetry as a result of his detailed observations. But Ammons, like Thoreau, is also cognizant of the limitations of the merely factual, of the danger "in forming too exact habits of observation." We shall see in the next chapter that Ammons shares Thoreau's "remedy" for this—"a free sauntering of the eye."[73] In addition to giving free rein to perception, Ammons, again like Thoreau, balances and corrects the tendency to focus too narrowly by seeing with the inner eye of the transcendentalist, discovering metaphysical truths in his observations and in the scientific materials he draws upon. This other kind of seeing, however, which Emerson perhaps would call "higher," always begins for Thoreau and Ammons with their literally looking out—often at the small or "microscopic"—and then seeing more deeply into the object of perception.

In encouraging the reader to see the world anew and in exercising vision in the most comprehensive manner, Walt Whitman anticipated the work of A. R. Ammons. Ammons, like Whitman, hopes to encourage in his readers broader scope and what Ammons calls a greater "openness" to experience.

Inasmuch as science widens our "sight of things" through sense-extending instruments like the telescope, broadens our understanding of nature through new discoveries, and provides analogies for deeper understanding of the self, Whitman and Ammons embrace it heartily. Neither poet expresses as many reservations as Emerson and Thoreau do in their comments on scientific thought and perception. Although Ammons in his long poem "Extremes and Moderations" deplores the technological devastation of the American environment, wrought indirectly by the advance of science, and Whitman in *Specimen Days* cautions against seeing too precisely ("You must not know too much, or be too precise or scientific about birds and trees and flowers")[74], neither Whitman nor Ammons hesitates to incorporate in his poetic vision the discoveries of science.

The extent to which nineteenth-century astronomy, chemistry, physics, and evolutionary theory find their way into *Leaves of Grass* has been well documented by Joseph Beaver in his book *Walt Whitman—Poet of Science*.[75] The extent to which evolutionary and ecological science finds its way into Ammons's verse has, at least in an initial way, been documented by Philip Fried.[76] It is not my purpose here to reduplicate their efforts but rather to suggest how both Whitman's and Ammons's thinking about science affects their verse and vision.

Fried suggested that Ammons incarnates the future poet Whitman described in *Democratic Vistas*, the poet who would produce a literature "consistent with science." He writes, for example, that Ammons "is following in Whitman's footsteps when he borrows ideas from evolution and ecology."[77] True enough. Yet in tracing evolution and ecology in Ammons's poems, Fried does not develop the comparison of Ammons to Whitman. What does this twentieth-century visionary poet-scientist share with his Romantic forebear, and in what ways do they diverge?

In his 1855 Preface, Whitman struck the tone of relations be-

tween poet and scientist that future American poets would have
to respond to. He writes:

> Exact science and its practical movements are no checks on the great-
> est poet but always his encouragement and support. . . . The sailor
> and traveller . . . the anatomist, chemist, astronomer, geologist, phre-
> nologist, spiritualist, mathematician, historian, and lexicographer
> are not poets, but they are the lawgivers of poets and their construc-
> tion underlies the structure of every perfect poem. . . . If there shall
> be love and content between the father and the son and if the great-
> ness of the son is the exuding of the greatness of the father there
> shall be love between the poet and the man of demonstrable science.
> In the beauty of poems are the tuft and final applause of science.[78]

Being a builder of bridges between peoples and continents,
Whitman included in his architecture of unity a strong link between the man of science and the poet. In order to prove that "the
anatomist, chemist, astronomer . . . are the lawgivers of poets,"
Whitman engaged in self-designed studies of these various fields.
He records in his early notebooks his own zeal to familiarize
himself with many sciences, encouraging himself "to read the
latest and best anatomical works. Talk with physicians. Study
the anatomical plates."[79] We read in Harold Aspiz's book *Walt
Whitman and the Body Beautiful* that if he had not been a poet,
Whitman would have become a physician, for that vocation
would have presented him with an ideal opportunity to integrate
objective knowledge with "emotional elements."[80]

Whereas Whitman's knowledge of anatomy was the result of
self-study, Ammons's scientific education, which includes college studies in chemistry, biology, and other sciences, is more
formal. Yet Ammons too is an independent reader of scientific
texts. However they may have come to their anatomical knowledge, both men in their evocations of bodily structure exhibit an
exactness of detail that in all likelihood would win the admiration of the anatomists of their day.

In addition to emphasizing his own willingness to draw on
scientific material for his poetry, Whitman's 1855 statement also
highlights the *love* he himself felt for the man of science and
the love that should be expressed between all future poets and
scientists. This was essential to Whitman's poetic program of
creating a new, more modern, more democratic and American
expression. Empiricism, for example, naturally appealed to
Whitman, the great experimenter, who was an intense observer
of the world around him and who, like the great early scientists,

upset conventional patterns of thought. To achieve a revolution
in verse, he would have to incorporate the latest in science,
which after all displaced the old with the new. In *Democratic
Vistas*, he outlined "a new founded literature," which would act
as a tonic for the stupor of an America gone sour, "a literature
underlying life, religious, consistent with science, handling the
elements and forces with competent power."[81]

What would this new literature "consistent with science" be
like? Whitman's own poetry is one of the best responses we have
to that question. His poems abandon standard iambic pentameter
in favor of longer, looser rhythms and line lengths. He forges
images, similes, and metaphors out of the facts of science. He
inveighs against authority, thus opening up truth to experimentation. These innovations helped to make his own verse consistent
with science—for often science too destroys old measures of the
world and questions previously untested authority. The ultimate
result of both science and his newly founded literature was to
free the average democratic person, as well as the future poets
of America, from the bondage of the past.

Ammons, like Whitman, feels love toward the scientist and
exhibits an accommodating vision, both flexible and broad
enough to embrace not only scientists, but also all other incarna-
tions of the modern American spirit. In section 125 of *Sphere* he
writes, "I want, like Whitman, to found / a federation of loveship"
including the "adman or cowboy, librarian or dope fiend, / house-
wife or hussy." When Ammons discovers that an astronaut is
writing poems, he cheers him on. The poet-astronaut is but another manifestation of the poet-scientist, who can integrate
things and feelings, and who can draw on both sides of the brain
to perform highly technical tasks and highly intuitive ones.

The love that Whitman and Ammons feel for science is based
on some very practical benefits they reap from it. First, Ammons,
like Whitman, discovers a rich new language in science. It was
Whitman who, in his *American Primer*, outlined the benefits of
encountering new fields of knowledge. He realized that "new
forms of science . . . may have something in them to need new
words."

> *Medicine* has hundreds of useful and characteristic words—new
> means of cure—new schools of doctors—the wonderful anatomy of
> the body—the names of a thousand diseases—surgeon's terms—hy-
> dropathy—all that relates to the great organs of the body.[82]

Whitman's magnetic attraction to the new words of medical science typifies the excitement he felt. This excitement was translated into the words that composed *Leaves of Grass*, which at the end of his career Whitman himself referred to as "only a language experiment." In section 9 of "I Sing the Body Electric," for example, the wonderful anatomy of the body is evoked by words that "relate to the great organs of the body"—"the lung-sponges, the stomach-sac, the bowels sweet and clean" (LOG, 100). This is but one instance among many where the words Whitman generated from his scientific readings found their way into his poems.

The most fundamental relationship, then, between the scientist and the poet was based on language itself. Whereas Whitman could write in the 1855 Preface that "in the beauty of true poems are the tuft and final applause of science," he would refine that statement in his poem "Song of the Answerer" to read "the words of true poems are the tuft and final applause of science" (LOG, 170). The fruition of science, then, was realized in the language of poetry. The same could in fact be said of A. R. Ammons's work, which draws on the vocabulary of science in an even more rigorous and extensive way than Whitman's to enrich its poetic diction.

In addition to supplying the poet with a rich new source of language, the scientist enables the poet to extend the scope of his considerations. Science uncovers laws of nature that poets turn into metaphors, opening up new vistas. Whitman defines love in terms of the law of gravity in "I Am He That Aches with Love"; he likens human evolution and progress to Newton's first law of motion in "Passage to India." Ammons subtly evokes the role of the poet as a "transducer" in his poem by that title, and in "Essay on Poetics" finds the one:many mechanisms of organisms parallel to the structure of poems.

As poets of science, Ammons and Whitman could not help but reflect the extensions of the visual sense science made possible in their respective centuries. F. O. Matthiessen, in *American Renaissance*, noted the extent to which vision in the nineteenth century had developed. He writes, "The special stress that the nineteenth century put on sight is evinced by some of its outstanding creations, the perfection of Herschel's telescope, the invention of photography, the development of open-air painting, the advancing power of the microscope."[83] Whitman, very much a man of his own time, as well as of ours, was inevitably influenced by these specific innovations and by the "visual" accent of the century.

The twentieth century in turn has further advanced the frontiers of the eye. The powers of the telescope have been amplified; new kinds of telescopes, like the "space telescope," have been developed; x-ray vision has been used in medical science to "photograph" the body in ways previously undreamed of. In addition to these technological extensions of vision, the science of behavioral optometry has arisen to correct and modify vision through developmental techniques. The art of photography that Matthiessen alludes to has been refined by the laser, and we now receive on our nightly news programs photographs from outer space. Advanced technologies for surveying the landscape from satellites have led to breakthroughs in anthropology and paleontology. The twentieth century, then, like the nineteenth, has witnessed a great emphasis on seeing—farther, clearer, more deeply. Whitman and Ammons respectively show a keen interest in particular developments within the field of vision and science. Whitman, for example, was fascinated by telescopes, and Ammons's poems reflect a firsthand knowledge of the more recent developments in astronomy.

Whitman's interest in astronomy was motivated by two related developments. The telescope, and the recordings made through it, enabled the poet, and indeed all Americans, to extend the range of their perceptions. Concomitantly, the poetic contemplation of the facts of astronomy would allow Whitman to develop in himself and in his readers the "cosmic perspective" that obsessed him throughout his life.

In "Salut Au Monde," after questioning himself: "What do you *see* Walt Whitman?" he replies:

> I see a great round wonder rolling through space,
> . . . .
> I see the shaded part on one side where the sleepers are sleeping, and the sunlit part on the other side.
>
> (LOG, 139)

Beaver has suggested that the verb "rolling" is used to conceive "of the two principal motions of the earth (rotation on its axis and revolution about the sun)."[84] The verb that interests me most, however, is the one that is repeated: "see." How is it that Whitman *sees* the earth in its cosmic perspective, as a planet revolving about the sun, half sunlit and half in shade? It may be, as Beaver has suggested, that Whitman's lines describe what the poet saw drawn commonly in nineteenth-century astronomy books. Or perhaps these lines were suggested to him by his visits to a planetarium. That Whitman typically sees the earth as it is seen here—in its astronomical perspective—is to suggest that its inhabitants are part of something grand. For when we begin to contemplate that our world is but one of many in a vast solar system, our sense of place expands. For Whitman, at least, the vastness of the solar system and the earth's position in it did not dwarf a person, but rather launched one into the vast unknown with all its wonder and beauty.

The precision and regularity of the earth's orbit elicits Whitman's wonder in "Who Learns My Lesson Complete?":

> It is no small matter, this round and delicious globe moving so
>   exactly in its orbit for ever and ever, without one jolt or the
>   untruth of a single second.
>
> (LOG, 394)

Whitman admires the regularity of the earth's orbit, just as Ammons does the orbits of all the planets in the concluding sections of *Sphere*. Ammons, in his twentieth-century rendition, encourages readers to attune their minds to the planets' "holy roads," in large measure so that they will approximate the greatness, harmony, and immortality Whitman admires of the earth. Moreover, Whitman's appreciation for the regularity of the earth's motion—it continually moves both in its orbit and on its axis "without one jolt"—reminds one of Ammons's "Spaceship," where the earth's regularity of motion is implicitly praised because it is the source of "equilibrium."

Ammons, like Whitman, also admires the principle of excellence manifest in the universe. He writes in section 62 of *Sphere* that "excellence, one of the forming principles of the universe, is ever radical"—it is radical because it is itself at the base and because it can reform the very *foundations* of the mind, providing coherent models of natural processes. Elsewhere in *Sphere*, Ammons echoes the sentiment Whitman expressed repeatedly in *Leaves of Grass*—that the manifestations of natural law are cause for wonder. Whitman expresses this sentiment thus in "Who Learns My Lesson Complete?"

> The great laws take and effuse without argument,
> I am of the same style, for I am their friend,
> I love them quits and quits, I do not halt and make salaams.
>
> (LOG, 394)

The nineteenth-century astronomer-poet characteristically admires the rectitude with which natural law expresses itself, and he links himself to the great laws by saying "I am of the same style." He does not bow down to them because in a very real sense he is (as an expression of the laws of biology, anatomy, chemistry) the great laws. Ammons expresses a similar appreciation for natural law in section 57 of Sphere. There he writes:

> when you come
> to know the eternal forces realizing themselves through form
> you will need to lay on no special determination to assent
>
> to what demands none
>
> (S, 36)

Like Whitman, Ammons admires both the rectitude and the wonder of "the eternal forces" ("the great laws") realizing themselves. Once we have knowledge of their realization through form (the planets, for example), an act of will ("special determination") is not required "to assent"—to approve and praise them. Like Whitman, Ammons also knows that the eternal laws demand nothing in return—no "salaams" please.

In his 1876 Preface "Leaves of Grass and Two Rivulets," Whitman emphasizes the "higher" function of science in his poems. Looking back on more than twenty years of work, he remarks: "Without being a scientist, I have thoroughly adopted the conclusions of the great Savans and Experimentalists of our time, and of the last hundred years, and they have interiorly tinged the chyle of all my verse, for purposes beyond."[85]

Whitman's digestive metaphor ("chyle") demonstrates how deeply science permeated his own thought and vocabulary. With the three words—"for purposes beyond"—he reaffirms the transcendental function of poetry infused with science. He explains further that modern poetry must give expression to the "vastness and splendor and reality with which Scientism has invested man and the Universe."[86] He challenges poetry to achieve what astronomy and the other sciences had accomplished—the expansion of our awareness of time, space, and self. Whitman seeks the total revivification of poetry through its attunement with the "Kosmic Spirit" he finds in nineteenth-century astronomy. Continuing on this theme he writes that modern poetry "must henceforth launch Humanity into new orbits, consonant with that vastness, splendor, and reality, (unknown to the old poems) like new systems of orbs, balanced upon themselves, revolving in limitless space, more subtle than the stars."[87] To launch the reader into new orbits, Whitman chose to mine images and concepts from nineteenth-century astronomy, physics, and geology to create a poetry that expresses the splendor of an expanding universe. In doing so, he established a legacy for poets to come. The enthusiasm he has for space and astronomy, however, has not been shared by all those who have come after him. I alluded in my introductory chapter to the difference between Whitman and Jeffers, the latter finding the space between the stars and the stars themselves neither comforting nor reassuring. We will see in chapter 4 that Robert Frost also recoils from the vast emptiness of the night sky. The enthusiasm Whitman has for the stars, however, is revived by Ammons, who follows his lead and mines twentieth-century astronomy for images and concepts in his attempt to launch humanity into new orbits. Ammons, who has access to a new set of facts made available by new, more powerful telescopes, discovers and makes use of the new "systems" Whitman alludes to. In Ammons a whole new set of astronomic phenomena is treated poetically—including novas, white dwarfs, the discoveries of new galaxies and stars, and recent theories concerning the evolution of the solar system.

Although I have emphasized the similarities between Whitman and Ammons, I do not mean to suggest that Ammons is a mere clone. Ammons, more frequently than Whitman, will contemplate the "downside" of astronomy—the emptiness, the wastefulness, the darkness of the heavens. These passages temper his Whitmanian transcendental enthusiasm. Although Whitman occasionally uses astronomy as a metaphor for his own inner anxieties, as he does in "Year of Meteors" when he compares himself to a meteor—"one equally transient and strange" (LOG, 238)—his accent, to be consistent with the self-confident persona he created in Leaves of Grass, is more often enthusiastic. Ammons, as a contemporary poet, must feel more pressure to moderate this tone occasionally if he is to be taken seriously. His contemplation of the waste and emptiness of stellar space may stem from his own uncertainties, but it also results in part from a necessity to present more than one perspective. On at least two occasions in Sphere Ammons feels the threat of meaninglessness derived from an astronomical perspective. In section 45, he evokes what appears to be our precarious position in the galaxy and "the extravagance of waste" manifest in planets either too hot or too atmospherically different to be habitable.

> we cooling here and growing on a far outswing

of the galaxy, the soaring, roaring sun in its thin-cool
texture allowing us, the moon vacant though visitable, Mars
not large enough to hold an air, Venus too hot, so much

extravagance of waste, how can the bluegreen earth look
purposeful, turn a noticeable margin to meaning:

(S, 30)

Here Ammons expresses dismay over the apparent wastefulness
in the cosmic design, leading him to wonder about the possibility
of meaning at all. The heaviness he feels here is later replaced
by an apperception of "freezing gulfs of darkness," not unlike
those he experienced as a child when his younger brother died.
He writes:

> it appears to those who have gone above our

atmosphere that the universe is truly a great darkness, light
in the minority, unsurrendered coals sprinkled in the thinnest
scattering, though, of course, light, even when seen from

afar, attracts the attention most: but out on the periphery
the lights are traveling so fast away their light can't get
back to us, darkness, in our dimension, finally victorious

in the separation:

(S, 72)

In these lines Ammons creates a very different feeling and view
than Whitman does when he describes himself "speeding with
tail'd meteors, throwing fire-balls like the rest." The impact of
Whitman's line, as Hope Werness has noted, is "excitement, the
expansive, bursting energy and absorption in swift cosmic
rhythms."[88] All this is muted by Ammons, who describes the
vision of those who have traveled above our atmosphere, where
one finds "light in the minority" and the stars appear to be fading
"coals," scattered in the vast darkness. Because these "coals" are
so distant from us and because their light cannot get back to us,
"darkness" seems to triumph. Yet this muting of the Whitmanian
vision is temporary, and by the end of the poem Ammons, like
Whitman, is ready to take off; he rejoices in the fact that the
earth floats—and our ride upon it "beats any amusement park
by the shore."

Ammons's subtle metaphor of the poetic process as one of *transduction*, whereby one kind of input energy (the facts of science) is transformed into a different kind of output energy, seems particularly apt when one thinks about how Whitman envisioned his relation to science. The poet is the transformer who endows the facts with a new *gloss*. One major result of the energy conversion will be an increased familiarity with scientific knowledge on the part of readers. Even William Wordsworth, much more hostile toward science than Whitman or Ammons, envisioned the poet as the "transducer" who would make chemistry familiar. In his Preface to *Lyrical Ballads*, he writes:

> The remotest discoveries of the Chemist, the Botanist, or Mineralogist, will be as proper objects of the Poet's art as any upon which it can be employed, if the time should ever come when these things should be familiar to us.[89]

For Whitman that time had quickly come to cast off the myths of the past and to integrate the discoveries of the present. Although his tone is more ecstatic than that of either Wordsworth or Ammons, he shares the notion that the poet alone is in a unique position to make the facts of science come alive—to *vivify* them—and thereby to endow life with new genius.

In today's era of unparalleled scientific explosion, Ammons writes in his editor's introduction to a *Chelsea* issue on science that "it is part of the result of a poem to personalize and familiarize, to ingest and acquaint—to bring feelings and things into manageable relationships."[90] This is more subdued, perhaps, than Whitman, who said in his 1855 Preface that poets should "indicate the path between reality and their souls." Ammons emphasizes the necessity of familiarizing us with modern science, of humanizing it, of making it less threatening by "ingesting" and "personalizing" it, all of which is essential if the average citizen and reader is to find some kind of reconciliation with an unquestionably scientific age. Although his tone is cooler than Whitman's, his goal more modest, he also sees the poet as the figure who can "transduce" the facts of science into something not only more manageable, but ultimately more illuminating.

The extent to which Ammons's poetry functions to modify

one's vision of the world will be the subject of the next two chapters. After analyzing how Ammons functions as a "vision therapist" in chapter 3, I will examine in the succeeding chapter how he further widens "scope" through his engagement with astronomy and biology.

3

Flex Your Eyes: Ammons's "Visual Calisthenics"

"Who knows the curious mystery of the eyesight?"
—Walt Whitman, 1855 Preface to *Leaves of Grass*

". . . there is no finality of vision."
—A. R. Ammons, "Corsons Inlet"

From his poetic annunciation in *Ommateum*, through the years of development when he wrote *Tape for the Turn of the Year* and *Corsons Inlet*, and in the subsequent books that were eventually compiled in *The Collected Poems 1951–1971*, A. R. Ammons has maintained a continuous fascination with vision. Much of Ammons's art stems from the keenly perceptive moment, the opening of vision to "events" and the subsequent rendering of events through language. Like Emerson before him, Ammons cherishes the hope that his work will enable the reader to "look at the world with new eyes."[1]

In his book *American Visionary Poetry*, Hyatt Waggoner reads Ammons as a visionary poet, that is, one whose poetry stems from "the act of seeing." Waggoner rightly places Ammons in the context of a tradition of poets whose work is generated primarily from the act of visual perception—from seeing the world "out there"—the phenomenal world that feeds the eyes, and through the eyes, the mind.[2]

Waggoner is careful to draw a distinction between the "visionary" who sees "better or farther, deeper or more truly, than we" and he who merely concocts, dreams, or hallucinates.[3] The visionary poet is not "mystical." The mystic's quest for an Absolute is inward—away from the immediately visible, in contrast

71

to Ammons, whose poems are energized by encounters with the world.

The major thrust and contribution of Waggoner's discussion is to reattach the word "visionary . . . to its root in vision—that is, at the most literal level, to the act of seeing, as in the expression he has 20/20 vision."[4] "Visionary" poems of the sort Waggoner describes depend upon how the poet literally ("physically") sees the world.

Research has replaced the old photographic model of vision with a more complex one. Vision is more than the ability of the eye to resolve detail—it is an act of cognition. What one sees is processed and interpreted in the brain. Waggoner quotes primarily theorists on this subject; however, behavioral optometrists have begun to apply this knowledge in their work with patients' vision. Dr. Richard Kavner, O.D., and Lorraine Dusky, in their important book *Total Vision*, succinctly summarize the significance of this latest research when they write that "what is perceived depends not only upon the nature of the object, but on the nature of the observer as well."[5] Kavner, a leading pioneer in contemporary vision therapy, explains that "our eyes are receptors of the brain. The eyes take in the data, channel them along neural impulses to the cortex, where the central control makes sense out of them and we see images."[6] Kavner adds that "the brain receives more sensory stimulation from the eyes than it does from any of our other senses."[7]

For behavioral optometrists like Kavner, the discovery that the eyes and the brain work together has had extremely practical implications, not the least of which is the treatment of visual problems through eye exercises. Kavner explains:

> . . . since vision is learned and occurs in the brain, to retrain (or recondition) that process we need to alter the environment, or the input. This could be done with a program of vision therapy that would guide what the eyes send to the visual cortex and eventually straighten out misperception. Then we could see better and understand more.[8]

The goal of vision therapy—to enable people to "see better and understand more"—coincides with one of the major goals of American visionary poets, perhaps first and best expressed by Emerson in his essay "The Poet." According to Emerson, the poet distinguished himself from others by his superior vision.

> As the eyes of Lyncaeus were said to see through the earth, so the poet turns the world to glass, and shows us all things in their right

series and procession. For, through that better perception, he stands one step nearer to things, and sees the flowing or metamorphosis.[9]

Ammons, whose poems trace nature's metamorphoses, works to fulfill Emerson's visionary aspirations for the poet. In the 1973 *Diacritics* interview, he describes heightened "focus" and "concentration" as the beneficial results of a visionary poem.

> To rehearse, to alert, to freshen, to awaken the energies, not to lunacy and meaningless motion, but to concentration and focus. That is the desirable state to which art should bring you, and to the extent that the poem becomes an image of this, and a generator of it, it is a desirable thing.[10]

Ammons's and previous visionary poets' insistence that poetry has the power to alter our perception of the world is analogous to the claim of behavioral optometrists that visual perception can be modified and enhanced. The subjective experience of feeling "more alive," "more keenly aware," "more perceptive," after reading a visionary poem may be enough evidence to suggest that it is influencing consciousness and the nervous system. The poet, like the behavioral optometrist, "alters the environment, or the input," by exposing the reader's attention to new and more significant patterns. In addition, both the visionary poet and the professional vision therapist share the goal of culturing for us "better, deeper, truer" perception.

Waggoner, who also has suggested that the visionary poet plays a therapeutic role, does not develop the implications of this role as it applies to Ammons. He discusses a few of Ammons's poems where the visual element is strong, but he barely touches on Ammons's motivation—to expand the poet's own scope and the visual scope of the reader. While Waggoner's hypothesis that visionary poets enable their readers to see better is correct, he falls short in his analyses of Ammons's poems of discussing *how* this is achieved.[11]

Ammons's technique of altering his readers' perceptions begins with opening himself up to the flow of natural "events" and then conveying the events in his poems. As Ammons describes them, the events function to break down rigidity in thought and perception. He states in an interview:

> The event in its power and unexpectedness is more material to be considered against the too narrow symmetry of a previous definition. What I try to do in my poems, essentially, is to resist my own obses-

sions and others', to dissolve those obsessions to some extent, and to replace them with a more complex, easy-going, tolerant mental scope.[12]

In attempting to resist his own obsessions, Ammons creates poems that unlock modes of perception and create a greater openness to the flow of experience itself. To achieve this, he repeatedly implores himself to move beyond "intellection," which is limiting and prone to a too "narrow symmetry." In *Tape for the Turn of the Year* he declares:

> I beg that my eyes that are
> open
> be opened, that the
>   drives, motions,
> intellections, symbologies,
> myths—lift,
>   expose me
> to direct
> sight:

                                                      (T, 34–35)

Ammons's desire may sound naive, for vision researchers have shown that there is no such thing as "direct," unmediated sight. Here, however, Ammons is primarily concerned with distinguishing "direct sight" from other kinds of cognitive processes ("intellections," "symbologies," "myths"). In his essay, "A Poem Is a Walk," Ammons writes: "Definition, rationality, and structure are ways of seeing, but they become prisons when they blank out other ways of seeing."[13] He distrusts philosophical abstractions that may "blind" us to certain truths or patterns.

His caution against "editorializing" in these lines from *Tape* sounds reminiscent of the early Imagists, who sought to eliminate "interference" between the world and their perception of it. Like the Imagists, Ammons seeks to liberate readers from conventional patterns of perception. He is not constrained by Imagist theory, however, the inconsistencies of which have been discussed by John Gage in his book, *In the Arresting Eye.*[14]

The Imagists believed objects triggered emotions in their perceiver. The poet's job was to find the "equation" to render the object "exactly" so the reader could experience the poet's initial emotion. Gage, building on the criticism of Kenneth Burke, describes this as "the fallacy of reciprocity." He writes, "our perceptions of feelings are not a function of the objects," as the Imagists

believed, "but a function of our own state of receptivity." Both
Burke and Gage conclude that "an image alone is insufficient to
control an emotion in a reader which is equivalent to that felt
by the poet who selected the image."[15]

For Ammons, the world is in too great a state of flux for it to
fit neatly into "equations." Reality is too slippery to be captured
in an "instant of time."[16] Ammons is also self-conscious in a way
that the Imagists were not about the "impositional remove" of
language from reality.[17] He is less prone to think that words can
"embody" things.[18] Instead, Ammons hopes to evoke the constant
flux in nature, inventing forms, especially in the long poems,
that accommodate maximum change.

In his poem "Clarity" he admires how a rockslide creates
new vision:

> After the event the rockslide
> realized,
> in a still diversity of completion,
> grain and fissure,
> declivity
> &
> force of upheaval,
> whether rain slippage,
> ice crawl, root
> explosion or
> stream erosive undercut:
>
> well I said it is a pity:
> one swath of sight will never
> be the same: nonetheless,
> this
> shambles has
> relieved a bind, a taut of twist,
> revealing streaks &
> scores of knowledge
> now obvious and quiet.

(CP, 274)

The poet here records the results of a subtle kind of metamorphosis achieved by forces that cause an entirely new visual configuration: "one swath of sight will never / be the same."
Although this particular change involves entropy and erosion
("a pity"), the poet finds his compensation in the results of the
transformation. In this instance, the rockslide, a "shambles," results in new discovery—"revealing streaks & / scores of knowl-

edge / now obvious and quiet." Surprisingly, "clarity" results from entropy, and knowledge is derived not from philosophical probing, but rather from the visual apperception of the discrete and the particular. The rockslide, in its power and unexpectedness, breaks the mold of a previous geological definition, and in that way functions as an "event" that is the source of new insight.

David Kalstone finds in "Clarity" an attempt by Ammons to give "visionary words like *clarity* a tumble." That is, "the poem deliberately belies its abstract title . . . scaling down the large questions of philosophy and romantic lyric to answers made possible by discrete and particular encounters."[19] These encounters are *visual*, and in "Clarity" the "scaling down" achieved is by virtue of a rearrangement in the visual field. Words like "clarity" and "knowledge," abstract and, according to Kalstone, "civilized" terms, receive new, more "earthy" meanings. "Knowledge" becomes "obvious" because it is visually apparent, literally on the surface, in this case on the earth's crust in the form of new patterns ("scores") of rock and dirt. This is not an ordinary or traditional definition of "knowledge," yet Ammons makes the reader discover it in the event of a rockslide.

While "clarity" is one of Ammons's poetic subjects, much of his work also attempts to correct nearsightedness. As a "vision therapist," there is good reason for Ammons's concern about myopia. Research shows that Americans are becoming increasingly myopic. Our vision of things has literally changed as the country has shifted from being agricultural to industrial to highly technological. According to Dr. Richard Kavner, a proponent of the near-work theory of myopia, "our eyes developed for long-distance viewing, to hunt and to farm, and not to spend hours staring at small marks on a page."[20] Today's occupations do not reward distance vision, as did the old tasks of farming and hunting. Instead, the kind of work that is most highly compensated in an information-based society requires intense concentration at nearpoint for long periods of time. Computer programmers, for example, must work for hours visually processing information at a very close range. Scientists, teachers, lawyers—all must spend hours each day, both while training for their professions and in its practice, reading, examining, and studying information at close range. The transition to an information age has been accompanied by a dramatic increase in nearsightedness.

According to the near-work theory, the effect of all this visual strain is directly experienced by the eye muscles. Kavner explains that:

> To see clearly at near-point, eye muscles strain to bring the focus together on the retina. Kept up for a long time, the muscles find a way to accommodate themselves to the job: they get locked into place. But then they lose the ability to loosen up when you want to look far afield—off into the distance—which is what the eye is more suited for.[21]

Much of Ammons's poetry is an attempt to reverse this process—to remind his reader to unlock the eye muscles so that they become less rigid, to loosen up vision so that one does not miss the "radiance" on the "periphery." His poem "Eyesight" is a parable of what can happen when one becomes too myopic. It is one of the many "fable poems" Ammons has written, where winds, mountains, or streams "talk" back to the poet. In this instance, the mountain teaches him something about sight.

> It was May before my
> attention came
> to spring and
>
> my word I said
> to the southern slopes
> I've
>
> missed it, it
> came and went before
> I got right to see:
>
> don't worry, said the mountain,
> try the later northern slopes
> or if
>
> you can climb, climb
> into spring: but
> said the mountain
>
> it's not that way
> with all things, some
> that go are gone

(CP, 388–89)

The poet has missed spring at the lower altitudes because he was simply unaware of it. Ammons does not explain why, but the title of the poem provides a clue. It signals, as do so many of his titles, that this is a lyric about sight. The poet's attention may have been caught up in close work, the eye's muscles locked in, so that in fact he has missed the great event of the year— spring—"it / came and went before / I got right to see." Ammons has failed to look up, to *see* beyond the range of a limited scope. The talking mountain resolves the dilemma, however, by directing the poet's attention upward and outward. That the poet can still "climb into spring," an action that would take him beyond the boundaries of narrow daily perception, suggests that it is not too late to catch up with the season's glory.

The phrase "climb" / into spring" signals a moment of release in the poem. Just as the ciliary muscles must relax and stretch ("unlock") for vision to accommodate to distance again, so too must the poet relax and stretch ("climb") beyond the constraints which caused him to miss spring. The poet is issued a warning, however:

> it's not that way
> with all things, some
> that go are gone

This parable instructs in a casual and delightful way about the hazards of nearsightedness. Ammons repeatedly warns himself and his readers against forms of vision that are binding, restrictive, and ultimately stifling.

His insistence on not getting too locked into near-point vision is reminiscent of Emerson. The transcendentalist's warnings over a century ago about the dangers and limitations of "narrow" vision have proved to be good optometry. Emerson knew, like the optometrists of today, that "if you bury the eye too exclusively on minute objects, it gradually loses its power of distant vision."[22]

If "Eyesight" warns of the limitations of myopia, Ammons's poem "Laser" concerns itself with a related problem—restricted peripheral vision. Too often those who do concentrated close work get so involved with their material that they begin to block out peripheral vision. Kavner writes that "people who block out peripheral vision tend to lose the ability to see what's going on outside a narrow and limited perspective, and this may come to be how they relate to the world."[23]

Ammons's poem "Laser" dramatizes the mind's need to break free from a too narrow vision of the world. He uses the laser

beam, an intensely focused, narrow beam of light, as a metaphor
to suggest a too constrictive scope:

> An image comes
> and the mind's light, confused
>
> . . . .
>
> gathers up,
> parallelizes, focuses
> and in a rigid beam illuminates the image:
>
> (CP, 187)

The three verbs that appear consecutively ("gathers up," "parallelizes," and "focuses") hold the reader's attention. The grip
these verbs have on the reader conveys the experience of contain-
ment Ammons so aptly suggests in the "laser" metaphor. The
"rigid beam" (of laser light) effectively illuminates the image,
but as the poem progresses the intensity of the beam's focus
blocks out possibilities not within its very narrow range. "The
mind tries to / dream of diversity" but the focused beam prevents
other possibilities from coming to light. The final two lines end
on a dismal note: "the head falls and / hangs and cannot wake
itself." The beam that gathers up and "parallelizes" has essentially paralyzed the seer; it is as if he has been exhausted by
the experience.

"Laser" is one of the few poems Ammons himself has commented on. He says, in his interview with David Grossvogel,
"that's what I'm talking about in that poem called 'Laser,' where
an image or representation is seen, and the mind is then locked
with it obsessively, and what the mind needs most is some other,
disorganized energy that it can use to break free."[24] Here Ammons acknowledges the close link between mind and vision—
what is seen "locks" the mind, just as "gathers up," "parallelizes," and "focuses" "lock" the reader. What is needed is some
other energy, some new input to free both mind and vision from
their too narrow concentration.

In drawing attention to the problem of "tunnel vision" and in
encouraging a broader latitude for perception, Ammons plays an
important role as "vision therapist." In other poems, particularly
"Corsons Inlet," he also flexes his own vision, effectively encouraging the reader to do the same.

In the poem "Space Travel," Ammons seems to discover the
latitude (or "space") so sorely lacking in "Laser." In actuality,
however, only the *illusion* of a broad perspective is created:

Go down the left
hand side of the yard,
a contrived bankslope,
down to the corner of
the lot, past the
forsythia bushes now
all green, and look
back up toward the house,
the lawn, the young
maple, the bushes along
the foundation & you can
practically work up
a prospect: vision adjusts:
feeling roomy is room
enough and many a
twenty-mile out-west view
thins to staging:
it's going to be all right
I think, for those
who wish to live, at least:
there are some who do.

(CP, 323)

The reader is given instructions about where to stand to best see the house. Walk to the very edge of the lot and look "back up"—"you can / practically work up / a prospect." Everything is "staged" by the landscapers to create the illusion of space. The bankslope is "contrived" to create the impression of a hilly terrain. The landscape has all the pleasant ornaments of suburban design. Ironically, one does not see an expanse of natural scenery, but merely the illusion of such. Vision does indeed adjust, just as it accommodates to prolonged near-point work. But in adjusting to the limiting "prospect" of a suburban plot, the eye is deprived of the wider expanses it needs for relief.

In the context of Ammons's ongoing concern with perceptual freedom, "feeling roomy is room / enough" is cleverly ironic. We have come to accept that merely "feeling roomy," as opposed to actually having room to move, is sufficient. The suburban plot, with its spatial limitations, symbolizes the "space" defining the range of many contemporary lives. Compared to the view the countryside offers ("twenty-mile out-west view"), the residential plot, surrounded by similarly sized plots, offers little room for distant vision. If, as Emerson knew, the eye demands the horizon, then the suburbs are not the place to look. The muted and highly qualified statements of the last lines suggest the adjustment made is at best merely satisfactory.

The title of the poem further underscores the poem's irony, the way space can be made to appear to "travel." "Prospects" change once one moves from the countryside to the suburbs. The root of "prospect" is *prospiciere*—to look forward—and while the nation once looked westward and forward toward greater "prospects," we now look backward over a "contrived bankslope."

The forms of both "Space Travel" and "Laser" are narrow and confining, reinforcing the constraint that is the subject of each. Neither poem offers much "space"; in "Space Travel" there are no stanza breaks whatsoever—the entire poem is squeezed into one narrow block of text. "Laser" is also uncharacteristically blocklike in its structure. While there is some breathing space between its stanzaic blocks, the overall impression is tight and narrow like the laser's beam. These constricting forms stand in stark contrast to poems like "Corsons Inlet," where the configurations defy limiting shapes.

Ammons, like Emerson, resists the city because the city diminishes vision. Sherman Paul, in his book on Emerson, *Emerson's Angle of Vision*, notes that for Emerson "the city was short-sighted business."[25] Emerson closely identified the near-pointed tasks of city work with the Understanding. He writes in his journal that:

> the City delights the Understanding. It is made up of finites; short, sharp, mathematical lines, all calculable. It is full of varieties, of successions, of contrivances. The Country, on the contrary, offers an unbroken horizon, the monotony of an endless road, or vast uniform plains . . . the eye is invited ever to the horizon and the clouds. It is the school of Reason.[26]

Ammons, over a century later, echoes Emerson when he states in an interview shortly after the publication of the *Collected Poems 1951–1971*: "I identify civilization (the City) with *definition.* . . . That's why I'm not in the city; that's why I am not an urban person. The city represents to me the artificial, the limited, the defined, the stalled."[27] He too links the nearsighted vision of city life with constrictive modes of thought and diminished intuition.

Ammons's attempt to move beyond the "mathematical lines" of urban life is best evidenced in his poem "Corsons Inlet." Ammons is above all a peripatetic poet, and he begins "Corsons Inlet" by walking away from the city.

> I went for a walk over the dunes again this morning
> to the sea,
> then turned right along
>   the surf
>   rounded a naked headland
>   and returned
>
> along the inlet shore:
>
> (CP, 147–48)

Both the direction of the walk and the form of its record defy "straightness." The varying lengths of the lines jut and curve down the page, evoking both the movement of the poet's walk along the inlet's shore and the uneven margins of the inlet itself. In reading them, the eyes must oscillate, swinging back and forth. In addition to engaging the reader in a beneficial visual exercise, the content of the poem points *out* toward nature, *out* toward the very flux of creation that Ammons believes must be experienced to avoid the contemporary myopia epidemic.

The activity of walking in "Corsons Inlet" is an exercise in eye-body coordination; the eye traces the events in nature as the body balances itself on the winding path. Ammons finds this walk "liberating":

> I was released from forms,
> from the perpendiculars,
>   straight lines, blocks, boxes, binds
> of thought
> into the hues, shadings, rises, flowing bends and blends
>   of sight:
>
> (CP, 148)

The poet has moved beyond the defined, described here in terms of the geometry of straight lines, into the "flowing bends and blends of sight." He evokes the difference between "hard eyes" and "soft eyes." Those who see with "hard eyes" tend to look for the hard edges of things. They tend to see people and objects as separate and not necessarily related. They constantly analyze and dissect experience by their way of seeing. Ammons, by contrast, is encouraging a "softer" approach, allowing one to see relationships, "blends of sight," flows of experience.[28] Both the eyes and the mind are now free to open up to the flow of "events" the poet celebrates in the rest of the poem.

The word "lines" is repeated as many as ten different times in the poem, and one learns that Ammons prefers the "curvy" to the "straight," the spontaneous to the rigid, when describing both the visual geometry of nature's lines and his own processes of thought. Ultimately he seeks to resist definitions, boundaries of thought, any kind of reductive philosophy. He keeps his attention on the flux in nature, which functions as the model of openness he hopes to experience and sustain.

"Corsons Inlet," like so much of Ammons's work, presents a record of the poet's vision, but Ammons is particularly resistant to summarize the significance of the many natural events recorded, for to do so would be to construct a box of thought against which the flow of the poem argues. He writes:

> I allow myself eddies of meaning:
> yield to a direction of significance
> running
> like a stream through the geography of my work:
>   you can find
> in my sayings
>   swerves of action
>   like the inlet's cutting edge:
>   there are dunes of motion,
> organizations of grass, white sandy paths of remembrance
> in the overall wandering of mirroring mind:
>
> but Overall is beyond me: is the sum of these events
> I cannot draw, the ledger I cannot keep, the accounting
> beyond the account:
>
>   (CP, 148)

The "eddies of meaning" Ammons allows himself are found in the myriad "events" of this and his other poems. Unlike Emerson, Ammons does not feel compelled to make these events fit into a paradigm. His use of "Overall" echoes Emerson's "Oversoul," but Ammons distances himself here from his major influence by refusing to engage in the kind of speculation that takes him beyond the physical world of sight.

Harold Bloom, in his article on Ammons and the Romantic Sublime, cites "Corsons Inlet" as a pivotal poem in Ammons's development, a moment when the poet resists his own intense desire for Transcendence. Bloom writes, "Ammons was losing his battle against himself until he wrote his most famous poem, 'Corsons Inlet.'"[29] Ammons opts for the vision of nature because he finds "direct sight" more liberating than the contemplation

of the Sublime. In Ammons's universe, the apperception of physical, manifest phenomena and processes yields pleasure and
sometimes pain. Despite the lure of the Transcendent, he resists
it. Ammons associates the "Overall" with closure, whereas freedom depends upon process and visible change.[30]

Much of this long lyric poem alternates between descriptions
of what Ammons sees on his walk and his reminding himself
not to draw conclusions from what he sees. There are no sharp
lines in nature; there should be no sharp lines of thought to hem
in consciousness. He employs words like "so" and "as" to make
gramatically parallel the proper relation between thought and
nature. Thus we read:

> as
>
> manifold events of sand
> change the dune's shape that will not be the same shape
> tomorrow,
>
> so I am willing to go along, to accept
> the becoming
> thought, to stake off no beginnings or ends, establish
>   no walls:

(CP, 149)

To "accept / the becoming / thought" is to be open to process,
and the continuously transforming sand dunes inspire him. The
shifting dunes are just one of the many manifold "events" in the
poem that have the capacity both to criticize restrictive mental
forms and to simultaneously function as examples of "becoming," encouraging a more "easy-going, tolerant mental scope."

The poet's walk leads to the discovery of fresh visual patterns
("every walk is unreproducible"), liberating him from stale
boundaries of thought and perception. For Ammons, the walk is
"the externalization of an interior seeking."[31] The many turns he
takes along the inlet's shore reflect his internal quest for freedom
and possibility.

While in the first half of "Corsons Inlet" Ammons argues per-
suasively against the "tyranny of straight lines," in the second
half he is careful to avoid endorsing chaos or anarchy. And although the inexactness of the waterline captures his attention
and is mirrored in the inexactness of the lines he uses to structure his poem, Ammons is careful not to endorse total ran-
domness. Instead, he eventually uncovers in his walk the paradox
of nature's mechanisms, which incorporate both order and ran-

domness. The flock of tree swallows he sees in the distance is
such a system.

>   the news to my left and over the dunes and
>   reeds and bayberry clumps was
>   fall: thousands of tree swallows
>   gathering for flight:
>   an order held
>   in constant change: a congregation
>   rich with entropy: nevertheless, separable, noticeable
>   as one event,
>   not chaos: preparations for
>   flight from winter,
>   cheet, cheet, cheet, cheet, wings rifling the green clumps,
>   beaks
>   at the bayberries
>   a perception full of wind, flight, curve,
>   sound:
>   the possibility of rule as the sum of rulelessness:
>   the "field" of action
>   with moving, incalculable center:
>
>   (CP, 150)

The words used to describe this flock of swallows coexist as
opposites: "constant" and "change," "order" and "entropy,"
"rule" and "rulelessness." Individual swallows can shift direction with the wind, swoop down for food or rest, and circle in
seemingly aimless patterns. Ammons finds such diversity "rich."
Yet he knows that this collection of swallows—this "congrega-
tion"—presents a unity to the mind that is "separable, noticeable / as one event, / not chaos." These swallows partake of the
same flux that Ammons finds in the sand dunes and in the other
natural events within the poem. Most of all they present him
with the kind of perception that is anything but constricting:
"full of wind, flight, curve, / sound." Yet for all the movement
the swallows suggest, they also present "the possibility of rule
as the sum of rulelessness." As a group they form a coherent
wholeness.
    As the poem moves toward its conclusion, Ammons has
learned to accommodate his vision, shifting it from far to near.
The reader follows him in these shifts and is encouraged to accommodate vision without straining or blurring. Contemplating
the marine life in the inlet, the poet observes that inside the
bellies of minnows must be "pulsations of order." But the min-

nows in turn are swallowed up by larger fish, the smaller order "feeding" the larger, illustrating the constant metamorphosis in nature.

In the final stanzas of the poem, Ammons resists trying to make too much sense out of all he has seen; to do so would be to create an unnecessary stop to processes that resist closure. Most of all Ammons does not want to diminish the reality of nature's events by imposing upon them a particular philosophical framework—"no humbling of reality to precept." Given "Corsons Inlet's" repeated emphasis on flux and curvature, it is not surprising for the poem to end with the poet's celebrating the fact that no perception is final. His credo is to resist at all costs a final "Credo," and in this sense the message of "Corsons Inlet" echoes what Ammons has said in the Foreword to *Ommateum:* that "forms of thought, like physical forms . . . are susceptible to change," and when one resists change the results are "costly and violent."[32] In the final stanza of the poem he reiterates his preference for "the looser, wider forces" of nature in contrast to "limited tightness."

In employing the words "see," "vision," and "scope" in the final lines of the poem, Ammons leaves the reader with a final reminder about *perception,* the vehicle *through* which the provisional nature of reality is experienced.

> I see narrow orders, limited tightness, but will
> not run to that easy victory:
>   still around the looser, wider forces work:
>   I will try
>   to fasten into order enlarging grasps of disorder, widening
> scope, but enjoying the freedom that
> Scope eludes my grasp, that there is no finality of vision,
> that I have perceived nothing completely,
>   that tomorrow a new walk is a new walk.
>
> (CP, 151)

Ammons enjoys the freedom of not having to reduce his perceptions to a single, unifying philosophical abstraction ("Scope eludes my grasp"). Instead he celebrates that "there is no finality of vision." And, in attempting to widen scope, he will move beyond the range of the natural eye to look through the telescope and microscope.

"Corsons Inlet" offers a corrective to a shortsighted age. Ammons makes a major statement about the nature of reality, thought, and perception, suggesting that we avoid perceptual and psychological rigidity in exchange for a broader, more open, more tolerant way of being in the world.

Throughout the *Collected Poems 1951–1971* one can envision Ammons down on hands and knees, inspecting flowers and plants, walking by waterfalls and inlets, observing the arcs of winds, measuring drifts of snow and the permutations caused by all kinds of weather. The visual component of these poems is strong. Like Whitman and William Carlos Williams before him, Ammons "looks lovingly at the commonplace and finds poetry there."[33] Although he has been discussed as a "philosophic" poet by Bloom, Hartman, and other critics, Ammons's clear and intense lyrics of the visual moment have won the praise of others, including Paul Zweig, who writes that these critics have "overlooked what seems to me to be his real achievement: the lyrical articulation of small moments of experience; his ability to organize shapes of language into an epiphany of movement, a frozen flood of perceptions which is visionary not because of any passionate metaphysics, but because of the sheer clarity of the poet's ability to recreate what he 'sees.'"[34]

Four additional selections from *Collected Poems 1951–1971*, when read together as a cluster, reveal some of the other characteristic and salient ways the poet visually interacts with his world. These poems have received little or no critical attention because, as Zweig has said, critics have neglected Ammons's shorter lyrics of the visual moment. In the first of these, "March Song," Ammons explores a group of cattails the moment they begin to change in early spring.

> At a bend in the stream by willows
> I paused to be with the cattails
>   their long flat leaves
> and tall stems
> bleached by wind and winter light
>
> and winter had kept them
>   edged down into the quiet eddy of the bend
> tight with ice
>
> O willows I said how you return
> gold to the nakedness of your limbs
>   coming again out of that country
> into the longer sun

> and Oh I said turning to the fluffy cattails
> loosened to the approaching winds of spring
> what a winter you leave in the pale stems
>   of your becoming

                                                    (CP, 44)

In the first stanza, Ammons surrenders himself to careful observation, much as Thoreau did in his walks outside Concord. The poet re-creates the image of the cattails as he perceives them after the long winter months. The language used to describe his perception is both clear and precise. The adjectives ("long," "flat," "tall") describing the stems and leaves of the cattails are appropriately simple, and the verb "bleached" evokes the whiteness winter has worked upon them. As the reader learns in the short second stanza of this poem, the cattails have been constricted by the strength of the season that hems in nature. This stanza's final line ("tight with ice") contracts to further suggest the constraint winter imposes upon the landscape.

"March Song," however, is about change, and the poem turns at the beginning of the third stanza as Ammons shifts his attention to the willows. Delighted by the change he sees in them, he remarks out loud: "O willows I said how you return / gold to the nakedness of your limbs." That the willows cannot literally answer does not daunt this poet, for he knows that what he *sees* is in fact what they "say," and the message is "becoming." Ammons celebrates the beauty of their transformation and puns playfully upon the word "return." The willows "return" to life by "returning" gold to their limbs.

Ammons characteristically registers his wonder with the vocative "O." It occurs at the beginning of the second stanza and in a variant form ("Oh") again at the beginning of the third. Traditionally used in religious hymns, as in "O God on high," the word "O" has been appropriated by Ammons to express awe. In "March Song," "O" marks the moment of great release, the point at which the poem turns from winter to spring, from the frozen "bleached" world to the world of color and movement. Like the shape of the letter "O," the seasons too form a circle— and the circle of natural events is about to release life from death. The "o" sound is repeated in the word "gold," which visually and dramatically signals the change that has begun.

When Ammons turns his attention from the willows to the cattails in the third stanza, remembering that they too will be transformed, he again utters "Oh." Perhaps the change in spelling occurs because "Oh" is now used as an independent interjection. It forces one to pause momentarily with Ammons before he turns again to the cattails. The poet addresses the cattails directly in the final lines, remarking upon the dramatic transformation they too have begun to experience, the first signs of which are the "pale stems" of their "becoming."

In "March Song," Ammons has fully participated in his perceptions. What he discovers beside the stream is "becoming," and although he never explicitly links himself with the cattails, the poet implicitly discovers in their awakening a symbol for rebirth. Ammons thus creates a vision of early spring, involving himself and the reader in the event.

In "The Yucca Moth," a later lyric in Collected Poems 1951–1971, Ammons more intimately links himself with what he sees.

> The yucca clump
> is blooming,
>   tall sturdy spears
> spangling into bells of light,
>   green
> in the white blooms
>   faint as
> a memory of mint:
>
> I raid
>   a bloom,
> spread the hung petals out,
>   and, surprised he is not
> a bloom-part, find
>   a moth inside, the exact color,
> the bloom his daylight port or cove:
>
> though time comes
>   and goes and troubles
> are unlessened,
>   the yucca is lifting temples
> of bloom: from the night
>   of our dark flights, can
> we go in to heal, live
>   out in white-green shade
> the radiant, white, hanging day?

(CP, 142)

In the first three lines, the poet as botanist carefully describes the physical characteristics of the yucca clump. In the fourth line, however, objective description is transformed figuratively—the plant's spears "spangle into bells of light." Here is evidenced the melding of objective and subjective description discussed in the previous chapter in connection with Thoreau. In this poem, more so than in "March Song," the literal observations of nature are figuratively transformed in the process of contemplation.

The poet-botanist becomes an even more active participant in this event in the second stanza. In a characteristic pose, Ammons literally pries into nature's private parts to see what he can discover. He raids a bloom and hangs out its petals, only to discover a moth inside. The botanist's bloom becomes the moth's "daylight port or cove," another instance in the poem where objective reality is transformed metaphorically.

Ammons concerns himself in the first two stanzas primarily with what he sees, whereas in the third stanza he reflects upon what he has seen. He observes, as have his Romantic predecessors, that nature manifests beauty despite "troubles" besetting the human world. This poem ends by posing a crucial question. The poet asks whether "we," like the moth, can find healing solace from "our dark flights" in the blooms of the yucca plant. Ammons likens himself and his reader to the moth, which takes shelter during daylight hours inside the plant's spears. The analogy is apt, for like the moth we too often need to recover from our "night journeys," albeit psychological ones. Like Whitman in "A Noiseless Patient Spider," another visionary poem that begins by simply seeing, Ammons convincingly and brilliantly discovers relationship between himself and an insect. Although Ammons ends "The Yucca Moth" with the crucial question unanswered, he presents the reader with sufficient evidence that one can recover in nature's company.

Indeed, Ammons's acceptance of the natural world and the positive energy he derives from it runs counter to much contemporary poetry, with its emphasis on despair and alienation. Ammons himself does not deny these emotions; he implicitly acknowledges them in "The Yucca Moth" by linking all of us to the moth's "dark flights." In Tape for the Turn of the Year, the poet struggles with destructive forces in nature and within the self. And in several other shorter lyrics he registers both anxiety and isolation. Yet ultimately Ammons takes a stand against these "darker" feelings and forces. Even when he takes as his subject the destruction one inevitably finds in the natural world, whether it be the passing of a season or the death of a hornet or bee at the onset of winter, Ammons almost always manages to reconcile himself to change. He struggles through the moments of personal despair and anxiety in his work that, as DeRosa has noted, he perceives as plateaus in an ongoing evolutionary process.[35] He writes in *Tape:*

> I believe that man is
> small
> & of short duration in the
> great, incomprehensible,
> & eternal: I believe
> it's necessary to do
> good
> as we can best define it:
> I believe we must
> discover & accept the
>   terms
>   that best testify:
> I'm on the side of
> whatever the reasons are
>   we are here:
>
>   (T, 98)

Ammons risks considerable criticism for his faith and optimism in an age of despair and doubt. In one sense, his poems can be viewed as experiments, attempts to discover "the / terms / that best testify." He knows that he can react emotionally to what he sees in different ways, but he *chooses* to react creatively, positively. He states clearly the choice that he makes:

> I can react with
>   restlessness & quiet
>   terror, or with
>   fascination &
>   delight: I choose the
> side of possibility:
>
>   (T, 99)

The poet expresses "fascination" and "delight" in "March Song," emotions registered by the expressive "O," a magical sound that recurs like a mantra throughout his work as he investigates the natural world on his myriad walks in and around Ithaca. In "The Yucca Moth," the poet registers his delight in a plant clump, only to discover a ray of relation between one of its inhabitants and himself.

In "Way to Go," the third in this group of four selected to

articulate and typify Ammons's lyrics of small moments of visual experience, the poet expresses his acceptance of the phenomenal world—*as it is*. This poem, ignored by critics, belies its surface simplicity and offers the reader much in the way of understanding Ammons's vision of reality.

> West light flat on trees:
>   bird flying
>   deep out in blue glass:
>   uncertain wind
> stirring the leaves: this is
>   the world we have:
>   take it

(CP, 169–70)

"Way to Go" has the unassuming quality of much Chinese poetry. It also contains a great deal of silent wisdom, partially derived from Ammons's use of the colon. The pauses the colons force one to take create a gap, or silence, before the next image is registered. These gaps become part of the message of the poem, for the silences between perceptions, and the silences underlying perceptions, are part of the vision the reader is asked to accept.

The spare clarity of its vision reveals a world of transient beauty. The light of sunset, the bird flying, the uncertain wind— are all transitory. If this is "the world we have," then it is the world of flux described earlier in "Corsons Inlet."

The poem's title also suggests its Asian tone and message. In colloquial usage, "way to go" is the verbal equivalent of a pat on the back, and in this sense Ammons is paying homage to the world itself, complimenting it ("way to go") on its lyrical simplicity. But Ammons is punning on the word "way." In Chinese philosophy, the "Way," which is the English translation of the "Tao," takes on special significance. Ammons acknowledges his debt to Taoism in the 1973 *Diacritics* interview, stating that "when I was younger, I read a good deal, finally coming to Lao-tse. . . . That's my philosophical source in its most complete version."[36] Read in the light of the *Way*, or Tao, this poem's transitory images evoke the first great principle of Taoism, "the relativity of all attributes."[37]

Taoism also teaches an accepting attitude toward nature. According to Arthur Waley, who has written an extensive introduction to Taoism in his book *The Way and Its Power*, Taoist literature teaches one to approach the phenomenal world with

lyrical acceptance, in contrast to resignation or mere acquies-
cence.[38] In the final two words of this little poem—"take it"—
Ammons brilliantly understates the notion that one should perceive and accept the world *as it is.* Holder, in one of the only
other critical readings of this poem, finds its conclusion terse,
even grim, ending in "sober acceptance." The ending is not stoic
resignation; rather, Ammons evokes through the poem's silences
and Asian delicacy an exquisitely clear appreciation of life.

"Way to Go" is much more than a collection of random images.
The poem exemplifes in its images and teaches through them
the "way to go," which is the way of openness, the way of affirmation. In this poem literal seeing leads to the most significant
kind of insight, and part of its wonder is the way the poet effortlessly transforms the visual moment into something more—into
a vision of life itself.

The fourth poem of this cluster, in a more self-conscious manner than the other three, calls attention to the process of perception as it functions in Ammons's work. In "Poetics," Ammons
values a special kind of seeing.

> I look for the way
> things will turn
> out spiralling from a center,
> the shape
> things will take to come forth in
>
> so that the birch tree white
> touched black at branches
> will stand out
> wind-glittering
> totally its apparent self:
>
> I look for the forms
> things want to come as
>
> from what black wells of possibility,
> how a thing will
> unfold:
>
> not the shape on paper—though
> that, too—but the
> uninterfering means on paper:
>
> not so much looking for the shape
> as being available

to any shape that may be
summoning itself
through me
from the self not mine but ours.

(CP, 199)

Ammons is interested in processes—how things "turn" and "turn out." The birch tree, the one concrete image in this poem, is not static, but "wind-glittering." The key verbs of both the first and the third stanzas, "spiral" and "unfold," insist on movement, and Ammons wants to be open to the directions things take "spiralling" and "unfolding" from their sources ("centers," "black wells"). In his book *Imagining the Earth,* John Elder writes, "Ammons opposes his vision of the world to what Whitehead called 'the static morphological universe': the world's order is dynamic, with process rather than things providing the primary reality."[39] In "Poetics" Ammons discovers the appropriate perceptive mode for this "turning" and "spiralling" universe. He seeks to make himself "available" to shapes and processes.

The difference between "looking for the shape" and "being available / to any shape that may be / summoning itself / through me" is the difference between straining the eyes to fixate on an object and relaxing them so that patterns and shapes move through consciousness. This is also the difference between acquisitiveness, which grasps at knowledge, and receptivity, which receives knowledge. "Available" derives from the Old French *valoir,* "to be worth." Thus to discover "value" one must become "available." Ammons chooses not to force vision but to make himself "available," acting as a conduit.

The distinction between "looking" and "being available" is Taoistic. For another of the major principles of Taoism teaches that to "grasp" things is to lose them. Ammons's distinction between seeking things out and letting them come "through" him is also reminiscent of Thoreau. In an 1851 Journal entry Thoreau talks about looking with less effort. "I must let my senses wander as my thoughts, my eyes see without looking."[40] Rather than "looking" to dissect and analyze, one must make oneself worthy of ("available" to) experience.

In his brief comments on "Poetics" Holder remarks that Ammons does not spell out "the self not mine but ours." But one strong possibility, given Ammons's Taoistic leanings, is that this shared self is the Tao itself, described in Arthur Waley's translation of the *Tao Te Ching* as:

> bottomless; the very progenitor of all things in the world.
>
> . . . .
>
> It is here within us all the while;
> Draw upon it as you will, it never runs dry.[41]

The Tao is the ultimate "black well," the "progenitor" of all processes. Ammons alludes to the unifying nature of the Tao when he describes it as "the self not mine but ours." Emerson speaks of it in "Self-Reliance," when he writes that "we first share the life by which things exist and afterwards see them as appearances in nature."[42] According to Fritjof Capra, "this ultimate essence underlies and unifies the multitude of things and events we observe . . . and cannot be separated from its multiple manifestations."[43] The shapes "summoning" themselves through Ammons's consciousness have a common source in the Tao, or what modern physics has identified as the unified field.[44]

The unassertive character of making oneself "available" to nature is Taoistic.[45] But the attentiveness to manifest processes in this poem is distinct from another kind of "seeing" that is also Asian. Capra notes "the emphasis on seeing in mystical traditions should not be taken too literally, but has to be understood in a metaphorical sense, since the mystical experience of reality is an essentially nonsensory experience. When the Eastern mystics talk about 'seeing,' they refer to a mode of perception that may include visual perception, but which always and essentially transcends it to become a nonsensory experience of reality."[46]

The world "out there," that feeds the eyes and mind, is an illusory world, and the Eastern mystic shifts attention inward to discover a more permanent and truthful reality. "The name for Taoist temples, *kuan*, originally meant 'to look,'" according to Capra. "Taoists thus regarded their temples as places of observation," whereby one could "observe" through meditation the Tao within.[47]

In the following section from *Tape* Ammons expresses caution about this other kind of "seeing":

> here are "motions"
> that play in and out:
>   unifying
> correspondences that
> suggest we can approach

> unity only by the loss
>   of things—
> a loss we're unwilling
> to take—
> since the gain of unity
>   would be a vision
> of something in the
> continuum of nothingness:
> we already have things:
>   why fool around:

(T, 23)

"Here" stands in contrast to the "continuum of nothingness." Here in the world of the senses is the play of the laws of nature, "motions" that Ammons is "available" to. While these "motions" may suggest unity, Ammons knows "we can approach / unity only by the loss / of things." Unlike the Taoist monks in their observatories, however, this is "a loss we're unwilling / to take." Ammons says we're afraid to lose the things we have for "something" unknown in the continuum of no-thing-ness. The implication is that the "gain of unity" may lead to a kind of vacuous experience, potentially frightening and disorienting.[48]

Ammons's characterization of "unity" as lying beyond the senses is apt. Capra adds, "The Eastern mystics repeatedly insist on the fact that the ultimate reality can never be an object of reasoning or of demonstrable knowledge. It can never be adequately described by words, because it lies beyond the realms of the senses and of the intellect from which our words and concepts are derived."[49] The Upanishads say about it:

> There the eye goes not,
> Speech goes not, nor the mind.
> We know not, we understand not
> How one would teach it.[50]

For Ammons, the key phrase is "there the eye goes not." As a poet who derives his greatest energy from encounters with the visible world, he is naturally cautious of transcending appearances. "Unity," as Ammons thinks of it, would make both the writing of poems and eye exercises, among other things, impossible. Despite his reservations, however, Ammons has at other times been strongly attracted "to the continuum of nothingness."

Richard Howard was the first to note what he calls a "dialectic" in Ammons's verse between "the abstractive tendency, the immaterialism that runs through all our native strain . . . and the private instances of the sensuous world." Howard adds that the Transcendental magnet, what he calls "the great soft whoosh of Being," has obsessed our literature "from its classical figures . . . down to Roethke, Wright Morris, Thornton Wilder," and Ammons.[51] Bloom, following on Howard's lead, finds instances in Ammons's work where the poet's attraction to Transcendence seems to dominate. This is countered by the experience of the more mature Ammons, who has abandoned "the savage will to transcendence . . . in order for life and poetry to go on."[52] Hyatt Waggoner speaks of this dialectic as "the tension between the Seen and the Unseen."[53]

In "Some Months Ago," the fifth selection in the *Ommateum* volume, Ammons bids "farewell" to the terrestrial world and steps out into "the great open."

> Some months ago I went out early
> to pay
>   my last respects to earth
>   farewell earth
>   ocean farewell
> lean eucalyptus with nude gray skin
>   farewell
>
>
>   Hill rain
> pouring from a rockpierced cloud
> hill rain from the wounds of mist
>   farewell
>
> See the mountainpeaks gather
> clouds from the sky
> shake new bright flakes from the mist
>   farewell
>
> Hedgerows hung with web and dew
> that disappear at a touch
>   like snail eyes
>   farewell
> To a bird only this
>   farewell
> and he hopped away to peck dew
> from a ground web
>   spider running out of her tunnel to see
> to whom I said
>   farewell
> and she sat still on her heavy webs

> I closed up all the natural throats of earth
> and cut my ties with every natural heart
> and saying farewell
>   stepped out into the great open

(CP, 4–5)

As the title suggests, the speaker's grand departure from this world occurred "some months ago." The poem recalls the process of taking leave, with the speaker paying "last respects to earth" and to a variety of other phenomena: ocean, eucalyptus, hill, rain, and so on. He bids each of these "farewell," and the refrain echoes in the reader's ears as the poet recalls cutting his ties "with every natural heart." The speaker puns on the word "farewell," not only saying good-bye but also expressing his wish that the things he leaves behind fare well.

Whitman's "Darest Thou Now O Soul" provides an illuminating comparison with "Some Months Ago." Like Ammons's poem, its movement is from the concrete to the abstract, from the seen to the unseen, from the defined to the unbounded. Whitman too speaks of a moment when "ties loosen," and one bids farewell to sensory experience.

> Darest thou now O soul,
> Walk out with me toward the unknown region,
> Where neither ground is for the feet nor any path to follow?
>
> No map there, nor guide,
> Nor voice sounding, nor touch of human hand,
> Nor face with blooming flesh, nor lips, nor eyes, are in that land.
>
> I know it not O soul,
> Nor dost thou, all is a blank before us
> All waits undream'd of in that region, that inaccessible land.
>
> Till when the ties loosen,
> All but the ties eternal, Time and Space,
> Nor darkness, gravitation, sense, nor any bounds bounding us.
>
> Then we burst forth, we float,
> In Time and Space O soul, prepared for them,
> Equal, equipt at last, (O joy! O fruit of all!) them to fulfill O
>   soul.

(LOG, 441)

Whitman's poem is more clearly about forthcoming death, rather than a nostalgic recollection of earth from a world beyond.

Whitman looks *forward* to his unknown region; Ammons looks *backward* to the world he knew. In Whitman's poem one dies to the body only to experience a more blissful, fulfilling state: "(O joy! O fruit of all!)." The great open beyond the boundaries of relative time and space is celebrated. Although the poet claims neither "map" nor guide to this "region" beyond, he expresses his delight in going "there."

Whereas Whitman is clearly speaking about death, Ammons's "great open" is purposefully ambiguous. The human voice of the poem suggests it has survived a departure from earth, one indication that the "great open" stepped into is not death itself. Read in the context of his other poems, the "great open" of "Some Months Ago" is Transcendental Unity. Ammons does experience transcendence at the end of his poem.

> I closed up all the natural throats of earth
> and cut my ties with every natural heart
> and saying farewell
>   stepped out into the great open

The speaker of Ammons's poem dies to the objects of perception, and the objects of perception also "die" to him—they go out of sight. Yet the reader is left wondering whether his departure is unequivocally a joyful release. Ammons describes the moment of release much more matter-of-factly than Whitman. The emotion in the speaker's voice is reserved for the objects to which he bids "farewell."

Robert Morgan's comment on "Some Months Ago" identifies the irony of Transcendence in Ammons's poetry. "The seer looks back with great affection to the things he has given up to reach his level of vision. The irony is that the gain of the open is the loss of the specific."[54] What is especially intriguing about this early *Ommateum* poem, however, is that the speaker is willing to move beyond the world of sense at all. In this poem, at least, he does not seem to be especially troubled by his transcendental status. Elsewhere within *Ommateum*, however, Ammons retreats from his encounters with the Unseen, which he refers to in his work by various names: "unity," the "One," the "Absolute," the "implicit," and simply "transcendence."

Of all Ammons's early poems, "Guide" most clearly dramatizes the poet's ambivalence about foregoing daily vision for some "higher" kind of reality. It is curious that Waggoner, who raises the issue of the tension between the Seen and the Unseen in Ammons's verse, should omit this poem from consideration, where that very tension is most prominent.

> You cannot come to unity and remain material:
> in that perception is no perceiver:
>   when you arrive
> you have gone too far:
>   at the Source you are in the mouth of Death:
>
> you cannot
>   turn around in
> the Absolute: there are no entrances or exits
>   no precipitations of forms
> to use like tongs against the formless:
>   no freedom to choose:
>
> to be
>   you have to stop not-being and break
> off from *is* to *flowing* and
>   this is the sin you weep and praise:
> origin is your original sin:
>   the return you long for will ease your guilt
> and you will have your longing:
>
>   the wind that is my guide said this: it
> should know having
>   given up everything to eternal being but
> direction:
>
> how I said can I be glad and sad: but a man goes
>   from one foot to the other:
> wisdom wisdom:
>   to be glad and sad at once is also unity
> and death:
>   wisdom wisdom: a peachblossom blooms on a particular
> tree on a particular day:
>   unity cannot do anything in particular:
>
> are these the thoughts you want me to think I said but
>   the wind was gone and there was no more knowledge then.
>   (CP, 79–80)

In the first two stanzas the poet's metaphysical "guide," the wind, describes "unity" through paradox: "in that perception is no perceiver"; "at the Source you are in the mouth of Death." The accumulative effect is to render "unity" formless, transcendental.

Examined closely, the wind's description is uninviting—there are "no entrances or exits / no precipitations of forms." The notion that "unity" is too far off—"when you arrive / you have gone too far"—suggests it may not be a desirable destination.

In the third stanza the poet's "guide" describes the necessity of breaking off from unity in order to exist at all:

> to be
>   you have to stop not-being and break
> off from *is* to *flowing* and
>   this is the sin you weep and praise:
> origin is your original sin:

According to Bloom, the Kabbalists taught that "every act of creation is also a catastrophe, a breaking-of-the-vessels," and "breaking off from *is* to *flowing*" is the equivalent of the Kabbalists' explanation of the breakup of the original Transcendental Unity or the Divine Light.[55] Origin is the wind's and Ammons's version of the fall—from a Transcendental reality into the manifest world—in Kabbalistic terms, from the hidden Godhead to the ten *Sefirot*, or manifest levels of creation. The material level of life is where the laws of nature are visible, where love and joy and sadness and all human emotions are experienced, where this poet lives and works.

The fall from Unity is of necessity an experience of duality. The gulf between seer and seen is the cause of sadness, but by virtue of such separation worldly vision is possible, bringing with it rich compensation. Rather than bridge this gap through meditative techniques, or "observations" in Japanese or Chinese temples, as for instance Gary Snyder has done, Ammons chooses to walk along the New Jersey coast or the Finger Lakes in upstate New York.[56] He "goes around places" ("gnaskor"), experiencing release from conceptual forms into the flowings and blendings of sight.[57] Ammons also reunites himself to the world through the unifying vision of science.

In this poem Ammons reconciles himself to his human limitations: "a man goes / from one foot to the other." This is the image of Ammons walking through the observable universe. The world around him is comprised of *particular* phenomena—"unity" broken apart into bits, pieces, and localized boundaries.

> wisdom wisdom: a peachblossom blooms on a particular
> tree on a particular day:
>   unity cannot do anything in particular:

What material creation offers that "unity" cannot is particular wisdom, that is, specific and observable phenomena ("parts" of creation) that bring delight and pleasure. Although the final two lines of "Guide" leave Ammons in doubt as to what to really think about the dichotomy between the "particular" and the "immaterial," between the Seen and the Unseen, the entire thrust of the wind's message has been to move him in the direction of the seen world.

DeRosa, who reads this poem in a Hindu context, finds the "Source" representative of Brahma—"wherein all variety and differences are swallowed up." She finds in the poem evidence of Ammons's typically Western fear of the loss of identity, in direct contrast to an Eastern point of view, which would not construe merging with the Source (be it Brahma, the Tao, or Pure Being) "as a loss of consciousness, but rather the giving up of particularity and limitation for wholeness and boundlessness."[58] Although the experience of unity would temporarily "annihilate" the perceiver, the ultimate goal would be to return from that experience freshened, more keenly perceptive to the world.

"Guide" dramatizes the differences between East and West in their approaches to enhancing vision. Eastern mystical texts teach that to enhance vision, one must transcend the world of the senses. Paradoxically, the loss of vision during meditation results in clearer vision afterward. In the West, the approach is open-eyed rather than closed-eyed. Behavioral optometrists strive to improve vision through eye exercises. Today, the Western approach of vision therapy is being applied in the East, where factory workers in China take breaks for visual exercise to relieve the strain of prolonged concentration.[59] In the West, Eastern forms of "observation" (meditation) are increasingly popular. Ammons manages to synthesize aspects of each tradition. He warns against narrow perception in ways that remind us of the behavioral optometrist. Although he resists transcendence, Ammons's spare clarity of vision and "availability" to natural processes are characteristic of haiku and other forms of Asian poetry.[60]

The dialectic "Guide" presents is one manifestation of a recurring subject in Ammons's verse—the one and the many. In this poem they appear to be mutually exclusive. And Ammons will continue to be cautious of the one as long as it obliterates the visual. Yet in other approaches to the one:many problem, Ammons does discover a synthesis, whereby the one and many coexist. In the previous chapter, for example, we saw that in *Sphere* Ammons converts the earth into a symbol of unity *and* diversity. In "Essay on Poetics" he admires the *cooperation* of one and many found in living systems and likens this to the structure of poems.

The challenge of discovering a satisfactory way of seeing is especially important to the next chapter, where the impact of astronomy on Ammons's vision is considered. The ever-expanding universe revealed by modern astronomy only widens the gulf between observer and observed, making us feel more isolated. Ammons, however, works to overcome this isolation. He discovers strategies to reconcile himself to what has been previously unseen—galaxies and stars out there on the edge of the universe.

4

Ammons's Telescopic and Microscopic Vision

"I know if I find you I will have to leave the earth
. . . .
And I know if I find you I will have to stay with the earth
inspecting with thin tools and ground eyes . . ."
—A. R. Ammons, "Hymn"

The twentieth century has witnessed an unparalleled exploration of space. As we push back the frontiers of the universe, our own earthly existence seems to get more precarious. As we explore the destiny of the cosmos, we naturally reflect inwards, asking ourselves what is our own destiny. Loren Eiseley, in *The Immense Journey*, writes that "in a universe whose size is beyond human imagining, where our world floats like a dust mote in the void of night, men have grown inconceivably lonely."[1] Eiseley's reaction is not atypical; this century has seen poets recoiling from the vistas opened up by astronomy. Robert Frost's "I Will Sing You One-O" expresses the loneliness reflected in the vast space around us. The poem begins with Frost being awakened in the middle of the night by the town's tower clock and steeple. A single knock indicates that the hour is one A.M. As the poem unfolds the poet thinks about what's "out there" beyond his window, and his own relation to the vast universe.

> In that grave One
> They spoke of the sun
> And moon and stars,
> Saturn and Mars
> And Jupiter.
> Still more unfettered,
> They left the named

And spoke of the lettered,
The sigmas and taus
Of constellations.
They filled their throats
With the furthest bodies
To which man sends his
Speculation,
Beyond which God is;
The cosmic motes
Of yawning lenses.
Their solemn peals
Were not their own:
They spoke for the clock
With whose vast wheels
Theirs interlock.
In that grave word
Uttered alone
The utmost star
Trembled and stirred,
Though set so far
Its whirling frenzies
Appear like standing
In one self station.
It has not ranged,
And save for the wonder
Of once expanding
To be a nova,
It has not changed
To the eye of man
On planets over
Around and under
It in creation
Since man began
To drag down man
And nation nation.[2]

The sound of the tower clock knocking its "One-O" in the midst of a winter storm turns Frost's mind to the bleakness of one-zero. The muffled grave sound striking out the hour reminds him of the named planets and the unnamed stars—"the sigmas and taus / Of constellations." The image of the universe handed us through the telescope reduces gigantic masses of gas and matter to "cosmic motes"—mere specks of dust. Seen from an astronomical perspective, our own planet is also a "dust mote in the void of night."

The "solemn peals" of clock and tower remind Frost of the

vast clockwork of the universe operating under natural laws. The interlocking mechanisms, however, provide him with little solace. He cannot bridge dichotomies between mind and nature, earthly time and heavenly time. Just as the town's tower clock and steeple are not perfectly synchronous (they ring out "one" after the other), so too is something askew between heaven and earth. Compared to the vast cosmic history, our own human history is tiny. Our chaotic movements contrast with the distant stars that appear stationary to the eye. Although Frost hints of integration in the universe, "I Will Sing You One-O" ends on a note of disintegration. The grave sound of "One" has filled his mind with thoughts of a vast, indifferent universe and the poet's loneliness within it.

Frost is skeptical of astronomy because its vision accentuates human futility and loneliness. In his poem "The Star-Splitter," he cannot understand why Brad McLaughlin has burned his house to acquire insurance money to purchase a telescope.

> We've looked and looked, but after all where are we?
> Do we know any better where we are,
> And how it stands between the night tonight
> And a man with a smoky lantern chimney?
> How different from the way it ever stood?[3]

Frost's rhetorical questions suggest astronomy has yielded nothing useful or different. The poet is bewildered by McLaughlin's attachment to an instrument that only hands over the image of a universe devoid of meaning. Moreover, Frost is unable to work through astronomy to find solutions to the problems that plague us on earth. Given the debacles of human history, his cynicism seems justified.

Robinson Jeffers, like Robert Frost, also discovers through the lens of astronomy support for his own dark notion of human insignificance. Jeffers, however, is not so skeptical about the investment we make in astronomy; he paid many visits to Lick Observatory, and his work reflects a detailed understanding of astronomical phenomena not found in Frost.[4]

Jeffers's brooding on human transience and frailty is especially evident at the beginning of his poem "Margrave." The poet climbs a tower and from atop its "marble-paved platform" observes the night deepening. He sees "new lights / glow over the sinking east rim of the earth" and contemplates how astronomy has shrunken our humanity.

The earth was the world and man was its measure, but our
   minds have looked
Through the little mock-dome of heaven the telescope-slotted
   observatory eye-ball, there space and multitude came in
And the earth is a particle of dust by a sand-grain sun, lost
   in a nameless cove of the shores of a continent.
Galaxy on galaxy, innumerable swirls of innumerable stars
   endured as it were forever and humanity
Came into being, its two or three million years are a moment,
   in a moment it will certainly cease out from being
And galaxy on galaxy endure after that as it were forever
. . . But man is conscious,
He brings the world to focus in a feeling brain,
In a net of nerves catches the splendor of things,
Breaks the somnambulism of nature . . . His distinction perhaps,
Hardly his advantage. To slaver for contemptible pleasures
And scream with pain, are hardly an advantage.
Consciousness? The learned astronomer
Analyzing the light of most remote star-swirls
Has found them—or a trick of distance deludes his prism—
All at incredible speeds fleeing outward from ours.
I thought, no doubt they are fleeing the contagion
Of consciousness that infects this corner of space.[5]

Jeffers's notion of the earth as a "particle of dust" echoes both
Frost and Eiseley. Before astronomy revealed this fact, the earth
really was the world and man its measure. Beginning with Copernicus, however, our centrality and the centrality of our planet
have been undermined. "Through the telescope-slotted / observatory eye-ball" the new configuration can be discerned with ever
greater clarity and intensity. As Jeffers describes the shrinking
of the earth and sun to mere "particles," he contrasts the long
history of galaxies and "innumerable stars" to humanity's much
briefer history. Jeffers writes that our "two or three million years
are a moment"—a brief flash. We will flare out long before the
universe itself either collapses or disintegrates. In both "I Will
Sing You One-O" and "Margrave," the stars and galaxies are but
a foil to human life, and in their light we appear shadowy, transient, ephemeral.

Jeffers, like Ammons in "Cascadilla Falls," distinguishes himself from nature because of his *consciousness*. Yet human a-
wareness is hardly an advantage in Jeffers's world; he often associates it with depravity. The knowledge the astronomer gains
through consciousness, if indeed he or she is not tricked by the
great distances light must travel to reach the eyes, is that the

"most remote star-swirls" are "fleeing outwards from ours." Here Jeffers alludes to one of the most important findings of early-twentieth-century astronomy, that other galaxies are flying away from us. He was, in all likelihood, familiar with the work of the astronomer Vesto Slipher, who between 1912 and 1928 "succeeded in obtaining spectra of the light from forty galaxies."[6] In his book *The Soul of the Night*, Chet Raymo recalls Slipher's work in an attempt to understand why the galaxies appear to be flying away from us.

> Slipher passed the light of the galaxies through a prism and examined the rainbows of their colors. The light of the galaxies was typical starlight, but the wavelengths of the light were slightly lengthened— shifted toward the red end of the color spectrum. The red shift of the galactic light implied to Slipher that the galaxies were moving away from us.[7]

The questions that Raymo asks about this discovery are the very same ones Jeffers must have asked himself, yet their answers are starkly different. "Are we such unattractive company?" Raymo asks. "Are we at the center of a cosmic repulsion?" Jeffers's answer to both these questions is a resounding *yes*. Yes, we are unattractive company—*yes*, we are witnesses to a cosmic repulsion: "no doubt they are fleeing the contagion / Of consciousness that infects this corner of space." Nevertheless, Raymo, and countless astronomers like him, have not been so personally affronted by the phenomena. He writes:

> Not only are the galaxies receding from us, but the velocities of recession are directly proportional to the distances of the galaxies. This is precisely the relationship one would expect if the texture of the universe were uniformly expanding—everywhere. The galaxies, it seems, are rushing apart. Space is inflating. Our galaxy is not at the center of this cosmic repulsion; residents of every other galaxy would also see their neighbors receding.[8]

In his poem Jeffers mistakenly attributes humanity with being the cause of "fleeing" stars. In actuality, Jeffers, an astute student of astronomy, probably knew what Raymo himself tells us—that our galaxy is not at the center of this cosmic repulsion. But Jeffers chooses to portray it as if we were to blame for the retreat. The gulf between mind and nature seems to widen.

In "Margrave" humanity repels nature; elsewhere in his poetry Jeffers uses astronomy to evoke the *indifference* of nature toward

man. In his long poem "Give Your Heart to the Hawks," Jeffers
has the character Fayne attempt to convince her lover that their
actions are ultimately unimportant:

> the earth, the great
> meteor-ball of live stone, flying
> Through storms of sunlight as if forever, and the sun that
>   rushes away we don't know where, and all
> The fire-manned stars like stallions in a black pasture, each
>   one with his stud of plunging
> Planets for mares that he sprays with power; and universe
>   after universe beyond them, all shining, all alive:
> Do you think all *that* needs us? Or any evil we have done
> Makes any difference?[9]

The earth, sun, stars, and planets exhibit brute power. By contrast
Fayne's actions and her lover's seem inconsequential. Fayne reasons that the world will go on "shining" even if her lover were
to murder his rival. That the universe does not need "us" is
reinforced elsewhere in Jeffers's poetry by astronomical images
that dwarf human desire and effort. Both Jeffers and Frost find
the dichotomy between mind and universe as revealed by astronomy unbridgeable. The more we seem to discover about what is
out there, the further the gap seems to grow between human
consciousness and the night sky.

Ammons, however, wrests out a way to celebrate the vastnesses
science hands us and manages to make us at home in the cosmos.
He is equally adept at journeying out to the farthest reaches of
the universe and at contemplating the cellular basis of life.
Through making his ascent and descent, Ammons achieves his
goal of "widening scope." Ammons, on occasion, will feel the
isolation and terror Frost feels in "I Will Sing You One-O." But
more often he reminds us of Whitman, whom Ammons invokes
in his long poem *Sphere*. Rather than remaining terrorized, Ammons is ultimately energized by ever-new spheres of astronomical thought and discovery. Whitman, in an amazing and
imaginative self-definition, referred to himself as "Walt Whitman; an American, one of the roughs, a kosmos"; he sets up the
integration of self and universe, an integration Ammons develops.[10]

Ammons's poem "Exotic" pays tribute to science for outreach-
ing other modes of inquiry.

> Science outstrips
> other modes &

> reveals more of
> the crux of the matter
> than we can calmly
> handle

(CP, 238)

The title "Exotic" reflects Ammons's own awareness that the poem's assertion is perhaps an "exotic" one, especially in an age where poets like Frost have resisted "assigning science preeminence."[11] Exotic, however, also means "outside of"—and crux means "cross," the essential inner element. Science, coming from outside, strips away more to get us to the crux, which, because it is beyond our senses, we literally cannot handle. What is discovered is so extraordinary, so richly entertaining that we cannot sit "calmly" by.

In order to go further with the implications of "Exotic," I want to draw on three of Ammons's longer poems, "Extremes and Moderations," "Hibernaculum," and Sphere. In these poems Ammons reflects on the gulf between mind and astronomical data and rediscovers a wholeness missing in the work of Frost and Jeffers. In looking at passages from these poems, I propose following the advice Ammons gives on how to read his book-length poem Sphere. In section 44 he explains:

> this measure moves
> to attract and hold attention: . . .
> dip in anywhere, go until the
>
> attractions fail:

(S, 30)

"Dip in anywhere" because Sphere and his other long poems take up various curvatures of mind quickly and then just as quickly drop them and take up some new arc of thought—as, for example, when in Sphere the poet quickly shifts his subject from the Apollo 16 blastoff to an outing with his son. Ammons himself cautions against reading his long poem linearly, following the particular curve of thought at that moment until it tails off and a new one begins. The form of Sphere is like the cosmos, turning in on itself, cycling, recycling; just as there is no place to "start" in the universe, so in the poem that imitates its vast structureless structure, its form in motion or motion in form.

Ammons's advice to "dip in anywhere" may sound unusual, but not from the poet who later, in section 138 of Sphere, declares,

"I'm sick of good poems, all those little rondures / splendidly brought off, painted gourds on a shelf." Ammons expresses disgust with the overly polished poem, the too refined touch (expressed in the French sounding "rondures"). The "painted gourd," an emblem of the "finished" poem, is unnecessarily cosmetic and therefore false, detached from its organic origins. In contrast, Ammons says, at the end of the section, "give me / the dumb, debilitated, nasty, and massive." His long poems resist the effete and genteel quality suggested by the image of "painted gourds on a shelf." Instead, they are at times and to varying degrees cumbersome, long-winded, chaotic, "massive," allowing him to break away from a too limited definition of a poem.

Geoffreys Hartman, in his *New York Times* book review of the *Collected Poems*, criticizes the poet's longer poems for becoming dangerously "all periphery and no center."[12] Even Bloom, who writes that "Ammons . . . defends his procedure by comparing the energy of his poems to the energy of nature," seems to agree with Hartman that some of these long poems "show rather more in common with nature's entropy than with nature's energy."[13] But that is just the point. In his long poems Ammons would prefer to err in the direction of the "debilitating" than to simply add more "painted gourds" to the shelf.

The unwieldy nature of Ammons's long poems may be one explanation for the paucity of critical commentary on them. Holder, in his book *A. R. Ammons*, does devote a chapter to the longer poems, in which he talks mostly about their themes. But a quick look through his selected bibliography of critical articles on Ammons, ranging from 1964 to 1975, shows that not one of over twenty critical essays is devoted entirely to any one of the major long poems.[14] Since that time Fried and De Rosa, in their doctoral dissertations, have filled this gap somewhat, devoting portions of their theses to discussions of key passages within the longer poems.[15] Recently, more critical attention has been given to Ammons's longer poems as evidenced by Cary Wolfe's 1989 article "Symbol Plural: The Later Long Poems of A. R. Ammons" and Gerald Bullis's article "In the Open: A. R. Ammons' Longer Poems."[16] Yet the existing criticism does not discuss the clusters of astronomical passages except occasionally in passing. By focusing on how Ammons widens scope, my approach illuminates just how significant these astronomical clusters are to Ammons's work.

The long poem "Extremes and Moderations" is considered his greatest ecological testimony, and although it does not reach for the stars to the same degree as "Hibernaculum" and Sphere do, it does create an important context for understanding one of the primary motives behind Ammons's use of astronomical facts: a widening of our perspective to get us out of our self-centered focus. It sets up the necessary distanced perspective that allows Ammons to assimilate astronomical data more fully in later poems.

The self-regulating mechanisms that sustain ecological balance are the poem's subject. The reader is presented with example after example of "moderating" natural laws balancing "extreme" tendencies. Ammons discovers in the earth's oceans, in the farthest reaches of the galaxy, and in the human physiology, "currents" that keep forces moving, so that balance is maintained and stagnation or death—both "extremes"—avoided. He tells us:

> go to look for the ocean currents and
> though they are always flowing there they are, right in place, if
> with seasonal leans and sways: the human body
> staying in change, time rushing through, ingestion,
>
> elimination: if change stopped, the mechanisms of
> holding would lose their tune: current informs us,
> is the means of our temporary stay:
>
> (CP, 334 – 35)

That the ocean's currents are always "right in place," allowing for some seasonal variation ("leans and sways"), is an astronomical truth. The sea's currents are all ultimately due to differential heating of ocean and atmosphere by the sun (hotter near the equator, colder at the poles). The eternal flow of oceans and atmosphere is a way to re-establish equilibrium.

Ammons swings the reader's awareness from the macrocosmic—ocean currents as astronomical phenomena—to that which is closer to home—human digestive processes. By discovering correspondences between the cosmos (macrocosm) and the individual (microcosm), he awakens in us a broad appreciation for the self-regulating mechanisms our bodies share with more cosmic phenomena.

For example, the ocean's currents share with bodily functions regularity. By virtue of their constant and regular processes the ocean (through its currents and tides) and the body (through ingestion and elimination) function and maintain equilibrium. One can see in bodily "extremes and moderations"—ingestion

being an "extreme," elimination being a "moderation"—the flow
of currents, the intake of water and the release, the rush of energy
and its relaxation. On a large scale the ecosystem has the capability to maintain its equilibrium through self-purifying mechanisms; ocean currents and digestive processes are but two
examples of the balancing act at work.

In a moment memorable for its candidness and for its lyricism,
Ammons directly implores the reader of "Extremes and Moderations" to "enter the currents."

> O city, I cry at
> the gate, the glacier is your
> mother, the currents of the deep father you, you sleep
>
> in the ministry of trees, the boulders are your brothers sustaining
> you: come out, I cry, into the lofty assimilations: women, let
> down your hair under the dark leaves of the night grove, enter
> the currents with a sage whining, rising into the circular
>
> dance: men, come out and be with the wind, speedy and lean, fall
> into the moon-cheered waters, plunge into the ecstasy of rapids:
> children, come out and play in the toys of divinity: glass, brick,
> stone, curb, rail are freezing you out of your motions, the
>
> uncluttered circulations:
>
> (CP, 335)

The inhabitants of the city are surrounded by the forces of
nature—glaciers, trees, boulders—and Ammons urges the urban
dwellers to break out of the glass and brick that hem them in.
The movement he urges is outward and upward. "Come out," he
says, "into the lofty assimilations." Frost in "I Will Sing You One-
O" remains inside looking out; he cannot "assimilate" his vision
of the night with his own humanity. Ammons, however, in a
Romantic gesture, urges movement beyond walls that hem us
in—to join with whatever is on the other side—to "assimilate"
with nature. Ultimately, he will manage to achieve through consciousness the "assimilation" he is encouraging here.

The city, for Ammons, as we have seen in chapter 3, represents
stasis, and in contrast to it he urges women, children, and men
to enter with abandon the "currents"—"the uncluttered circulations." We have been cut off too long from the nourishing energies of a nature both wild and passionate. These "currents" and
"circulations" are the cosmic swirls found in rivers and oceans,

in the biosphere, and in the farthest reaches of the galaxy. By plunging "into the ecstasy of rapids," we lift ourselves out of the plateaus of urban life and participate in the more exhilarating current of nature. We gain new perspective as we experience the cosmic dance—the "circulations" of wind, "speedy and lean," of tides and "moon-cheered waters," of planets in their orbits around the sun. Once again the key word is "currents"; Ammons implores his readers to move beyond the artificial into a world of flux, into space, where both the body and the eye have room to explore.

His advice is particularly apt for seeing the radiance of the night sky. The night's dazzling brilliance is obstructed by the city's artificial light and pollution. The result is that we have "lost the faint lights." One must move beyond the confines of "glass, brick / stone, curb, and rail." According to Raymo:

> On the darkest, clearest nights thousands of stars are visible to the naked eye. In addition to stars, there are other naked-eye wonders available to the careful observer who is far from city lights: star clusters, at least one galaxy, nebulas, the Milky Way, the zodiacal light. But the typical urban or suburban observer might see only a few hundred of the brightest stars, and none of the more elusive objects. We have abused the darkness. We have lost the faint lights.[17]

Ammons urges the city-dwellers to move beyond constrictions on their vision in order to regain these "faint lights."

As the poem progresses, he accumulates more and more evidence in support of his thesis—that the laws of nature are self-regulating, that the best we can do is not to interfere with them, that we should in fact attune ourselves to them. Ammons is not overly optimistic about our ability to achieve harmony, however; he repeatedly presents examples of land desecration, chemical pollution, and ecological chaos resulting from greed and short-sightedness. In contrast to these images of desecration—"bleak scald of lakes, underground poisonous tides, air litter / like a dusk"—he continuously returns to the unadulterated forces of nature beyond the confines of the city. At one point in the poem he declares:

> I have found the world
> so marvelous that nothing would surprise me: that may sound
> contradictory, the wrong way to reach the matter-of-fact: but
> if you can buy comets sizzling around in super-elongated

orbits and a mathematics risen in man that corresponds to the
orbits, why, simple as it is finally, you can move on to glutinous
molecules sloshing around in the fallen seas for something
to stick to: that there should have been possibilities enough to

include all that has occurred is beyond belief, an extreme the
strictures and disciplines of which prevent loose-flowing
phantasmagoria:

(CP, 339)

Ammons expresses no trace of Jeffers's brooding on human consciousness. Instead he expresses admiration, even awe, for human
intelligence that can translate the physical events into mathematical equations. That comets, or what the Greeks called "long-
haired stars," orbit the sun closely enough for us to observe them,
that in their orbits they do not "switch our magnetic poles" so
as to upset the oceans' currents, that humanity in its inventive-
ness has derived a mathematics that corresponds to the orbits,
are indeed the source of "marvel." Given all that has happened
in the evolution of the universe, nothing would surprise this
poet. For if indeed one observes "comets sizzling around," incredible as they appear, one can go on to accept the equally
incredible as commonplace—the origin of life in ancient seas—
"glutinous / molecules sloshing around in the fallen seas for
something / to stick to." Ammons expresses his amazement over
how much has worked out. One recalls Whitman's awe before
the universe when he writes, toward the end of "Song of Myself":
"It is not chaos or death—it is form, union, plan—it is eternal
life—it is Happiness."[18] The creation is not, as Ammons here
states: "loose-flowing / phantasmagoria"; the "strictures and disciplines" through which natural laws express themselves are too
intelligent to be merely haphazard.

In "Extremes and Moderations," Ammons evokes a precari-
ously balanced world, one whose cosmic forces are self-regulating, but which are susceptible to artificial disturbances. The
major causes of disturbance—pollution, ecological "tinkering,"
improvements "marked uncertain," all kinds of artificial ma-
nipulation—cause Ammons to lament at the end of the poem:

extreme and moderation is losing its quality, its effect: the
artificial has taken on the complication of the natural and where
to take hold, how to let go, perplexes individual action: ruin
and gloom are falling off the shoulders of progress: blue-green

globe, we have tripped your balance and gone into exaggerated
possession: this seems to me the last poem written to the world
before its freshness capsizes and sinks into the slush: the
rampaging industrialists, the chemical devisers and manipulators

are forging tanks, filling vats of smoky horrors because of
dollar lust, so as to live in long white houses on the summits
of lengthy slopes, for the pleasures of making others spur and
turn: but common air moves over the slopes, and common rain's

losing its heavenly clarity: if we move beyond
the natural cautions, we must pay the natural costs, our every
extreme played out: where we can't create the room of
playing out, we must avoid the extreme, disallow it:

(CP, 340)

The poet expresses horror and indignation over the misman-
agement of the planet. Progress is a curse, the ruin and gloom
caused by disturbances of the natural balance. In Ammons's
view, as in the estimation of many environmental activists, the
"rampaging industrialists" are to blame. Their error is to place
greed—"dollar lust"—ahead of their concern for ecological
balance.

Ammons knows that we have reached a critical point in the
history of the planet ("blue-green globe")—its continued despo-
liation will eventually destroy it. Thus, he writes his poem at
what he perceives as a critical threshold, just before the world's
"freshness capsizes and sinks into the slush." Those who move
beyond the "natural cautions" must ultimately reap the "fruits"
of their actions, a world where "extremes and moderations" are
no longer in balance, where "common rain's / losing its heavenly
clarity." "Common rain" is both *ordinary* and *commonly* shared
by us all. Its ordinariness, however, seems all the more "heavenly," given the recent concerns over acid rain, with dissolved
sulphuric acid, dust, and ashes in its droplets.

Those who desecrate the earth because of "dollar lust" are
suffering from extreme shortsightedness, preventing them from
seeing beyond their very narrow scope. They have failed to realize the truth of Ammons's ecological position, expressed best in
section 138 of *Sphere*: "touch the universe anywhere you touch
it / everywhere." As a result they are unaware or unconcerned
about the consequences of their actions. Ammons, while point-
ing a finger at the industrialists, knows we are all susceptible to
this disease. He uses the pronoun "we" to implicate us all in the

impending disaster: "blue-green / globe, we have tripped your balance and gone into exaggerated / possession." "Exaggerated possession" can be defined in many ways. In one sense, it is obsession with ownership, with acquiring material things—"white houses on the summits / of lengthy slopes." Ammons, of course, is not alone among contemporary poets who with increasing indignation in the 1960s condemned the kind of greed that breeds disrespect for the environment.[19] In another, more profound sense, "exaggerated possession" is a narrowing down of the visual field so that one becomes focused on the self to the exclusion of the world outside. The failure to look up, out, and around results in a tunnel vision, criminal on a planet where we are all interconnected.

The shortsightedness of those in power, those who fill the vats with smoky horrors, is particularly alarming because the effects of their actions so directly influence the environment. Clearly Ammons's desire to widen scope is in part his response to and corrective for the shortsighted vision of those who abuse the environment. The evidence he accumulates testifies to nature's checks and balances, broadening the reader's vision of how things work when unimpeded.

Unlike Frost, Ammons believes that astronomy has a purpose. Its cumulative effect is to culture in us what Carl Sagan refers to as "a sense of cosmic perspective—living out our lives on a tiny hunk of rock and metal circling one of 250 billion stars that make up our galaxy in a universe of billions of galaxies."[20] It was Sagan who astutely observed that the ecological conscience, to which Ammons appeals in "Extremes and Moderations," was fueled by space exploration in the 1960s and 1970s. Sagan writes in his essay "Space Exploration as a Human Enterprise":

> The current resurgence of interest in the ecology of the planet Earth is also connected with this longing for a cosmic perspective. Many of the leaders of the ecological movement were originally stimulated to action by photographs of Earth taken from space, pictures revealing a tiny, delicate, and fragile world, exquisitely sensitive to the depredations of man—a meadow in the middle of the sky.[21]

One proof of Sagan's thesis is that The Whole Earth Catalog, largely devoted to raising ecological consciousness in the early 1970s, portrayed on its cover just such a photograph of the earth floating in space.[22] To see the earth as a floating "meadow"—as Sagan has seen it, and as Ammons, and before him Walt Whitman, have seen it—requires a shift in perspective; one must either visualize the planet as an orb among others, or actually make the voyage in a spaceship, or see photographs of the earth taken from outer space. Ammons strives to achieve this kind of shift in scope by his use of astronomical facts. The astronomical passages in Ammons's poetry often confirm what his colleague, Carl Sagan, at Cornell University writes in the Preface to his book *The Cosmic Connection*—that "the deflation of some of our more common conceits is one of the practical applications of astronomy."[23]

In another of Ammons's long poems, "Hibernaculum," he imaginatively makes a descent through the layers of the earth.

> I look to the ground for the
> lost, the ground's lost: I see grime, just grime, grain,
>
> 7
>
> grit, grist: the layers at thousand-year intervals
> accumulate, reduce to beginnings: but I see the nightwatchman
> at the cave's mouth, his eyes turned up in stunned amusement
>
> to the constellations:
>
> (CP, 353)

Ammons "sees" in his mind's eye one of the earliest astronomers—"the nightwatchman / at the cave's mouth." The poet displays his sense of play in the pun describing this ancient astronomer who keeps "watch" at the cave's mouth—on the *look-out* for trouble but also on the *look-up* at the night sky. His reaction to the constellations typifies Ammons's own reaction—"stunned amusement." The vision is indeed "stunning"; the constellations are both astounding and strikingly attractive. For this earliest nightwatchman, for Ammons, and for hundreds of thousands of people who make their way annually to planetariums, the constellations also please and entertain. Ammons will build on this experience elsewhere in "Hibernaculum" and in the book-length volume *Sphere.*

"Hibernaculum" refers to a place of winter residence. Written when "the days shorten down to a / gap in the night," this long poem provides him with a shelter for winter. Ammons's first long poem, *Tape for the Turn of the Year,* also provided him with a "place" to spend the winter. If on occasion the rapid fire of commentary on a wide array of topics in both poems seems exasperating, one must keep in mind that his meditations provide him with the necessary diversion to survive the blustery season.

The poem's lining, like the winter quarters of a hibernating animal, gives him all the protection he needs.

In section 18 of this winter meditation, Ammons contemplates the earth, the platform from which the stars are observed. He finds in the earth's predictability, in its continuous and orderly revolution around the sun, a spiritual center:

> our immediate staying's the rock but
> the staying of the rock's motion: motion, that spirit!
> we could veer into, dimpling, the sun or into the cold
>
> 19
>
> orbital lofts, but our motion, our weight, our speed
> are organized here like a rock, our spiritual stay:
>
> (CP, 357)

The earth is indeed a gigantic rock—its solidity is our most "immediate staying"—and it provides us with direct support for our actions. We walk, we grow food, we observe the other planets—essentially we live here by virtue of this "rock" so firmly planted beneath our feet. While the "rocklike" and seemingly solid, even stationary, quality of the earth supports or "stays" our human activity, what supports the earth itself is motion, spinning at 800 miles per hour, traveling nearly 190 million miles in its yearly journey around the sun. The steady rotation of the earth on its axis creates its own "staying" power. We are reminded of the law of equilibrium that Ammons more subtly alludes to in "Spaceship," and of the "staying change" he talks about in "Extremes and Moderations." In all three instances "motion" is a spiritual force, a vital principle, and a dynamic power.

Ammons characteristically appeals to astronomical fact to evoke intelligence at work in the universe. The *intelligence* of the earth's motion, for example, ensures that collisions are avoided. If our planet were to bump into the sun, the consequence might indeed be perceived as "dimpling." The earth would leave a depression (like a "dimple") on the sun's surface. Ammons playfully invents the verb "dimpling" here to describe such a consequence. The earth, however, will not "dimple" the sun, nor will it swerve off "into the cold orbital lofts"—potentially as dangerous. Instead, "our motion, our weight, our speed / are organized here like a rock, our spiritual stay." Again, by repeating the pronoun "our," Ammons insists on *our* close link to the planet, as if in some way we share a similar destiny. The key word in this phrase, however, is "organized." The laws of nature that structure "our" (our own and the earth's) motion, weight, and speed have been "organized" in just such a way that these kinds of catastrophic collisions do not occur. The result is that we feel secure—solid as a "rock" on what is actually a floating, spinning ball.

In the previous passage, Ammons also alludes to the great classical Copernican controversy—whether or not the earth moves at all. The followers of Ptolemy, of course, believed the earth was stationary—"the staying of the rock." Copernicus's followers believed in the earth's motion; the planet revolved around the sun. The controversy, of course, has long been over; nevertheless, Ammons adds his own poetic gloss to the issue by posing "the staying of the rock's motion." The earth derives its stability from its mobility. Ammons also refers to the earth's motion as "that spirit!" Galileo, the first astronomer to document Copernicus's theory, was censored and ultimately forced to recant on religious grounds. His telescopic observations confirmed that the earth did indeed revolve around the sun, but the church felt that his findings were contrary to Scripture. In an age of science, however, Ammons turns the situation around, discovering *spirit* in scientific fact.[24]

In section 29 of "Hibernaculum," Ammons catalogues several experiences and perceptions, culminating with "the Pacific Ocean," described as "a small sweep through the arc / of the galaxy, one arm of the spiral in particular." Normally, one does not think of the Pacific as "small" in any way. It is the earth's largest body of water (70 million square miles), extending from the Arctic to the Antarctic and from the Americas to Asia and Australia. Yet seen from a cosmic perspective, the Pacific Ocean *shrinks*, and becomes "a small sweep through the arc / of the galaxy."

The shift in perspective renders "small" that which was before considered "enormous." The effect is to redefine scope and geography; one becomes connected to a much larger field of experience. The ocean, of course, has become one of the primary waste dumps for industrialists. One justification, perhaps, for its pollution is that the oceans of the earth are so vast. Yet seen from an astronomical point of view, their vastness shrinks, their seemingly endless and exhaustless nature is transformed into a mere "sweep."

Elsewhere in "Hibernaculum" Ammons meditates on the kinds of discoveries made possible by new, more powerful telescopes. One such dramatic discovery is the "sighting" of two previously unknown galaxies. He learns of this, as does the average citizen, through the news media. Ammons himself culls his knowledge of astronomy from many different sources—including newspapers and books. Doubtless, Ammons, like Jeffers before him, has also spent time looking up at the night sky through the lenses available in the observatory. He must also have spent time looking at recent photographs from outer space. Here, however, he reports on what he has read:

the other night the paper said two nearby

106

galaxies, hidden by our Milky Way, have been found, sight
having made other kinds of sight hunting, eating, loving
had no use for, some high conditions of burning: oh, yes,

we're in the explosions and we're going to see them out
and no other course could be half as interesting: falling
back can't help us now, returning to nature's lovely

subtle mechanisms: forward to the finish, of course, the
way it's always been or to a knowledge how to avoid the
finish: the possibility seen through to its perfect end:

(CP, 386)

For Ammons, the sighting of those galaxies is further evidence of human evolution. We have transcended the more elemental human activities of "hunting, eating, loving." "Sight," or advances in telescopic vision, have in fact made for new kinds of vision. What we "see" now are "some high conditions of burning," a reference to the formation of galaxies billions of light years away. Ammons knows that the evolution of galaxies, including our own, involves several explosions or nuclear reactions. Robert Jastrow and Malcolm Thompson describe this process in their book *Astronomy: Fundamentals and Frontiers*:

A galaxy in the process of formation, before any stars have formed in it, is called a protogalaxy. In the course of time the protogalaxy contracts and its density rises, as a result of the continuing inward force of its own gravity. Throughout this time, pockets of gas continually form and dissolve in the swirling and eddying motion within the cloud. Whenever the density of one of these pockets of gas is high enough, it turns into a protostar. The protostars contract and heat up until nuclear reactions begin at their centers, at which point they turn into stars. When many stars have been formed, the protogal-axy becomes a galaxy.[25]

In the evolution of galaxies, a critical moment occurs when nu-clear reactions transform protostars into stars, which ultimately form galaxies. The "high conditions of burning" Ammons refers to are the "conditions" that make possible the "nuclear reac-tions" essential in the evolution of galaxies.

He goes one step further, however, in asserting that "we're in the explosions"; Ammons knows that the Milky Way, our galaxy, is also the consequence of an actual cosmic explosion. Astrono-mers themselves are uncertain whether "the formation of galax-ies may have been limited to the early years of the Universe, or it may have been a process stretched out over a long span of time and, perhaps, still continuing today."[26] If the process is ongoing, our presence here guarantees our participating "in" the explo-sions, for they would be contemporaneous with our existence. But even if our galaxy is no longer forming, Ammons is correct to assert that "we're in the explosions," for other galaxies, perhaps neighboring ones like those recently sighted, are still exploding, and our proximity to them makes his statement just as true.

In this passage Ammons engages the reader in the process of cosmic evolution. He knows, for example, that in fact man will "see" out the evolutionary process. "See" is a reference both to new astronomical tools and technologies that enable us to better understand cosmic evolution and to our ability to adapt and persevere, to "see" things out, to "evolve." According to him, "no other course could be half as interesting"; that is, cosmic evolu-tion and all the surprises it holds is of supreme interest.

Ammons's fascination with cosmic evolution may in fact de-rive from his understanding of what were two competing cosmol-ogies. The Big Bang theory, which explains that the universe originated with an initial cosmic explosion, also contends that eventually "the galaxies themselves will grow dimmer and even-tually fade out entirely. In the end, the Universe is devoid of matter, energy, and life."[27] On the other hand, the "Steady State" theory of the universe, now discredited but still current at the time Ammons wrote this passage, is not nearly so pessimistic. Its founder, Thomas Gold, contended that hydrogen, essential for the formation of new stars, is continuously created out of noth-ing, ensuring that the universe renews itself in perpetuity. "Ac-cording to this cosmology—the Steady State theory—the

Universe has been unchanged and will remain unchanged throughout eternity."[28]

Ammons, in these lines from "Hibernaculum," suggests that we cannot advance our cause by devolving to simpler life forms, but that we must move forward to the finish. In proposing two alternatives—"the / way it's always been or to a knowledge how to avoid the / finish"—he is alluding to these two cosmologies, which predict very different courses for the universe. The Steady State theory presents the likelihood of the universe continuing "the way it's always been"; the Big Bang theory predicts the eventual fading out of galaxies, compelling humanity to develop "a knowledge how to avoid the finish." Just as scientists have learned to avoid other unpleasant alternatives through technology, Ammons suggests that possibly the inevitable "crunch" predicted by the Big Bang theory can also be avoided. Consequently, humanity would be able to realize its potential—"the possibility seen through to its perfect end." The unfolding of the drama is bound to be of supreme interest to astronomers and to the rest of us. (Only recently have astronomers discovered new evidence, detection of electromagnetic radiation, called microwaves, to support the Big Bang theory.)

Of all of Ammons's long poems, *Sphere: The Form of a Motion* "reaches for the stars" in the most persistent way. It has, as De-Rosa notes, "handfuls of cosmic and galactic particulars," ranging from Ammons's continual fascination with the earth as a floating orb to his ongoing obsession with other planets and galaxies.[29] Given this, it is surprising no one has commented on the relation between the poem's title and its fascination with astronomy. As I noted earlier, the ancients referred to the night sky and its stars as the *celestial sphere*, and although Ammons is concerned with the multiple associations of his title, one of the most important must be the image of the heavenly sphere composed of myriad spheres of energy and light. Even contemporary astronomers, when cataloguing celestial objects in their positions in the sky, think of all the heavenly bodies as lying on the inside surface of a sphere, still called the celestial sphere.

Within the poem itself Ammons describes our pear-shaped planet, the earth, as an "oblate spheroid," and he celebrates, as Whitman himself did, its "floating dimensions." The subtitle of the poem—"the form of a motion"—is equally suggestive. DeRosa points to the paradoxical nature of this phrase, the apparent contradiction between form (which suggests fixity) and motion. She astutely observes that "this quality of formful motion is, however, the composition of the universe and its 'matter,' as far as theoretical physics has been able to determine."[30] The notion of "formful motion" also has rich astronomical possibilities, the most salient of which is evidenced by the image of the "floating orb," celebrated elsewhere as a "staying change."

What is this seemingly endless poem—"1,860 lines long, with only one full stop in it"—about? The very form of the poem itself, with its many open-ended sections, its seemingly countless arguments and shifts in focus, from the astronomical sublime to the poet's own personal and mildly satirized health habits—"my / potassium-laced diet (jiggers of orange juice) will free me / from episodes of irregular heartbeats"—seems to defy the notion that it is about anything at all, except perhaps whatever is running through the poet's mind at any particular moment. Indeed, he declares right at the outset that "often those who are not good for much else turn to thought / and it's just great." The inexhaustibility of the mind to contemplate just about anything does seem in large measure, or mismeasure, depending on your sympathy for the wanderings of Ammons's mind, to be what *Sphere* is most about. Given this, however, Ammons does appear to return to a set of recurring subjects even as he indulges himself in the inexhaustibility of thought.

Sphere, like the earlier "Essay on Poetics," spends a good deal of time talking about the nature of poetry. Toward the midpoint of the poem, Ammons reflects on the purpose of poetry by comparing it to hypnosis, only to distinguish the two as he probes their effects on consciousness.

hypnosis
is induced by focusing the attention: the trinket swings
or spins before the eyes, the normal flood of distractions

67

that keeps one awake is drained, and the mind sinks into
simplified ease: the poem, its rhythm, is exclusive and hypnotic,
too, but the poem keeps enough relevant variety going to interest

the mind from sleep but enough focus to disinterest it in
external matters: a hypnotic focus, then, that is awakening,
a focus of controlled fullness, not over-exclusiveness: but

the purpose of the motion of a poem is to bring the focused,
awakened mind to no-motion, to a still contemplation of the

whole motion, all the motions, of the poem: this is very

different from hypnosis: a descent into the subconscious
(tentacles maybe into the unconscious) is prepared for not by
blotting out the conscious mind but by intensifying the alertness

68

of the conscious mind even while it permits itself to sink,
to be lowered down the ladder of structured motions to the
refreshing energies of the deeper self:

(S, 40)

That poetry takes the mind in a vertical direction, enabling it to
experience "the refreshing energies of the deeper self," has been
a concern of Ammons dating at least as far back as 1967. In a
paper delivered to the International Poetry Forum in Pittsburgh,
Ammons concluded that "poetry leads us to the unstructured
sources of our beings. . . . Poetry is a verbal means to a nonverbal source. It is a motion to no-motion, to the still point of
contemplation and deep realization."[31] Ammons echoes this sentiment in a 1986 interview, where he says: "There are so many
things that happen in a poem that are nonverbal, not just verbal.
And I think finally the nonverbal assimilations are the things
that really draw us to the poems and to the poets."[32] The "sinking" effect created by its rhythms likens poetry to hypnosis,
which also causes the mind to transcend the "normal flood of
distractions," but poetry, unlike hypnosis, allows the mind to
stay awake, conscious of itself, even as it "sinks." The poetic
experience of transcending described by Ammons has two kinds
of benefits: the holistic experience of all the poem's motions,
and secondly, the revitalization of the mind.

Sphere, however, is more than simply a meditation on its own
purposes; it is also a continuation of Ammons's quest to fathom
the "one-many" paradox. Before discussing the astronomical
passages in the poem, I would like to consider briefly Ammons's
discovery of unifying correspondences in the natural world. In
section 9 he probes the underlying cellular unity of all life:

though the surface is crisp with pattern still we know
that there are generalized underlyings, planes of substratum
lessening from .differentiation: under all life, fly and

> dandelion, protozoan, bushmaster, and ladybird, tendon
> and tendril . . . is the same cell:
>
> (S, 14)

Beneath discrete and multitudinous surface patterns are underlying unities. His "descent" through the world of physical phenomena is parallel to the "sinking" experienced by the mind in
the act of reading the poem. Both lead to greater unities. Moreover, Ammons's descent to discover underlying unities mirrors
the tendency of modern physics, mathematics, and physiology
to explain phenomena in terms of the most fundamental components. Ammons does not insist, however, that the whole can be
known solely from its parts, a kind of "reductionism" both he
and many scientists would oppose. After contemplating the cellular basis of such disparate things as the "fly" and the "dandelion," he goes on to acknowledge:

> I could not say, then, that the earthworm is not
> my radical cousin, and I could not say that my veins entering
>
> along the cell walls disresemble the transportative leaf:
> I mean, if one speaks of mysticism, it makes good science,
> which is the best part of science, that it makes mysticism
>
> discussable without a flurry:
>
> (S, 15)

The mystical traditions of the East have more typically concerned themselves with what Ammons suggests in these lines
and states elsewhere in *Sphere*—that we are "unmendably integral with the universe." Yet Ammons arrives at this conclusion
through the facts of biology and botany. Ammons's assertion is
in itself revealing. He leads us to believe that his real attraction
to science is that it "makes mysticism / discussable without a
flurry." If some of the statements of mysticism can be given a
scientific interpretation, then they are open to quantifiable experiment and are therefore discussable.[33] Ammons does not explain what he means by "mysticism," but within the context of
this passage one can surmise that "mysticism" implies the unity
of all things. Here Ammons discovers this unity in structural
correspondences.

Calvin Bedient, in his review of *Sphere* in the *New York Times
Book Review*, has criticized Ammons's "*reasonable* approach to
Romantic 'spirituality.'" Bedient takes issue with Ammons's

"colonizing for poetry the structural models of science." Rather than perceiving Ammons as a direct descendant of Whitman, he regards the latter-day poet as a weaker mutation of the once visionary strain. Bedient calls Ammons "an intellectual's Whitman, afoot with a laboratory vision that, for all its abstract vocabulary, and however palely, he lectures and tweaks into poetry."[34] Bedient's statement is unfortunate, demeaning both Whitman and Ammons. In calling Ammons an "intellectual's Whitman," he suggests there is a lack of intellectual content in Whitman, when in fact much of Whitman's use of science is every bit as informed and accurate as Ammons's, albeit Ammons has access to a new set of scientific facts. Moreover, Bedient suggests that the twentieth-century poet has somehow shrunk the Whitmanian vision into the laboratory, whereas Ammons actually sustains and expands the Whitmanian fascination with outer space. Lastly, Bedient finds the language of science in Ammons's poems abstract, overly rhetorical, somehow twisted or pinched forcibly into the poem. Although Ammons's scientific diction occasionally lapses into abstractness, in most instances it is precise, concrete, and visually suggestive.

Ammons, in section 47 of *Sphere*, explores in detail what Whitman intuited long ago in his poem "When I Heard the Learn'd Astronomer." Whitman's poem has often been mistakenly read as disavowing strong intellectual interest in astronomy and science. Rather than reading it as a rejection of the facts and figures in the astronomer's lecture, we can view the poem as Whitman's affirmation of the personal, immediate, and direct apperception of those facts and figures:

When I heard the learn'd astronomer,
When the proofs, the figures, were ranged in columns before me,
When I was shown the charts and diagrams, to add, divide, and
     measure them,
When I sitting heard the astronomer when he lectured with much
     applause in the lecture-room,
How soon unaccountable I became tired and sick,
Till rising and gliding out I wander'd off by myself,
In the mystical moist night-air, and from time to time,
Look'd up in perfect silence at the stars.

                                                    (LOG, 271)

It is easy to see how the poem might be read as a repudiation of the calculations of astronomers, given their "sickening" influence on the poet. Typically, the ending of the poem, when Whitman walks out into the "mystical night-air," has been read as the poet's attempt to revive himself after the stuffy lecture. Beaver notes that the poem has been "most popular as a piece of evidence showing Whitman's impatience with science." Beaver himself counters this argument by emphasizing that Whitman was at an astronomer's lecture in the first place, and that "he was looking at charts and diagrams," just as he had on numerous other occasions.[35] Yet this interpretation does not do justice to the poem either. Hyatt Waggoner, in his reading, seems to come close to the truth: "when the poet walked out and 'look'd up in perfect silence at the stars,' he was not repudiating objective knowledge in favor of pure subjectivity but was acting out his need to experience for himself the personal dimension of knowledge."[36] Having listened to the astronomer's explanation of the vastness of the heavens, Whitman moves beyond the proofs to a direct vision of the night sky. His walking out on the lecture is a criticism of the astronomer for stopping short of what he should do with the facts—absorb them. By "rising and gliding out," Whitman renders the astronomer's objective impersonal description personally meaningful.

Whitman also subtly demonstrates his own scientific insight when he describes looking up at the stars "from time to time." The phrase should not be limited to its colloquial sense—that is, intermittently, or occasionally. Rather, the words suggest in a precise and technical way the gap in time between our looking at the stars and the origination of the light we see from them—traveling an unimaginable distance to reach us. Whitman knows that a lecture cannot replace experience, but he also knows that experience alone does not replace facts. Rather, his experience of the night sky is enriched by facts. Having listened to the astronomer's lecture, and having absorbed the facts, Whitman's gaze into the night sky is well informed—he not only sees, but he also knows what he sees.

Ammons, in one of the more dramatic moments in *Sphere*, explores in detail the astronomic possibilities of what Whitman alluded to in the last lines of his poem. Contemplating the speed at which light reaches us from various stars, he writes in sections 47 and 48:

                                        we are as in a
cone of ages: each of us stands in the peak and center
of perception: around us, in the immediate area of recent

events, the planets make quickly-delivered news and the sun

acquaints us of its plumes eight minutes old: but then
the base widens dropping back and down in time through

the spinal stars of spirals and deepens broadening into
the core of our configuration with its ghostly other side:
and then the gulfs and deepenings begin and fall away

48

through glassy darkness and shadowy mind: antiquity on
antiquity the removes unveil, galaxies neighbors and foreign
cousins and groups of galaxies into the hazy breadths and

depths the telescope spells its eye to trace: but here
what took its beginning in the farthest periphery of event,
perception catches the impact of and halts to immediacy,

the billion-year-old flint light striking chemical changes
into the eye: behold: the times break across one
another like waves in surfy shoals and explode into the

white water of instantaneous being: each of us stands in
the cone of ages to collect the moment that breaks the
deeper future's past through: each of us peak and center:

(S, 31–32)

Ammons uses the image of the light cone to evoke the great distances light must travel to reach us and to celebrate human perception at the "peak and center" of the cone. "The planets make quickly have delivered news" because they are relatively near—it doesn't take their light very long to reach us. The "plumes" of the sun, of course, also arrive relatively soon—just "eight minutes old"—but as the base of the cone widens we drop back and down in time because light will travel greater distances over increasingly longer times in order to reach our eye. The deeper we look into space through a telescope, the farther back in time we go, and Ammons works his way back "through / the spinal stars of spirals," a reference to our galaxy and its myriad stars, and then back to "the core of our configuration." Subsequent layers of "antiquity" are unveiled as we look farther and farther into space—light from nearby galaxies, their more distant "cousins," and still other galaxies clustered into groups reach us over increasingly greater distances and spans of time, until eventually we "reach" the "hazy breadths"—suggestive of the time when the galaxies were first beginning to form. (Even as I write this,

new galaxies are being discovered—new antiquities are unveiled.) With the words "but here," Ammons stunningly turns
our attention from the unveiling of antiquities to what happens
"here"—from space time to earth time.

>   but here
>   what took its beginning in the farthest periphery of event,
>   perception catches the impact of and halts to immediacy,
>
>   the billion-year-old flint light striking chemical changes
>   into the eye:
>
>   (S, 32)

The light from distant stars and galaxies find its destination in
the human retina (spherical in shape), where it strikes "chemical
changes into the eye." Having traveled vast distances (a light year
is the distance that light travels in one year, about 6 trillion
miles) over incredibly long periods of time, the "flint light"
comes to a stunning "halt." The impact of light being arrested
by human consciousness testifies to the power of our perceptive
mechanisms:

>   the times break across one
>   another like waves in surfy shoals and explode into the
>
>
>   white water of instantaneous being: each of us stands in
>   the cone of ages to collect the moment that breaks the
>   deeper future's past through: each of us peak and center:
>
>   (S, 32)

Ammons likens the light's arrival to ocean waves crashing; the
waves meet and intersect in the shoal; likewise the light beams
meet and intersect in a moment of our "instantaneous being."
We are the ultimate processor of all that light; we stand, viewed
from the side, at the peak and, viewed from the top, at the center
of the cone. While Ammons's description evokes the awe one
must feel looking out at a star in another galaxy a million light
years away, it also celebrates human perception and consciousness that "absorbs" the light. Ammons's celebration of consciousness as the synthesizer of all that light stands in stark
contrast to Jeffers, who in describing a similar phenomenon accents the negative—that the sources of light are retreating from
depraved human consciousness.

Ammons has explored the resonance of Whitman's phrase "from time to time" in all its richness, without shrinking the Whitmanian vision. Moreover, his account of the light cone is physically precise without seeming unnecessarily abstract. Rather than being haunted by the Whitmanian ghost, as Bloom would have us think, Ammons builds upon the greatness of his poetic father ("the greatness of the son is the exuding of the greatness of the father"), in just the way Whitman said the poet should build upon the scientist's achievement.

In a later passage Ammons seems intent upon reversing the lens or "mirrorment," so that the earth is seen from outer space:

> from other planets,
> as with other planets from here, we rise and set, our presence,
> reduced to light, noticeable in the dark when the sun is
>
> away: reduced and distanced into light, our brotherhood
> constituted into shining, our landforms, seas, colors
> subsumed to bright announcement: we are alone in a sea that
>
> 150
>
> shows itself nowhere in a falling surf but if it does not
> go on forever folds back into a further motion of itself:
> the plentitude of nothingness! planets seeds in a coronal
>
> weaving so scant the fabric is the cloth of nakedness:
> Pluto our very distant friend skims a gulf so fine and far
> millions and thousands of millions of years mean little to—
>
> how far lost we are, if saving is anywhere else: but light,
> from any distance or point we've met it, shines with a similar
> summation, margin affirmational, so we can see edges to the
>
> black roils in the central radiances, galaxies colliding in
> million-year meetings, others sprung loose into spiral
> unwindings: fire, cold space, black concentration:
>
> (S, 77)

From some distant planet the earth would appear to rise and set, just as from here other planets appear to rise and set. "Our presence," if we were standing on Mars, would be "reduced to light"—that is all we would see, no details. And just as planets are seen only in the nighttime because the sun is too bright in the daytime, so too would the earth's light be discernible from some distant planet "only when the sun is / away." Then our "sphere" becomes just a speck of light, all the things that bind us together "subsumed to bright announcement." In a similar way, when we look up at the night sky to see Mars it is reduced to a little red speck of light. The sea that "we are alone in" is, of course, the vast universe, which "if it does not / go on forever folds back into a further motion of itself." Here again Ammons alludes to the two competing theories, one that holds that the universe is open and will "go on forever," the other that it is closed and will collapse, folding back into itself—"the plenitude of nothingness!" This phrase, rich with Eastern philosophical connotations (e.g., the Tao is a fullness that is empty), also aptly suggests the tremendous potential in the collapsed or empty state of the universe—for out of its collapse, astrophysicists speculate, the universe may in fact re-create itself. The planets appear to be "seeds in a coronal," points on a wreath or circlet (the circle of creation, collapse, and re-creation) connected by nothing but the vast spaces between them. Pluto, the ninth and farthest planet from the sun, "our very distant friend," "skims" the incredible distance by reflecting the light of the sun back to us.

Ammons evokes a vast and mysterious universe, building to an utterance that is at once both despairing and hopeful—"how far lost we are, if saving is anywhere else." If we look beyond ourselves for "saving," then we will be truly lost. Because the universe is expanding, it is going to get farther and farther away, and our sense of being alone or lost in it may increase. Besides, there is no evidence that there is intelligent life in other places with the knowledge to save us. However, if we turn within to our truest self, the self that is awakened and refreshed in the act of reading Ammons's poem, "salvation" may be possible. Given that so much of what is out there is bleak and dark, the light that travels to connect and meet us is "affirmational." The passage ends with Ammons alluding to galactic collisions and spirals, evoking the combustion taking place out there in "cold space." These may be superlarge black holes in centers of galaxies.

What do these and the other astronomical passages within Sphere and his other long poems suggest about Ammons's use of astronomy? In two earlier sections from Sphere Ammons expresses horror before the vastness and apparent wastefulness of the universe. In the "light cone" passage, however, he celebrates the centrality of human consciousness, the ultimate processor of all that light. In "Hibernaculum," and elsewhere in Sphere,

Ammons takes pleasure in launching us into new orbits. The shifts in tone between loneliness and integration, despair and hope, reflect a range of reactions to the knowledge astronomy has given us. Perhaps Ammons's own ambiguous reactions reflect the complex truth that he is both a "nature poet," at home in the vast play of the cosmos, and "a poet of human loneliness within the natural order."[37] Elder, who compares Ammons to Wordsworth, finds that in them both "poetry is the medium, within which mind and nature interfuse."[38]

The new astronomy indeed reveals landmarks for Ammons's thought. When the poet says in *Sphere*, "we are not half in and / half out of the universe but unmendably integral," he asserts a truth demonstrated by how light from distant stars meets the human retina. Elder notes: "For Ammons, integral can mean both isolated and reunited."[39] This is particularly the case with Ammons's use of the facts of astronomy. They function to reunite us; astronomy teaches us of the vulnerability of our planet, ourselves, and our universe. We must cooperate—"reunite"—if we are to sustain life on this "floating meadow." Ammons cheers on the astronauts and revels in the discovery of two new galaxies because space exploration further extends the range of our "unmendably integral" connection to all that is out there.

Yet even as Ammons celebrates the technology that extends our vision and its newly discovered facts, he also occasionally reflects our isolation, our loneliness in an ever-expanding universe—"we cooling here . . . on a far outswing / of the galaxy." From this perspective we appear as an insignificant something on an insignificant speck going around an insignificant star in a very average galaxy somewhere in the middle of the universe. When, in section 45 of *Sphere*, he describes "so much / extravagance of waste," he presents another side of what astronomy brings us. Mars's gravity is too weak to hold an atmosphere. Venus is too hot—shrouded with clouds—creating a "greenhouse effect" of 700 degrees kelvin on its surface. In comparison to "the gross destructions that give life"—supernovae that seed the galaxy with heavy elements and simple molecules allowing new stars and planets to be born, the activity of our own creative imaginations ("mirrorments, astonishments of mind") seems unimportant. These sentiments echo Jeffers and confirm Frost's intuition that what is out there is hardly worth the effort. The sense of being off-key, lonely, isolated, reminds the reader of Frost's "I Will Sing You One-O." But Ammons resigns himself to neither disintegration nor separation from what is out there.

He passes through the darkest nights to achieve illumination. Ammons manages to discover, at least in *Sphere*, and *through* its creation, the "interpenetrating spiritual float," without which "heaviness weighs down." What is that "interpenetrating spiritual float"? It is the poem itself with its interpenetrating stanzas that evoke the very dynamism the heavens exhibit, and its rhythm which, according to Ammons, "sinks" the mind and refreshes it. He is also buoyed by reality's "great fugue, a holy unity," which is the mysticism modern science reveals—"the radiance glimpsed in the cooperative lives of a cell as well as in the long reach of the galaxies."[40] Each of us is inescapably part of the universe, "attached" to the earth by the force of gravity, yet floating free on this star that is itself adrift in the solar system. In the concluding section of *Sphere*, Ammons celebrates both our attachment and our freedom, our gravity and our weightlessness.

> to float the orb or suggest the orb is floating: and, with the
> mind thereto attached, to float free: the orb floats, a bluegreen
> wonder: so to touch the structures as to free them into rafts
>
> that reveal the tide: many rafts to ride and the tides make a
> place to go: let's go and regard the structures, the six-starred
> easter lily, the beans feeling up the stakes: we're gliding: we
>
> *are* gliding, ask the astronomer, if you don't believe it: but
> motion as a summary of time and space is gliding us: for a while,
> we may ride such forces: then, we must get off: but now this
>
> beats any amusement park by the shore: our Ferris wheel, what a
> wheel: our roller coaster, what mathematics of stoop and climb: sew
> my name on my cap: we're clear: we're ourselves: we're sailing.
>
> (S, 79)

Ammons concludes his 79-page poem, with its 155 sections, on an exuberant note: "we're sailing." The diction in this passage clearly emphasizes *lightness*. "The orb is *floating*," the motion of the sphere is *gliding*, we can *ride* the rafts—and at its very end—"we're *sailing*." The astronomer, of course, can verify all this levitation, and the poet half-mockingly, half-playfully, challenges skeptics to ask him.

Ammons here celebrates the most revolutionary discovery of astronomy—that the orb (our "spaceship") is floating. The mind "attached" suggests just how "unmendably integral" world and mind are. We are anchored to the landscape, this "bluegreen wonder." Here, in this last stanza, the appeal is to the joyful appreciation of "structures" and to our own levitation. "Let's go and regard the structures," he tells us, "the six-starred / easter lily, the beans feeling up the stakes." To regard them is to look at them attentively; Ammons as naturalist cannot resist the temptation to examine ("see"), and his interest in astronomy can be viewed as an extension of his unceasing curiosity.

Our ride upon this raft must end, of course, just as perhaps the universe itself will one day wind down, but for now, at least, Ammons is as giddy about the possibilities as a kid in an amusement park. For Ammons, the universe is a grand amusement park, yet even more entertaining. His at-home-ness in it shines through in these final lines. The earth—our "Ferris wheel"— turns us physically as we ride the different "forces." The earth as "wheel" also brings to mind the wheel of fortune, as we experience the ups and downs of our ride here ("our roller coaster")—moments of at-one-ness and times of loneliness. The Ferris wheel also evokes the vast wheel of karma, which dictates our getting off and perhaps on again, as well as the notion that all our individual actions return to us, which is, after all, one of the lessons of these long poems. The image of the Ferris wheel, lit against the darkness above it, appears as a kind of huge star, an appropriate image for the conclusion of Sphere.

At the end of Sphere, Ammons expresses a desire to enjoy both the ride upon this star and the sights it offers—from our time to distant star time. Like that kid about to spend a day in an amusement park, Ammons playfully, and a bit proudly, declares: "sew / my name on my cap." Ammons, has rediscovered Whitman's spirit. And it is this spirit of integration and celebration that ultimately triumphs over feelings of isolation and loneliness. His bravura is reminiscent of Whitman, just as all the floating reminds us of the last section of "Song of Myself." Yet Ammons remains firmly anchored to the orb at the end of his poem, whereas Whitman prepares to leave the body. Ammons "is sailing with us, floating along." The vehicle for his destination is the earth itself, the form of a motion enabling us to float free and to remain firmly grounded.

Even as he celebrates the experience of floating at the end of Sphere, Ammons tells us to go and "regard" terrestrial structures. He is interested in origin, process, evolution, and distribution of living organisms, and his poems often sound like the notes of a biology watcher. In his early poem "Hymn," Ammons signals that his quest will be not only upward and outward toward the heavens, but also downward toward the earth. His interest in the cosmos is complemented by his interest in the microscopic "event." "Hymn" is an early Romantic lyric in which Ammons unabashedly goes in search of the kind of knowledge he has learned from reading Asian wisdom. He is in search of the elusive "you" that is "everywhere partial and entire / . . . on the inside of everything and on the outside." For his quest to be complete, he knows he must engage both telescopic and microscopic perception. He reminds himself:

> And I know if I find you I will have to stay with the earth
> inspecting with thin tools and ground eyes
> trusting the microvilli sporangia and simplest
>   coelenterates
> and praying for a nerve cell
> with all the soul of my chemical reactions
> and going right on down where the eye sees only traces
>
> (CP, 39)

Ammons's intention to inspect with "thin tools" (microscopes, magnifying glasses) manifests in a variety of ways in innumerable poems after "Hymn." His work is especially influenced by biology and genetics, where "thin tools" have extended our perception in as dramatic a manner as advances in telescopic instrumentation. In "Mechanism," for example, he explores both the origins and functions of a goldfinch. He "sees" beneath the surface of its skin to consider "the chemistries, platelets, hemoglobin kinetics" that sustain life. He also considers the "unique genes" that originate life and tells us to honor them: "molecules that reproduce themselves, divide into / sets, the nucleic grain transmitted / in slow change through ages of rising and falling form" (CP, 78). Only after he has made his biological descent does he return to the surface—to the whole bird that "flashes black wing-bars / in the new-leaving wild cherry bushes by the bay."

The journey beneath the flesh of this not very great songster illustrates a scientific truth often overlooked in critical interpretations of the poem. Most commentators focus on the wonder Ammons evokes for biological processes, and indeed the internal chemistries are wondrous. At the heart of "Mechanism," however, is the poet's knowledge that the goldfinch is "unconscious of the billion operations / that stay its form." The gastric transformations, the maintenance of body heat, the self-adjusting chemistries are *autonomous*. They work on their own schedules according to their own laws. The goldfinch does not control them, nor is it conscious of them. Much the same can be said of human digestion, which Ammons describes in *Tape for the Turn of the Year*. The exchanges in blood, lymph, food, waste, and water are marvelously autonomous.

Ammons's celebration of autonomous function and reproduction in "Mechanism" is an early example of his continuous interest in these subjects. John Elder writes that "the genetic metaphor is of special value to Ammons because of his poetry's delight in sexuality and his conviction of the crucial value of tenderness."[41] The tenderness Elder detects in Ammons's poetry is closely linked to the poet's interest in "the precious least," be it the mold under a leaf or the tiny mitochondria that are the power plants of cells. In his "Essay on Poetics," Ammons explains his fascination with "tiny sets and systems of energy." This passage is parenthetically sandwiched between a meditation on the distribution of elmworms and a consideration of tree pollination:

> I have come lately to honor gentleness so:
> it's because
> of my engagement with
> tiny sets and systems of energy, nucleations and constructs,
> that I'm unnerved with the slight and needful
>   of consideration:
>
> (CP, 306)

The "needful of consideration" are, of course, the elmworms, elm seeds, maple seeds, and dandelion seeds he manages to weave into his poem. The elmworms and the tree seeds, though vulnerable, are powerful catalysts for change.

The cell, as both an image and a metaphor, captures Ammons's attention and figures in many of his longer poems. He is particularly fascinated by biological necessities, and in *Tape for the Turn of the Year*, he plays these necessities off his own wandering mind, which tends to lose contact with physical reality. The beauty of the body's functioning is that it frees the mind to explore, but it also constantly reminds us that our thoughts and lives are dependent on our bodies:

my "mind" is trying to
keep every cell
    in my body
happy: yes, it says, we
understand that you need
so-and-so but we're
    temporarily (we hope)
out of that and are having
a substitute manufactured—
this will be released to
    you as soon as
possible: be sure to alert
your receiving dept: it
gets an alarm from a group
of injured or invaded cells:
we are
sending several divisions
    & several kinds of
    divisions to help you:
and so on:
catalysts, enzymes &
membranes, functions,
trades & forces, the
in-coming, out-going:
this mind that I turn
outwardly—how thin by
        comparison—
the body releases from
inner concerns and
gives few commands: get
food, water, sex: then
reality brings its
interference in
and the simple outward
mind, complicated by
postponements, symbols,
    prerequisites, proofs,
    nearly loses in
metaphysics &
    speculations its
contact with the
original commands: get
food, water:

(T, 19–20)

Ammons knows that the body's internal systems—cells com-
municating with each other simply by touching, organelles send-

ing messages to other organelles—compose as delicate an ecosystem as any he explores along the Finger Lakes of upstate New York. Ammons likens the vast interlocking internal network of cells and organs to a factory, with a receiving department, "divisions," and "groups." The cells are the life-sustaining forces within this system, and they must be kept "happy." The right "materials" must be supplied so interactions can proceed smoothly, exchanges in blood can continue, internal and external flows can remain balanced. It is the job of the mind to hear the body's signals—to get food, water, sex—whatever is needed to sustain cellular health. And the body in turn "releases" the mind once its internal needs are met.

Ammons's respect for complex, life-sustaining, physiological systems is remarked upon several times in *Tape for the Turn of the Year*. By comparison, the mind that he turns outwardly seems "thin." Ammons, of course, is overstating the point—for the brain that enables us to think is another highly complex physical system. He must be thinking of the apparent ease with which our thoughts turn "outwardly." Densely complex internal "catalysts, enzymes & / membranes" are what free the mind. The simple outward mind, however, cannot wander too far without the body signaling its commands: "get / food, water, sex."

One is tempted to read this passage as a late-twentieth-century version of biological determinism. Yet the emphasis is not on how we are driven by biological necessity, but rather on the interdependence of body and mind. Ammons, throughout his work, is careful not to get too carried away with his tendency to philosophize, to create ever new saliences of thought. Whenever he engages his mind too much in the direction of "metaphysics & speculations," he tries to pull himself back to physical things. In this passage, he again reminds himself and his reader of the physical basis of life.

The ability of cells to multiply and reproduce excites Ammons. He often divides reality into centers and peripheries, moments of stability and change discovered in living systems. In *Tape for the Turn of the Year* he discovers center and periphery in the circular lichen spotting a tree trunk.

> there
> is a center
> where with threads the
> lichen knits in, the
> "holding-on" point

> that gathers stability
> from bark: and there
> is
> the outward multiplication
> of forms (cells & patterns)
> to an unprescribed
> periphery
> that marks the
> moment-to-moment edge
> of growth:

(T, 112–113)

The lichen is similar to the spider Ammons describes in his earlier poem "Identity." Both the lichen and the spider create holding points at their centers and spin their "webs" in diverse patterns along the periphery. The outward multiplication of the lichen's cells represents growth, change, possibility. But if deprived of water and light, the cells will die. The "edge / of growth" marked by the cells' multiplication is just one of the many "edges" Ammons explores in his work. Elder writes that "Ammons everywhere reflects on the edge between poetry and the natural world."[42] Here he is fascinated by the precarious "edge" between order and entropy in living cells.

Ammons is also interested in how cells transform energy. He emphasized earlier in *Tape for the Turn of the Year* the importance of supplying heterotrophic cells with the right materials. These cells, found in the human body and in higher animals, require a supply of carbohydrates, protein, and fat, which are the constituents of cells and tissues. Ammons is also interested in another class of cells that get their energy from sunlight. These cells are called "autotrophic"; principal among them are the cells of green plants. On the final day of the old year in *Tape for the Turn of the Year*, Ammons takes up the subject of energy transformation. It seems a particularly appropriate topic on the day that sees one year out, and with its "turning," ushers in the next. Ammons asks:

> what is the
> subcellular machine
> in the eye that
> converts
> radiant to electrical
> energy?
> in the chloroplast,

                    radiant to chemical
                            energy?
                            how do fireflies
                            turn
                            chemical into
                            radiant energy?
                            the nerve,
                    chemical
                    into electrical energy?

                    mechanisms: necessary
                            exchanges:
                            worked out & perfected
                            (proved
                            practical) long
                    before we stood
                    by the shores of
                    incredibly ancient sea:

                                                        (T, 140)

The key to all Ammons's questions about energy transformation is the same—highly specialized cellular mechanisms. The
conversion of light (radiant energy) into glucose (chemical energy) in photosynthesis, for example, is conducted by chloroplasts, the cytoplasmic structures that distinguish the cells of
green plants. Ammons does not explain how the chlorophyll
molecule within the chloroplasts reacts when a ray of sunlight
strikes the green plant. That is not his purpose. Rather, through
his questioning he hopes to awaken the reader to the amazing
kinds of energy transformations that are taking place around us
all the time.

He returns to a favorite theme when he puts his own gloss
on these questions—many of these transformative mechanisms
predate human existence. Like Robinson Jeffers, Ammons finds
cause for celebrating nature's independence from man. Yet in
Ammons we rarely find the harsh rebuke of humanity that we
do in Jeffers. Ammons's aim is not to put us in our place, but to
remind us of how much has already been worked out through
evolution.

Since Robert Hooke first looked through a primitive microscope and recognized and named cells over three centuries ago,
our understanding of them has grown tremendously. Ammons
acknowledges this explosion of knowledge in "Essay on Poetics."
After his futile attempts to "measure" a tree, he exclaims:

"Books / by the hundred have already been written on cytology," and quotes from one such book at the end of his long poem. Ammons appreciates the complexity of a cell's functioning:

. . . in an elm tree there are twelve quintillion cells,

especially in the summer foliage, and more takes place by way
of event, disposition and such in a single cell than any computer
we now have could keep registration of, given the means of deriving

    the information:

(CP, 308)

He knows that "even the most primitive cell is an immensely complex and highly integrated piece of biological machinery."[43] The cell also corroborates one of Ammons's persistent beliefs, that the "great" can be found in the "small." He learns in his many dialogues with mountains and streams that he should pay more attention to the humble and the inconspicuous. The discovery that microscopic cells contain marvelously diverse "worlds" and "mechanisms" gives him pleasure. If a computer cannot keep track of the myriad operations of a single cell, then Ammons himself cannot be expected to keep track of the operations of the entire elm tree. The cell's complexity further reinforces his notion that at times "it's necessary to be quiet in the hands of the marvelous."

Just as the natural state of the eye is to be in motion, so too is the natural state of the cell. Ammons's poetry is an attempt to make us comfortable in a pulsating universe, and to achieve this his scope must range the periphery of the galaxy as well as the membranes of cells. Moreover, he is moved by the cooperative nature of cells. A cell's internal parts work together to produce a single, smoothly operating unit. Many cells together, of course, work to produce a smoothly operating organism. The mutual give and take, the balance between one and many, appeals to Ammons. The cell is also an essential unit in a hierarchy of wholes. Ammons lists this hierarchy toward the end of "Essay on Poetics."

        subatomic particle
        atom
        molecule
        cell
        tissue
        organ

organ system
organism
species
community
living world

(CP, 311)

This list moves from the subtle to the gross, from the less expressed to the more expressed values of creation. Because the cell is the basic unit of all living matter, Ammons returns to it with great frequency. He knows that "if the whole is to be living, the molecular components must be organized into a specific variety of larger microscopic bodies; and these in turn into actual, appropriately structured cells."[44] Both the poem and the cell are "ideal organizations" because they achieve the proper balance and flow between their many discrete parts and the whole that they themselves represent. Moreover, in Ammons's scheme of things, both the cell and the poem are necessary to life. The cell, of course, is an essential building block for all material life, and the poem provides both needed "rest" and "pleasure" to inquiring minds.

While "Essay on Poetics" ends with a hierarchy of wholes, Ammons begins Sphere with a celebration of proliferation—"the haploid hungering after the diploid condition." In surrendering himself to the "hetercosm joyous" of Sphere, he appropriately begins by evoking the sexual basis of life. Although his mind wanders in this poem, Ammons periodically pulls himself back to the cell as image and metaphor. This process mirrors what he spoke of earlier in Tape for the Turn of the Year—the mind effortlessly turns outward, but it must also return to its biological support.

The barriers between mind and body become more transparent in Sphere, just as the gulf between the stars and ourselves is made to seem less imposing. The cell, for example, brings to mind an underlying unity ("under all life . . . is the same cell") that makes dichotomies superficial. Just as human consciousness processes the light of distant stars, so too does Ammons's own consciousness discover in the cell a way to transcend differentiation. He does not literally say that the same underlying cell is identical for all life, but that all of life does in fact have a cellular basis. This is an important chord in the "fugue of unity" that is the subject of Sphere.[45]

Because we are all connected in some way, when we "touch the world in one place we touch it everywhere." To illustrate this point in *Sphere*, Ammons describes what happens along the peripheries of grass blade cells when a grackle flies overhead.

> when the grackle's flight shadows a streak of lawn, constellations
> of possibility break out, for example, the multitude of
> grassblade shadows subsumed in a sweep: for example, an aphid
>
> 76
>
> resting in bugleleaf shade must think lost his discretion of
> position: (his feelers notice, his eyes adjust): an ant
> struck by the flashed alteration stops, the friction of which
>
> event gives off a plume of heat, a small invisible boom:
> myriad chloroplasts circling the cell peripheries kick out
> of photosynthetic gear and coast in a slough and many atoms
>
> of carbon and nitrogen miss connection:
>
> (S, 44)

The repercussions of the bird's shadow are far-reaching. Both the aphid and the ant are temporarily disoriented by the loss of sunlight. Moreover, the process of photosynthesis itself is temporarily disrupted by the grackle's flight, which casts into shade the chloroplasts along the cell peripheries of the grassblades. The phrase "kick out" is wonderfully appropriate to describe the disruption of the cells' normally smooth functioning; it also illustrates Ammons's willingness to use colloquial speech to describe technical processes.

Ammons's attentiveness to the exceedingly small—ant, aphid, chloroplasts—derives from his notion that "in the simple event / is the scope of life." This is, of course, the discovery of the early microscopists. Their writings marvel at the teeming life found in the most minute specimens. Leeuwenhoek, who examined an infusion of macerated peppercorns under the microscope, was ecstatic over his observations of spirilla, the "little eels," in pepper water:

> This was for me, among all the marvels that I have discovered in nature, the most marvellous of all; and I must say, for my part, that no more pleasant sight has ever yet come before my eye than these many thousands of living creatures, seen all alive in a little drop of water, moving among one another, each several creature having its own proper motion: and even if I said that there were a hundred

thousand animalcules in one small drop of water which I took from the surface, I should not err.[46]

To redeem the small, to discover value in the seemingly insignificant, to find the hidden secrets of the least particular have been the dreams of both the biologist and the Romantic poet. William Blake had praise for those who could "see a World in a Grain of Sand." John Clare went out to the fields stooping for birds' nests to discover hidden beauty. Emerson, in "The Poet," declares, "small and mean things serve as well as great symbols." And Whitman, in *Leaves of Grass*, exuberantly supports the exceedingly small.

> I believe a leaf of grass is no less than the journey-work of the
>   stars
> And the pismire is equally perfect, and a grain of sand, and the
>   egg of the wren,
>
> . . . .
> And a mouse is miracle enough to stagger sextillions of infidels.
>   (LOG, 59)

Ammons, in the tradition of these great Romantics, celebrates the slight and undervalued. Like Whitman, he cheers on the underdog. His particular contribution to the tradition stems from combining the insights of the biology watcher with the sympathy of the Romantic poet.

Ammons's concern for "the precious least," down to the cellular basis of life and the "unsmirched atom," also spills over into his compassion for the downtrodden. In section 17 of *Sphere*, he says:

>   I
> know my own—the thrown peripheries, the stragglers, the cheated,
> maimed, afflicted (I know their eyes, pain's melting amazement),
>
> the weak, disoriented, the sick, hurt, the castaways, the
> needful needless: I know them: I love them: I am theirs:
>   (S, 18)

The "needful of consideration" extend beyond elmworms, elmtree seeds, and chloroplasts to include society's misfits. All this of course directly echoes Whitman, who in section 16 of "Song of Myself" says, "I am of old and young, of the foolish as much as the wise." Later, in section 125 of *Sphere*, Ammons invokes his predecessor: "I want, like Whitman, to found / a federation of loveship." The widening of scope to include "events" of distant stars and galaxies, along with the microscopic activities of cells, develops in Ammons sympathy with all of creation. By encouraging himself to see beyond a limited scope, he learns to see in the most profound way. His vision embraces those who are on the periphery of society—the homeless and the afflicted. The ultimate benefit of widening scope is the breaking down of artificial barriers so that one can "assimilate" the cosmic lights, the cellular whirlwinds, and the "needful needless." This then is the achievement of Ammons's all-embracing vision.

5

Persistences

"In debris we make a holding as / insubstantial and permanent as mirage."

—A. R. Ammons, "Persistences"

Ammons reached the culmination of a major phase of his American poetic success with the publication of *Sphere* in the mid-1970s. His *Collected Poems: 1951–1971* was the winner of the National Book Award for Poetry in 1973, and *Sphere: The Form of a Motion* won the Bollingen Prize in Poetry in 1975. Since then he has continued to produce prolifically. Between 1975 and 1987 (the year Ammons published *Sumerian Vistas*), he published six volumes of new poems and two retrospective editions of selected poems, one devoted to his longer poems and the other to shorter lyrics published between 1951 and 1977.[1]

In these new volumes, Ammons continues to develop his concern with "widening scope." I would like to focus primarily on *Diversifications, The Snow Poems,* and *A Coast of Trees*—all important and fascinating for different reasons. *Diversifications,* coming after the heady years of prizes and national acclaim, begins the latter phase of Ammons's career and for that reason holds a special place as a transitional volume. *The Snow Poems* is perhaps Ammons's most unusual and problematic book, the one that has met with the greatest critical hostility. *A Coast of Trees,* published in 1981, won the National Book Critics Circle Award for Poetry. I will spend less time on the two thin companion volumes that follow it, *Worldly Hopes* (1982) and *Lake Effect Country* (1983), which seem to me less distinguished and less interesting than the others. I have reserved examination of *Sumerian Vistas* (1987) and *The Really Short Poems of A. R. Ammons* (1990) for the concluding chapter.

Although the title *Diversifications* suggests the poet will attempt to "diversify," many of the poems in this volume are reminiscent of *Uplands* and *Briefings*. They are for the most part short, spare lyrics where the poet, as in those earlier volumes, registers natural phenomena in close detail. (The most notable exception is "Ars Poetica," where Ammons chides would-be poets, presumably his students, for being too concerned with publishing instead of with the process of writing.)

Ammons's bittersweet resolve to forego transcendence in the earlier poem "Guide" is addressed again in the first poem inaugurating the post-*Sphere* phase of his career. To eliminate any confusion about its subject, Ammons titles the poem "Transcendence."

> Just because the transcendental,
> having digested all change into
> a staying, promises foreverness,
>
> it's still no place to go, nothing
> having survived there into life:
> and here, this lost way, these
>
> illusory hollyhocks and garages,
> this is no place to settle: but
> here is the grief, at least,
>
> constant, that things and loves
> go, and here the love that
> never comes except as permanence.
>
> (D, 1)

The incessant drive and energy that characterized *Sphere*, the long lines and even longer stanzas, are missing here. Instead, Ammons returns to a three-line stanza frequently used in his earlier poems, employing a diction that is simple and clear. He speaks with the authority of middle age, and indeed the poem is a reassessment of a topic that has preoccupied him for some time. Once again, as he did earlier in *Tape for the Turn of the Year* and in "Guide," Ammons contrasts the "transcendental" with "here." "It's still no place to go," he says of the transcendent, "nothing / having survived there into life." Ammons associates transcendence with a "foreverness" that "swallows up" all change and signs of life.

Yet in this poem Ammons acknowledges the Hindu belief that "here," or what is perceived to be manifest "reality," is in fact an illusion, or "maya." The Hindu concept of maya delineates that what most people perceive as reality, the manifest world of relative appearances, is an illusion. The true reality lies within and is transcendental, experienced as one's own eternal self. This world is both fallen and untrue, according to Hindu scripture.[2] Ammons echoes this point of view when he refers to "here" as "this lost way," where hollyhocks and garages are "illusory." Ammons's selection of objects—*hollyhocks* and *garages*—may initially seem puzzling and a bit arbitrary. Yet hollyhocks, with their long, noble stems and multicolored flowers, are illusory, appearing bright and majestic for only a season, then vanishing. Garage means, in its roots, to preserve or protect—it is a temporary storage place for things that move (cars) and get sold every few years. The poem, however, provides a stay against constant loss—it is a storage place (like a garage) for transitory hollyhocks and other natural phenomena Ammons records.

Despite its illusory appearance, the world of human interaction and observable phenomena is preferred by Ammons. "But here is the grief" that jars him sweetly because it grounds him "here" in a world of things and emotions. "Here the love that / never comes except as permanence." Such love is Ammons's rebuttal to those who retreat from this world, for love ties the poet and his reader into a world of shared human experience. Ammons repeats the word "here" in three out of four stanzas, reinforcing his preference for this world, though it be fallen and illusory, over a transcendental reality. The emphasis on *here* also refers the reader to the space of the poem, where illusory love and grief become "permanence."

Indeed, Ammons has always seemed to fight an impulse to lift himself out of his body, to give himself up to the great swoosh of Pure Being, to surrender once and for all to the Sublime. This hesitancy, or ambivalence (and it is an ambivalence—why else would he need to so resist Pure Being if he were not simultaneously attracted to it), is caused primarily by Ammons's need to exercise vision in a physically observable universe. In a poem named after one of his most influential predecessors, "Emerson," Ammons articulates the differences and similarities between the two poets in the context of transcendence. The argument reflects the poet's need to clarify once and for all important and perhaps misunderstood relationships.

> The stone longs for flight,
> the flier for a bead, even
> a grain, of connective stone:
> which is to say, all
> flight, of imaginative hope or
> fact, takes accuracy from stone:
>
> without the bead the flier
> released from
> tension has no true
> to gauge his motions in:
> assured and terrified by
> its cold weight, the stone
>
> can feather the thinnest
> possibility of height:
> that you needed
> to get up and I down
> leaves us both still
> sharing stone and flight.

(D, 15)

In this parable, the "flier" and the "stone" represent the will to transcend and the desire to remain material. The "stone" longs to defy the force of gravity that keeps it grounded, and the flier seeks to be connected to the "stone" so that he or she does not disappear into the stark emptiness. One cannot exist without the other, and indeed each longs to fulfill itself by integrating with its opposite.

Ammons likens Emerson to the stone wanting to get off the ground. "Terrified by its cold weight," as indeed Emerson felt when estranged from Nature and the Sublime, the stone "longs for flight." Emerson's record of his own "flights" occurs at the beginning of *Nature*, in his essays (especially "Self-Reliance" and "The Over-Soul"), and in his journals. To escape the boundaries of self, the weight of one's own terrible limitations, Emerson sought Universal Being and in this way uplifted himself and others. Ammons suggests that his own dilemma is just the opposite, needing to get "down" rather than up. Like the flier who endangers himself without some "connection" to the ground, Ammons may feel threatened by his own transcendental "flights." Whatever the causes, Ammons likens himself to the flier who longs for a bead; he needs in some way to ground himself.

DeRosa, in her reading of this poem, is skeptical of Ammons's conclusion that he needed to somehow "get down," to quit what she calls the "transcendental habit." She adds that such a statement "does not take into account the intensity of his contradictory need to 'get up' there with Emerson, which, once fulfilled, precipitated his hunger to return to the world. . . . It would be more accurate to say he needed both the flight and the return, that when he had one, he inevitably needed and longed for the other."[3] To a certain extent her comment is justified. Elsewhere, and especially in Sphere, Ammons seeks a unity through his stellar encounters and his contemplation of the underlying cellular basis of life. This unity, however, is a cognitive reality and does not require the poet to surrender either his vision or his individuality. While it is true that Ammons is very much a poet of the Sublime, he prefers to approach it through the understanding of science. Then he can maintain his own self-control, which is what the flier in "Emerson" fears losing most. It seems too harsh a rebuke of Ammons to label his conclusion in "Emerson" "inaccurate, simplistic, and deceptive," as DeRosa does. There is no plausible reason why Ammons would misrepresent himself here, and DeRosa herself admits that the poem reads as a "self-evaluative summary."[4]

Besides reassessing his relationship to the transcendent and to his transcendental forebear, Ammons fills Diversifications with a good many nature poems that have been the hallmark of his career. In "Insouciance," he has the reader looking again at flowers and seeds. Casual in tone, precise and clear in its description, "Insouciance" has all the characteristics that critics like Zweig have admired in Ammons.

> You notice
> as
> the flowering spike
> of the
> forget-me-not
> lengthens
> with flowering it
> leaves
> behind a drab notation (namely
> seeds even
> smaller
> than the flowers)
> which does not
> say
> forget me not

because
it means to
be back

(D, 2)

This skinny and delicate poem reminds one of the "flowering" poems of William Carlos Williams. Indeed, the way the lines run on, one to the next, suspending us briefly at line's end but without coming to a full stop, reflects the influence of Williams. Ammons takes pleasure in the process by which the "forget-me-not" enacts its name, leaving behind small seeds that ensure it will not be forgotten. Ammons's descriptions of natural processes are often analogical descriptions of his poetic processes. In this instance, his careful process of observance leaves behind small lines, its own "drab notation."

The first two words of the poem command the reader to look— "You notice." Or they can be read more casually, as if Ammons is speaking of what he has just seen. Either way, the poem offers praise of the world of sight, as do so many of Ammons's and Williams's lyrics. One is reminded of "March Song" and "The Yucca Moth," poems where Ammons first sees and then transforms the visual into signs of renewal.

In "The Make" Ammons exhibits what has too often been ignored by critics—his keen sense of humor. One does not think of Ammons as a comedic poet, but within the corpus of his work one can find many humorous moments.[5] "The Make" uses humor pointedly to express the poet's desire to free himself and his art from the burden of subject matter, theme, and other cumbersome conventions expected of poetry. Ammons simply wants to cut loose such baggage in "The Make," a slangy title suggesting the creative act in all its reckless abandon.

How I wish great poems could be written about nothing
you know just sitting around a comet coming
leaves falling off a bush in a cliff
ducks flipping their tails, a driblet spray,
the universe turning over or inside out
small prominences in the ocean wind-smoothed into waxen scallops
how I wish there could be the most exciting line ever going nowhere
or traveling making money spending it messing around
a warp in pure space just a warp unwarping
a stone losing three molecules into a brook's edge
or the point of a leaf trying to fall off by itself
how I wish that instead of poetic tensions there could be dreaming

shales of mind spilling off (with a little dust rising) into deep cones
a gathering and spinning out
into threads some so fine the mind rescues them with imagination
little bits of lightning when the wind bends them through the light
how I wish there could be such poems
about nothing doing nothing

                                                                    (D, 32)

Ammons widens scope here in the most playful way, opening himself up to the possibilities of writing about nothing, freeing the poetic line from its burden of going somewhere and doing something. If a function of humor is to enable one to *see* things differently, then Ammons clearly uses his humor here to encourage himself and his readers to see poetry in a different light. The freedom and élan expressed in "The Make" indicate that Ammons's successes have not gone to his head. He still cannot take himself too seriously. Indeed, one major thrust of his poetry has been to free us from our ego-bound view of the world, our own narrow scope, so that we may enter the more playful currents of the cosmos. "The Make," in fact, does just that, shuttling us back and forth, randomly, gaily, between the advent of a comet and ducks flipping their tails. Relaxed, obviously enjoying the freedom that he has earned, Ammons engages in fantasy—"traveling making money spending it messing around"—and he allows himself the joy of writing nonsense: "a warp in pure space just a warp unwarping."

Just as its lines alternate between contraction and expansion, so too does the poem both deflate and expand. "The Make" deflates serious expectations of a poem, opting instead for a playful definition that incorporates anything and everything in whatever way it pleases about nothing at all. Simultaneously, the poem expands the possibilities for poetry itself, once conventional expectations are dismissed.

But all is not levity in *Diversifications*, and in "History" Ammons once again takes time to clarify a long-standing belief, that "history is a blank."

                    The brine-sea coupling
                    of the original
                    glutinous molecules

                    preserves itself all
                    the way up into our
                    immediate breaths:

we are the past
alive in its
truest telling:

while we carry it,
we're the whole
reading out of consequence:

history is a blank.

(D, 27)

Science has shown that human hereditary material derives from the original building blocks of life that interacted in the earth's oceans. In the first stanza, Ammons describes the "coupling" of sticky ("glutinous") molecules, which resulted in the production of larger, more complex molecules—nucleic acids. The same basic twenty-three amino acids, which in turn formed proteins, are fundamental to all of life on earth, including human life. (Thus, our very breath is just proteins replicating themselves.) Indeed, the entire "history" of life can be traced on the level of proteins. On this same point Carl Sagan writes at the beginning of *The Cosmic Connection:*

> These molecules, remarkably enough, are the ones of which we are made: The building blocks of the nucleic acids, which are our hereditary material, and the building blocks of the proteins, the molecular journeymen that perform the work of the cell, were produced from the atmosphere and oceans of the early Earth. We know this because we can make these molecules today by duplicating the primitive conditions.[6]

As Ammons has told David Grossvogel, "the whole history of the planet earth is in your body at this moment."[7] Ammons is attracted to this idea for several reasons. First, it documents the "cosmic connection"; we literally embody the same "stuff" that originally formed life on earth. Moreover, as Sagan himself points out, the molecules that clung together in ancient oceans fell there out of the atmosphere. Thus we can trace our lineage back not only to these molecules jostling about in cosmic seas, but also to the inner parts of the solar system from which these molecules originated. Ammons interprets these facts to mean that "history is a blank," that everything is eternally present.

In 1972, when Ammons discussed this idea with Grossvogel in the *Diacritics* interview, he had not yet published "History."

He may have already written it, however, for Ammons refers to the poem's last line in making his point.

> I have another view of history that means more to me. I have written a little poem about it which I have never published, whose last line is "history is a blank." Whatever you see when you look out of the window at any particular moment is history—is the truest history surviving into the immediate moment. The whole history of the planet earth is in your body at this moment, and so on. So that I don't have to structure it into time periods. Perhaps this is another reason why I do not have problems with the anxiety of influence, because I believe that what is here now, at this moment, is the truest version of history that we will ever know. Consequently, I have as much right to enter it with all the innocence of immediacy as anyone else possibly could.[8]

Ammons makes this argument to explain why he does not feel Harold Bloom's "anxiety of influence" when confronting his poetic forefathers. In the process, he provides a theoretical basis for many of his own poems that begin with literally seeing. If what one sees at any particular moment is "history," then one will naturally write poems that take their inspiration from what is literally present and observable. Ammons, time and time again, enters the world with the "innocence of immediacy," and his attentiveness to nature's particularities serves the wider purpose of "history"—to assimilate, to learn, to become wise through inquiry.

Diversifications, published in 1975 on the heels of Ammons's national acclaim, was a modest volume with many good poems, but it lacked the energy, innovation, and exuberance of *Sphere*. Ammons's poetic career has been marked by periods of great innovation alternating with periods of his settling into the writing of shorter lyrics. *Tape for the Turn of the Year*, at the time Ammons's most daring formal experiment (written in 1963–1964), was followed by several volumes where the poet appeared to retreat from the openness and freedom that characterized *Tape*.

After the publication of *Uplands* and *Briefings* Ammons turned again in the early 1970s to the long experimental poem. Although "Essay on Poetics," "Extremes and Moderations," "Hibernaculum," and *Sphere* all appear tightly structured by a regular stanzaic pattern (the tercet in "Essay" and *Sphere* and the quatrain in "Extremes and Moderations"), in practice the poems defy many formal conventions. Ammons invites the reader of *Sphere*, for example, "to dip in anywhere," suggesting the nonlinear character of the poem's form and thought. His other long poems can be read similarly, without needing to progress from beginning to end. When compared with his shorter lyrics, these long poems risk much more.

In his article "A. R. Ammons and *The Snow Poems* Reconsidered," Michael McFee contrasts the positive reception given these earlier long poems to the reaction to *The Snow Poems*. At the heart of *The Snow Poems*, writes McFee, is "Ammons' deep anti-formalism," which apparently the poet has pushed to an extreme even at the risk of alienating avid supporters.[9] To illustrate the poem's "anti-formalism," McFee quotes from a poem with the oddly configured title "Ivy, a Winding)":

> imagine!
> writing something that never forms a
> complete thought, drags you
> after it, spills you down, no barrier
> describing you or dock lifting you up:
> imagine writing something the CIA would
> not read, through,
> the FBI not record or report,
> a mishmash for the fun-loving,
> one's fine-fannied friends!
> imagine, a list, a
> puzzler, sleeper, a tiresome business,
> conglomeration, aggregation, etc.
> nobody can make any sense of:
> a long poem, shindig,
> fracas, uproar,
> high shimmy uncompletable

(SP, 17–18)

Coming toward the beginning of this long volume, these lines serve warning that the poet will not be offering the stanzaic boxes that help maintain a semblance of order amidst entropy in his earlier long poems. Instead, and by his own admission, Ammons will be serving up a "mishmash," so subversive that even the CIA and the FBI will ignore it. Ammons's stated intention to subvert (overthrow) meaning, to write "something that never forms a / complete thought," is the expression of his "long-standing predisposition 'to prefer confusion to over-simplified clarity, meaninglessness to neat, precise meaning, uselessness to over-directed usefulness.'"[10] In *The Snow Poems* he pushes this impulse further than he ever has before.

McFee refers only in a general way to the lack of critical support for the volume.[11] Bloom is unusually reticent about this book. Two of Ammons's most avid supporters, however, have very negative things to say. Waggoner describes *The Snow Poems* as "a thick book of verse that I find both trivial and dull." He faults the poet for retreating from his earlier "visionary" encounters with the world. Dismissing the volume as an unfortunate blemish on an otherwise exemplary career, Waggoner writes of *The Snow Poems:* "In a world in which the seen has lost its natural radiance and the unseen has become 'unbelievable,' poetry comes to seem as empty as hope."[12] DeRosa, who in her thesis has great praise for Ammons, is equally harsh. She complains that much of the material should have been edited out and rebukes what she considers the "mental garbage of *Snow Poems*"—all the seemingly purposeless talk about the weather, the many reminiscences having little to do with the present moment, and the foolish wordplays and disconnections in logical thought. She is most upset, however, by what she detects as "weariness and indifference" from a poet "who has never known the mountains or the sea to withold response or truth and who has always believed in the power and potential of his own world."[13]

One of the more unusual features of the volume is Ammons's attempt to write two poems simultaneously. In many instances he begins a poem at the left margin of the page, and another "poem" appears as a sidebar down the right-hand side. Of the double columns Ammons says: "They are intended to be playful; they can be read one at a time, but with an awareness of the other column, the other perspective."[14] In "Poetry Is the Smallest," Ammons's attempt to write a "definition" of his craft, he uses this technique in a modified format. The poem begins innocently enough:

Poetry is the smallest
trickle trinket
bauble burst
  the lightest   f
windseed leaftrip   r
snowdown   e
poetry is the breaks   e
the least loop   d
from   o
    the general curvature   m
into delight

poetry is
the slightest   f
hue, hint, hurt   r
  its dance too light   e
not to be the wind's: e
yet nothing   d
becomes itself   o
without the overspill   m
of this small abundance

(SP, 81)

In the text on the left-hand side Ammons identifies poetry with
the slight, the delicate, the refined. This has been one of his
stances throughout his career—that small loops of creation offer
discoveries and aesthetic rewards. The reader need not struggle
through a "mishmash" to determine the significance of these
lines. And one tolerates, even enjoys, the message in the sidebar
as Ammons's own commentary on what he has written. "Freedom" expresses his feelings about what is said on the left-hand
side; Ammons also associates "freedom" with the process of
writing poetry; the poem's unusual typography also demonstrates his willingness to shatter conventional expectations and
to use the entire page in unpredictable and "free" ways.

The poem proceeds in a breezy tone, recording Ammons's discussion with a mountain, one of his favorite "confidants," on
the ramifications of associating poetry with the small. After this
discussion and an aside on the weather, Ammons concludes the
poem in a fashion that has earned the disdain of Waggoner and
DeRosa. He writes, presumably to give another example of poetry
as the smallest "trickle trinket":

poet friend of mine's   still his fat wife's
dick's so short   radiant every morning:
he can't pull it long enough   he humps well, probably,
to pee straight with: stringing her out far and
not to pee on   loose on the frail hook:
anybody by surprise   and, too, I notice she
sideways, he hunkers   follows his words
into the urinal so far   closely like one who
he looks like, to achieve,   knows what a tongue can do
relief:

(SP, 82)

These lines do more than violate some readers' notions of pro-
priety. In the context of the poem, they simply appear to be in

bad taste. DeRosa objects to the "graffiti" of *The Snow Poems*, and surely these lines are an example of that, albeit relatively mild graffiti. Moreover, she, like Waggoner, objects to Ammons dragging into the book uninteresting and essentially private information about personal friends. Indeed, this revelation seems to lack discretion. Surely, American poets have talked about sex before in a powerful and imaginative way. Ammons, like Whitman before him, is not a genteel poet. He has demonstrated skill and exuberance in describing internal bodily processes and the sexual basis of life. The problem here is that Ammons's revelation goes over like a bad joke. Too many of *The Snow Poems* have the same effect on the reader. One hears oneself remarking again and again, "Gee, I wish he hadn't said that!" More than one reviewer has asked where Ammons's editor was at the time.[15] The poet, apparently, was feeling either reckless or fearless; of course, it is impossible to know why he let so much of what sounds like "unedited journals masquerade as poems."[16]

In an attempt to excuse Ammons's performance in the volume, DeRosa writes that "these poems may only be expressions of a creative dormancy and self-doubt, a low point in the poet's creative and imaginative bio-rhythm."[17] That may be true, or one may view them as an experiment in which Ammons tests to an extreme some of his career-long preoccupations. For example, the use of sidebars to create the effect of "simultaneity" is, as DeRosa herself admits, a "radical fulfillment of Ammons' youthful intention to shatter 'classical fields.'"[18] In addition to smashing the integrity of the line as a unit of poetic form, the book works like an ambiguous figure drawing. Looked at in one way, *The Snow Poems* appears to be a collection of individual poems. Each one has a title, although the titles themselves are arbitrary. The first line of each poem is lifted from the text to function as a title. From another perspective, the book is more like *Sphere*, a single long poem. It moves through a seasonal cycle, beginning with autumn, spending a long time recording the poet's musings during another snowy Ithaca winter, and concluding, ever so tentatively, with the signs of early spring.

Ammons has always had a penchant for recklessness. In an earlier poem, "Lines," he talks about his passion for "Lines flying in, out: logarithmic / curves coiling / toward an infinitely inward center: lines / weaving in, threads lost in clustral scrawl" (CP, 104). *The Snow Poems*, with its horizontal and vertical lines, seems to be a fulfillment and a celebration of Ammons's concept of poetic freedom. In addition, Ammons has always believed that poetry should be play, and in *The Snow Poems* he allows himself free rein to write playfully about "nothing doing nothing." In "Early October," one of the first poems of the volume, he derives his joy from the effects of adding "y" to a series of adjectives. The spelling distortion has a pleasing effect, and the string of adjectives is like names called out in a children's game.

> Early October,
> fally, papery, yellowy
> watery, raggedy, high
> skimmy clouds, brooky
> (last week's rains,
> now run off, brookly,
> cool glass flowing,
> metal over slate sweeps)
> I'm at fifty Octobery

(SP, 14)

The poem, however, turns serious as Ammons contemplates that "in a short time all here will / clear and go." The leaves still hanging on trees will, of course, drop. Frost and snow will soon bite into the landscape and remove many signs of visible life. Ammons, at fifty, sounds like a man thinking about death, although at the end of this poem he turns his back on the subject ("why speak of that now") to "recall honey" and reflect on "the inner light of wine."

In turning to some of the other bright moments in the volume, one discovers that Waggoner's criticism of *The Snow Poems*—that they reflect a retreat by Ammons from his earlier "visionary" encounters with the world—is not entirely accurate. Many of the poems in this volume, especially those dealing with snow and winter (they compose a large proportion of the text), derive their inspiration and their success from Ammons's vision, a discriminating perception in a season whose whiteness tends to blend everything together. Instead of yielding to the blankness of winter, the white haze that seems to encompass places like upstate New York, Ammons manages to discover in the permutations of snow a radiant world.

The snow, of course, is a familiar image of winter, and the critical approaches to the volume that see this book as a "winter" in an otherwise sunny career may not have looked closely enough at the poetic possibilities of snow. The crystal lattice of water molecules giving the snowflake its structure appeals to a poet attracted to the elegant complexity of cells. Thus it would be wrong to associate Ammons's preoccupation in this volume with snow as a sign of middle-aged despondency. While it is true that one sign of deteriorating sight is to see "snow" or "floaters," Ammons's perception shows no sign of wear and tear. His poems about snow fall into three groupings: poems illuminating the aesthetic possibilities of snow, poems tracing the transformative power of snow, and poems celebrating the possibilities inherent in the thawing of snow. Often, however, the distinguishing characteristics of these groups overlap.

In "The Perfect Journey Is" Ammons goes out for a walk to see for himself, not listen to secondhand information (as Waggoner suggests he does in this volume).

> I went
> to walk between the pine
> colonnades
> up the road on the hill and there
> hill-high in dry cold
> I saw the weaves of glitterment
> airborne, so fine,
> the breeze sifting
> figurations from the snow
> reservoirs of the boughs
>
> (SP, 138)

"The weaves of glitterment" blown from the boughs of the pine tree represent the aesthetic possibilities inherent in the snow. Here, the interaction of weather (snow, breezes) and landscape (pines) transforms Ammons's walk into a revelation. The mode of discovery—the walk leading to a visual revelation—is vintage Ammons. The "sifting / figurations" he notices provide him with a spark during the otherwise dreary season. If, as Ammons says in the first two lines of the poem, "the perfect journey is / no need to go," then one can interpret this to mean no need to go south to escape the dead of winter, for winter, like middle age, provides its own rich compensations. The best journey is one with no purpose, no anticipated goal or end, such that the process itself is everything. Peter Matthiessen, in his book *The Snow Leopard*, refers to this kind of walking as "gnaskor," or "going around places," as pilgrimages are described in Tibet.[19] Ammons, like Matthiessen, is attentive to the transformative power of the landscape and discovers in his aimless winter walk the pleasures of merely circulating.

In one of the transitional poems that mark the end of one

season and the beginning of another, Ammons takes delight in the blends of weather and landscape. At the end of a long snowy afternoon, the sun appears. Ammons reflects in "No Matter":

> so it snowed and snowed
> the wind blew and the
> flakes flew
> and it added up to a
> passing
> the lily shoots
> hold scoops and sloops of
> snow
> (keep off the grass)
>
> . . . .
>
> I hope winter will not
> end like a Beethoven symphony
> with big bams and
> flurries into June but that
> it will ease off
> like something by Debussy
> so you will hardly miss it
>
> (SP, 238–39)

The snow resting in lily shoots reveals the aesthetic possibilities inherent in the gap between seasonal scores. The euphony achieved by sound repetition in the first of these stanzas suggests that Ammons is enjoying the effects of this transitional time. Nevertheless, he hopes the music of the future will begin to sound more like Debussy than Beethoven. This poem, like the previous one, offers a counterpoint to the jagged edges and disconnections elsewhere in the volume.

As an agent and symbol of change, the snow is attractive to Ammons. Snow opens up and transforms the world in unexpected ways. Ammons also acknowledges that snow is a burden and a nuisance. But more often he is interested in how snow carves a new landscape out of an existing one. In doing so, it releases mental and visual prisons, widening scope. Perhaps this explains why snowstorms are often accompanied by anticipation and excitement. The capacity of snow to build and transform is perhaps best accounted for in the poem "Snow of the."

> Snow of the
> right consistency,
> temperature, and

> velocity will
> fall in a lee
> slope
> building out over
> space a
> promontory of
> considerable
> reach in
> downward curvature:
> and snow
> will do this
> not once
> but wherever possible,
> a similarity of effect
> extended
> to diversity's
> exact numeration
>
> (SP, 139)

In "Clarity" Ammons identifies knowledge with the discovery of new patterns. Here too he celebrates, albeit more quietly, the transformation of the landscape. The eye in each case traces change. The conditions must be right, however, and at the poem's beginning Ammons places special emphasis on just the right combination of elements. Creation of any kind, whether poetry, sandcastles, or as in this instance snow promontories, depends on the fortuitous combination of materials. Once the initial conditions are correct, almost anything is possible. The "building out over / space a / promontory" is the work of the weather. What was unmanifest potentiality becomes manifest. And according to Ammons, "snow / will do this / not once / but wherever possible." Again, the natural processes Ammons attends to suggest his own creative processes. His poems build a shelf of words over space, wherever possible, one for each diversity or event. Attentive to the possibilities inherent in measurement—temperature, velocity, curvature—Ammons seizes on the data to construct his own "downward curvature," the vertical drop each poem takes. The ceaseless possibilities confirm that "there is no finality of vision," one of the central truths of Ammons's work.

His preoccupation with the weather in this volume, however, has come under attack. Hayden Carruth, in a disparaging review, comments, "I have never read so much verse about the weather in my life."[20] DeRosa sees this as a further sign of Ammons's diminishing powers. She views his "weather reports" as a tactic to generate material when the imagination has dried up. She writes: "We talk about the weather when we are self-conscious or embarrassed, when we are looking for distractions, and when we want to break the awkward silence of having nothing at all to say."[21] This may be true, but if one views *The Snow Poems* as a cousin to *Tape for the Turn of the Year*, then the poet's musings about the weather justify themselves as part of his ongoing daily record of winter in each. One way to survive winter is to confront it imaginatively. Ammons does not simply report the weather; he goes outside to discover it for himself and to turn it into the language of his poems.

Because *The Snow Poems* move through four seasons, there is ample opportunity for the weather to change. Ammons is especially fascinated by the transitions between seasons and those characterizing a single day. In "Snowed Last Night a Lot but Warmed Up," he describes the process of "unsnowing" and uses the occasion to dig up soil for the indoor plant collection he received at Christmas. The poem's casual description of a day's activity is typical of *The Snow Poems* and *Tape for the Turn of the Year*, where many of the "poems" sound like entries in a daily journal. The poem begins, as so many of these do, with a report of the latest weather.

> Snowed last night a lot but warmed up:
> today has been cloudy
> unsnowing and up to 40 maybe 45:
> icicles have dived off eaves:
> the hemlocks
> which keep fine clumps
> are unsnowed
> tipsy with breeze
>
>   (SP, 88)

Ammons relies on the weather as a way of "warming up," a way into the writing of a poem. If a complaint can be made about this technique, it might be that he repeats it so often that it becomes monotonous. Ammons, however, has a way of redeeming the mundane repetition of the weather by inventing imaginative ways of describing it. Here he thinks of "thawing" as "unsnowing," and suddenly the process itself becomes more interesting, as if what *was* were somehow dematerializing.

In the second stanza he shifts to personal recollection. DeRosa and others have complained about the trivial personal details that clutter this volume; there is an overabundance of confessional material that is of little interest to the reader. But in this

poem the personal is played off against the cosmic, and Ammons
achieves the integration between self and world he has longed
for and achieved elsewhere.

> I got a plant collection
> for Christmas, jars, cups, liqueur & other glasses,
> potted and planted,
> but I'm doing tiny plants
> I like my loyalty
> and their precariousness
>   the big round yew
>   has five thick floes
> indoor green   of snow on top
>   too central
>   to angle off, fall
>   away
>
>   (SP, 88)

Ammons's loyalty to tiny plants is not a surprise, given his
predilection for "tiny sets and nucleations." Here the spatial shift
to the right signals to the reader that the poet is going to shift
his thinking momentarily, away from the self and back out to the
landscape. He achieves the shift gracefully, however, not dis-
rupting the flow of the poem. The exceptional placement of the
lines describing a yew that shows no sign of "unsnowing" is
justified by the exceptional state of the tree. It is "out of line"
with all the thawing that is going on around it.

The balance of the poem describes how Ammons takes advantage of the temporary thaw to get out peat moss from the garage
and to dig up some soil to mix the two for his newly acquired
jars and cups.

> then I dribbled bits
> into my finestemmed glasses
> and reluctant jars
> poured dabs of water in
> to settle the roots
> and left them to heaven
>
>   (SP, 88–89)

Again, this is the perfect analogue for what Ammons does with
his poems—into reluctant and elegant forms he pours dirt and
peat moss and hopes they will grow. Ammons, continually attentive to transformative exchanges, is himself an agent of transfor-

mation, turning his natural encounters into the rich loam that fills his work.

Like Thoreau before him, Ammons is industrious, self-reliant, and economical. He achieves integration of self and landscape, but in such a relaxed manner that one hardly notices what has been accomplished. His interest in the weather further aligns him with Thoreau, who of all American writers perhaps best saw and described the poetic possibilities of thawing at the end of *Walden*.

Although *The Snow Poems* met with almost unanimous disapproval, the next volume was greeted by a chorus of praise. In *A Coast of Trees*, Ammons is more consistently in control of his material. His experimentation with the sidebar is gone; gone too are the doodlings in margins and the objectionable ramblings about the most inane events. Instead, every single poem in this volume is finely honed, as if the poet were signaling to his critics and readers that whatever had gotten into him in the previous volume was now gone. Waggoner speaks of this as "a volume of recovery." He writes: "Ammons has never written so well as he does *A Coast of Trees*." It "reads both like a return and a fresh start, as though the poet had gotten his second wind."[22] *The Snow Poems*, however, were not as horrible as Waggoner contends. And *A Coast of Trees*, following on the heels of the more unwieldy volume, continues Ammons's characteristic pattern of shifting from long, experimental poems to collections with shorter, more finely trimmed lyrics.

As it turns out, the longest of the poems in this volume, "Easter Morning," stands above the rest. Helen Vendler, in her review of *A Coast of Trees*, refers to it as a "classic poem . . . a new treasure in American poetry."[23] "Easter Morning" is different from Ammons's other poems, yet in its resolution is similar to all that he has written, echoing the ending of "Corsons Inlet." The poem's uniqueness stems from Ammons's willingness to talk openly about personal loss, something rare for a poet who has for the most part glued his attention to the world beyond the self. Occasionally in the past Ammons has returned to North Carolina, his native state, and written a few memorable poems about his boyhood experience there. In *The Snow Poems* Ammons does include a lot of personal details, but these are often little more than trivial accounts of daily activities and moods. The personal reserve and reticence of an entire career seem to break in "Easter Morning," with the poet standing in a family churchyard recalling the deaths of aunts, uncles, parents, and his younger brother.

> when I go back to my home country in these
> fresh far-away days, it's convenient to visit
> everybody, aunts and uncles, those who used to say,
> look how he's shooting up, and the
> trinket aunts who always had a little
> something in their pocketbooks, cinnamon bark
> or a penny or nickel, and uncles who
> were the rumored fathers of cousins
> who whispered of them as of great, if
> troubled, presences, and school
> teachers, just about everybody older
> (and some younger) collected in one place
> waiting, particularly, but not for
> me, mother and father there, too, and others
> close, close as burrowing
> under skin, all in the graveyard
> assembled, done for, the world they
> used to wield, have trouble and joy
> in, gone . . .
>
> (CT, 19–20)

How poignantly he speaks of them all as if their presences were still felt in a world they no longer know. This is the mature and contemplative Ammons on Easter morning, confronting the emptiness of a universe he alludes to only briefly in *Sphere*. For a moment, it seems as if there will be no recovery, no vision that can redeem the horrible facts of the graveyard.

> now
>
> we all buy the bitter
> incompletions, pick up the knots of
> horror, silently raving, and go on
> crashing into empty ends not
> completions, not rondures the fullness
> has come into and spent itself from
> I stand on the stump
> of a child, whether myself
> or my little brother who died, and
> yell as far as I can, I cannot leave this place, for
> for me it is the dearest and the worst,
> it is life nearest to life which is
> life lost: it is my place where
> I must stand and fail,

> calling attention with tears
> to the branches not lofting
> boughs into space, to the barren
> air that holds the world that was my world
>
> (CT, 20–21)

Standing on his brother's grave, Ammons cannot separate himself from the flesh and spirit it contains. Something has died within him that he can never recover. His cry, a momentary release of personal tension, is only a temporary resolution, for Ammons confesses he cannot leave this place. It is too horrible and yet too dear to him; chilling yet vibrant in a way only a survivor can feel in the midst of the dead. By contrast, the natural world that has rewarded him so richly seems barren, empty of hope.

Given the long anguish of the poem, it is difficult to imagine a resolution that does not harm the emotional intensity of what has been said. Yet sight itself rescues this poet from his greatest abyss, and like the two great birds he sees overhead, Ammons rises in a moment of transcendence. Despite the buried dead in the graveyard and the likelihood of our all "crashing into empty ends," Ammons does recover:

> still it
> is a picture-book, letter-perfect
> Easter morning: I have been for a
> walk: the wind is tranquil: the brook
> works without flashing in an abundant
> tranquility: the birds are lively with
> voice: I saw something I had
> never seen before: two great birds,
> maybe eagles, blackwinged, whitenecked
> and -headed, came from the south oaring
> the great wings steadily; they went
> directly over me, high up, and kept on
> due north:
>
> (CT, 21)

As in "Corsons Inlet," Ammons celebrates the visual offerings of the natural world and derives from them inspiration to write, to live, to survive. The new configurations, the "events" overhead, dramatically replace a too narrow scope that managed temporarily to paralyze the poet. Ammons is, as Vendler has said, "true to himself in ending 'Easter Morning' with the natural fact of bird-instinct, seen in a new configuration, rather than with the transcendent resurrection of the body in spirit."[24] His fear and despair disappear as his eye traces the flight of the two great birds, circling, coasting, "looking perhaps for a draft." It was, as the poet says, "a sight of bountiful / majesty and integrity." Elder pointed out that "for Ammons integral ('integrity') can mean both isolated and reunited."[25] Reunited with his dead relatives on Easter morning, Ammons feels intensely lonely. Yet he is re- united with the world of the living by the changing patterns registered on his retina. His discovery of something "never seen before" releases him from his isolation and binds him to the world. The changing patterns, the dance of movement that is at the core of Ammons's visual poetics, enable him to achieve an "interpenetrating spiritual float" when he most desperately needs one.

> the having
> patterns and routes, breaking
> from them to explore other patterns or
> better ways to routes, and then the
> return: a dance sacred as the sap in
> the trees, permanent in its descriptions
> as the ripples round the brook's
> ripplestone: fresh as this particular
> flood of burn breaking across us now
> from the sun.
>
> (CT, 22)

The entire volume oscillates between moments of despair and of hope. Many of these poems reflect Ammons's awareness of death and register his own sense of diminishing abilities, yet others celebrate life and demonstrate his still keen and illumi- nating vision.

In "Distraction," Ammons pokes fun at himself and his dimin- ishing powers of perception. He contrasts his younger "crazy years," when he had the energy to get up and pursue the "uni- verse relentlessly," with the present, when even his "anklebones hurt / when I stand up." This is Ammons during a moment of middle-aged fatigue remembering that he used to inquire:

> of goat
> and zygote,
> frill and floss,
> touched, tasted,
> prodded, and tested and as
> it were kept the

whole thing going
by
central attention's
central node:

(CT, 24)

He has been our poet-naturalist, down on hands and knees,
prodding, keeping it all going through his ever-attentive eye, the
central node of his attention. Yet the zest and curiosity that pro-
pelled Ammons in his younger years appear to be gone. Instead,
as he informs the reader in the second stanza, he is beginning
to show signs of forgetfulness and no longer understands how
his attention could keep the universe going.

in fact,
sometimes
a whole green sunset
will wash dark
as if it could go
right by without me.

(CT, 24–25)

The universe, he finds, does not need him. Just as significantly,
Ammons no longer feels capable of being at the right place at
the right time. He is like a reporter grown tired of the beat, no
longer rushing out to catch the newsbreaking event as it happens.
Something may be distracting him, which he hints at in his reference to two "small obligations" dropped off by the mail truck
that afternoon. To be distracted is to lose focus, to have one's
perception diminished. Vision has been central to his world, and
here he is saddened by its loss.

Perhaps the primary "distraction" in Ammons's life is death
itself, or at least the thought of it, which lurks behind so many
of the poems in this book. In "Rapids," for example, he looks up
at the night sky only to contrast the ephemeral nature of his own
existence with that of the universe. He sounds here more like
Jeffers or Frost. Missing is the exuberant tone that characterized
so many of his sightings in Sphere.

I can
look up at the sky at night and tell
how things are likely to go for
the next hundred million years:
the universe will probably not find

a way to vanish nor I
in all that time reappear.

(CT, 26)

The syntax of the final lines leads the reader to believe that Ammons, like the universe, will find a way not to vanish. The reader is temporarily suspended by the pause taken at the end of each line, believing that at least in spirit, if not in flesh, Ammons will find a way to perpetuate himself. The truth is revealed in the last line, and its impact is more severe given that he has temporarily led the reader to believe otherwise. Ammons's sense of play is not always good-natured, and here his enjambement and word-play take a dour turn.

In "White Dwarf" the poet likens himself to a star in its final evolutionary stage.

> As I grow older
> arcs swollen inside
> now and then fall
> back, collapsing, into
> forming walls:
> the temperature shoots
> up with what I am not
> and am: from
> multiplicities, dark
> knots, twanging twists,
> structures come into sight,
> chief of these
> a blade of fire only now
> so late, so sharp and standing,
> burning confusion up.

(CT, 23)

"White dwarfs," or "residual stars," are actually the remains of larger stars that have gotten rid of great quantities of matter by passing through a nova stage.[26] The collapsing and the heating up of temperature Ammons alludes to are part of the process by which a star is transformed. In likening himself to these rare stars, Ammons suggests that he too is undergoing a "burning up," a kind of "molting" that promises not renewal but ultimate disintegration. But even in this stage of disintegration, there are flashes of brilliance before the cold end.

Although "White Dwarf," "Easter Morning," and "Rapids" record Ammons's preoccupation with the extinction of his own creative vision and life, *A Coast of Trees* also contains many affirmative poems. As David Lehman has said, "the tug between elegy and praise defines the special quality" of this volume.[27] Ammons's willingness to confront the darkness of the universe, no matter how black and gloomy it may become, does not culminate in a dark and brooding vision. As long as his consciousness can remain open to the majesty and integrity of the earth, he can recover and still offer praise. Much of what Ammons stands for can be found in the concluding lines of "Vehicle."

> meanwhile my
> body knows the wind and
> calls it out,
> and dust and snow,
> the running brook,
> praise themselves seen in
> my praising sight.
>
> (CT, 17)

In "Strolls" Ammons assimilates visual "feasts of disposition." He admires nature's gift to sparkle independent of an observer.

> The brook gives me
> sparkles plenty, an
> abundance, but asks
> nothing of me:
> snow thickets
> and scrawny
> snowwork of hedgerows,
> still gold weeds, and
> snow-bent cedar gatherings
> provide
> feasts of disposition
> (figure, color, weight, proportion)
> and require
> not even that I notice:
>
> (CT, 11)

Disposition, or arrangement, is one of Ammons's primary concerns. In "Essay on Poetics" he registers the figure, color, weight, and proportion of both an elm tree and its worms; in "Strolls" the emphasis is on nature's kindly "disposition," the abundance so freely given. Later in this short lyric, after sighting the "near-quartermoon / sliding . . . / into color at four four-thirty," Ammons writes: "alone, I am not alone." Apart from human company, Ammons nevertheless feels kinship with the

natural world. He remains solitary, yet united. "Strolls" reinforces Wendell Berry's impression of Ammons as a "nature
poet," one whose art "has an implicit and essential humility, a
reluctance to impose on things as they are, a willingness to relate
to the world as student and servant, a wish to be included in the
natural order."[28]

"Getting Through" (one of six poems in A Coast of Trees with
brooks as their central image) is about a brook's persistences.
Ammons, like the brook, manages to persist, to discover a way
around another obstacle. The darkness that occasionally engulfs
him never lasts long enough for vision to be clouded permanently. In "Corsons Inlet," Ammons said of himself: "I allow
myself eddies of meaning: / yield to a direction of significance /
running / like a stream through the geography of my work" (CP,
148). The many brooks in A Coast of Trees remind one of Ammons's earlier promise to run meaning through his work like a
stream. Here is "Getting Through":

> The brook has worked
> out the prominences of
> a bend so as to find
> curvature's sliding
> speed and now thaw
> or shower can reach it
> to shell the shale out
> from an overhung ledge:
> the ledge bends way
> over as if to contemplate
> its solution in a spill:
> right now I think
> the skinny old arborvita's
> roots may be holding everything
> together: but when the spill
> comes the brook will have
> another heap
> in its way, another
> shambles to get
> through or around: or
> over: how much time does
> a brook have: how much
> time a brook has!

(CT, 13)

Ammons explores the poetic implications of edges again—in
this instance, between brook and shore. The brook is both silent

and forceful, working persistently around and through the
prominences of the shore. Ammons deftly uses line breaks to
hold the reader temporarily and then release him, enacting both
the thought of the poem and the process of the brook as it is
suspended momentarily before working its way forward. The
brook, in its own patient manner, carves out new configurations
along its banks. In the process, it may even create obstacles for
itself, spills of shale and dirt and heaps of debris. Yet it finds a
way around, a way to persist. In a volume where the poet contemplates death frequently, the brook is a symbol of continuity and
persistence. The ample time the brook has to make its way down-
stream seems almost endless when compared with the pressure
of time felt by the poet.

In "Country Music" Ammons listens to the "lolling timeless /
music" of a brook as it absorbs melting snow and surges ahead,
and in "Strolls" he says the brook "gives me / sparkles plenty."
While the brooks promise hope, the wind whistles shrilly in
many of these poems, foreboding destruction. In "Weather-
Bound," for example, a strong southwesterly wind prevents vulnerable moths from flying where they want to go. Caught in a
draft they cannot fight, the moths fly pitifully backward, and are
eventually grounded in a brutal death. Unlike the brook, the
moths that meet their death are caught in a current they cannot
overcome. This is the negative side of nature's own persistence,
which, like time, can be unremitting and recalcitrant.

The "persistences" in evidence throughout this volume are
nearly always discovered through the poet's visual encounters
with the natural universe. Although the brooks and birds and
flowers of these poems have symbolic overtones, their naturalistic facts absorb the reader as they do the poet. In "Persistences,"
however, the final poem of the volume, the outward reality is not
nearly so important as the psychological inscape it symbolizes.
The poem summarizes what has obsessed Ammons throughout
this collection—ruin and renewal, death and rebirth. In the first
half, the wind whirls through the insides of an abandoned temple, symbolic of the poet's psyche. The wind "nuzzles into al-
coves and porticoes"; restless, it sweeps aside the ruinous
remains. The wind

> leaks and brushes away again
> restless with what
> remains a while:
> the theorem of the wind

> no pigment, wall, or word
> disproves: propositions
> scatter before it,
> grow up in brier thickets
> and thistle thickets:
>
> (CT, 51)

Nothing can "disprove" the logic of the wind, which coldly and systematically smashes all that stands in the way of its own inexorable laws. This is not only nature's wind, but also the wind of time that ultimately destroys life and has taken so many of Ammons's own family. It is the wind of age that makes the body creak and dries up the brook of the imagination. Yet Ammons, in what is the poem's and the book's final stanza, engages in a creative act:

> still, from our own ruins,
> we thrash out the
> snakes and mice,
> shoo the lean ass away,
> and plant a row of something:
> we know,
> we say to the wind, but we will
> come back again and back:
> in debris we make a holding as
> insubstantial and permanent as mirage.
>
> (CT, 52)

On the verge of ruins, the temple (of body and mind) still stands. Ammons, returning as the temple's caretaker, performs the necessary purification, ridding the structure of the animals already preying upon it. In a gesture both humble and profound, Ammons and the entire circle of his readers bow "to plant a row of something." It does not matter what—the symbolic significance of the gesture signals both persistence and renewal. Although he recognizes the wind as a destructive force, Ammons cannot end his poem or book on that note:

> in debris we make a holding as
> insubstantial and permanent as mirage.

The roots of whatever is planted dig in and "hold" the soil, promising visible signs of life, just as many of these poems exemplify Ammons's own staying power. Ammons's willingness to create something positive out of debris is consonant with his attentiveness to small bits and pieces of creation, often rough and broken, that find their way into his poems. "Clarity" illustrated just how much can be recovered in a heap of rock fragments. Significantly, the poems themselves are the "holding" Ammons makes. They are permanent mirages, encoding in print enduring temples of thought and praise. Mirage, in its root, means to look at, and Ammons—through his looking closely at nature—brings it into focus and makes it appear immediate and nearby. He links the reader with him in this sacramental act, suggesting that *we* must all persist, to find (in the words of an earlier poem in this volume) "the reality we agree with" (CT, 6–7).

A *Coast of Trees* was followed by two slim volumes, *Worldly Hopes* and *Lake Effect Country*. The first of these is a continuation of Ammons's "experiments in the minimal."[29] For the most part the poems are brief (often no longer than seven or eight lines) records of close encounters with the landscape. Because of their brevity and their spare, natural imagery, many of these poems remind one of haiku. "Winter Sanctuaries" has the feel of haiku, while also being similar to William Carlos Williams's early poetry. In "Poem" Williams takes pleasure in tracing the movement of a cat climbing over the top of a jam closet: "first the right / forefoot / carefully / then the hind."[30] Ammons, like Williams, restricts himself to a visual record of motion, letting the kinesthetic movement carry the poem.

> The squirrel, bunching branches,
> knits a billowing raft
> from twigends and, riding air, lifts
> one paw to pull in a tip
> where shaken maple seed cling.
>
> (WH, 42)

Many of the poems in this volume are content to achieve what Ammons does here, a pleasing evocation of the natural event. One poem stands out. "Hermit Lark" is an important poem in Ammons's canon because it provides such a wonderfully apt self-definition. Coming as it does toward the end of a long career, it illuminates his past and flashes hope for his future. More modest than "Out of the Cradle Endlessly Rocking," "Hermit Lark" nevertheless echoes Whitman as the writer confirms his personal identity through listening to a bird.

Shy lark! I'll bet it took a while to get you
perfect, your song quintessential, hermit lark,
just back from wherever you winter: I learn my real

and ideal self from you, the right to sing
alone without shame!
water over stone makes useless brook music; your

music unbearably clear after rain
drops water breaking through air, the dusk air
like shaded brookwater, substanced clarity!

I learn from you and lose the edginess I speak of
to one other only, my mate, my long beloved, and
make a shield not so much against the world,

though against its hardest usages, as
for tenderness's small leeways: how
hard to find the bird in the song! the music

breaks in from any height or depth of the spiral
and whirling up or down, jamming, where does it
leave off: shy bird, welcome home, I love your

song and keep my distance: hold, as I know you
won't, through the summer this early close visitation
behind the garage and in the nearby bush:

you will pair off and hiding find deeper
shyness yet: be what you must and will be:
I listen and look to found your like in me.

                                        (WH, 25–26)

This poem, like the lark's song, is quintessential Ammons. The
hermit lark, in its shyness, in its lyrical expressiveness, mirrors
the poet. Ammons has always been a solitary singer, exploring
the edge between mind and landscape, discovering as he does
here the images for his own feelings. It is the hermit bird's song
that captures Ammons's attention, "unbearably clear after rain."
"To sing / alone without shame" has been Ammons's primary
"persistence," roaming the woods and Finger Lakes of his region.
The hermit bird is a harbinger of clarity; its song purifies the air
and its presence helps the poet to understand himself more
clearly.

Ammons learns about his real and ideal selves from the bird—

both merge in the image of "the solitary singer." Whitman is in the background here: "O you singer solitary, singing by yourself, projecting me."[31] The bird's song soothes Ammons, smoothing out the rough edges of his world. And, like the bird's song, Ammons's poems provide a shield against the "hardest usages" of the world, creating a place of "tenderness's small leeways." What makes the "hermit lark" so poignantly beautiful is that in it the poet discovers the perfect image of himself: "I listen and look to find your like in me." The eye, the mind, and the senses are all satisfied, at least momentarily, before the bird's visitation ends. He tells the bird: "Be what you must and will be." True to his own best nature he is prepared to let go of that which has most intimately revealed him to himself.

In *Lake Effect Country*, the companion volume to *Worldly Hopes*, Ammons continues to let go of the desire to be "somebody" ("The Only Way Around Is Through"), and of the illusion that things "hold" still ("We, We Ourselves"). Many of the poems attest to his own presence ("I'm here, too") and his praise of nature ("we love it here"). The final poem of the volume, "Meeting Place," self-consciously addresses itself to the "meeting place" between self and nature, between eye and landscape, that has been the central focus of his attention.

> The water nearing the ledge leans down with
> grooved speed at the spill then,
> quickly groundless in air, bends
>
> its flat bottom plates up for the circular
> but crashes into irregularities of lower
> ledge, then breaks into the white
>
> bluffs of warped lace in free fall that
> breaking with acceleration against air
> unweave billowing string-maze
>
> floats: then the splintery regathering
> on the surface below where imbalances
> form new currents to wind the water
>
> away: the wind acts in these shapes, too,
> and in many more, as the fall also does in
> many more, some actions haphazardly
>
> unfolding, some central and accountably
> essential: are they, those actions,
> indifferent, nevertheless

ancestral: when I call out to them
as to flowing bones in my naked self, is my
address attribution's burden and abuse: of course

not, they're unchanged, unaffected: but have I
fouled their nature for myself
by wrenching their

meaning, if any, to destinations of my own
forming: by the gladness in the recognition
as I lean into the swerves and become

multiple and dull in the mists' dreams, I know
instruction is underway, an
answering is calling me, bidding me rise, or is

giving me figures visible to summon
the deep-lying fathers from myself,
the spirits, feelings howling, appearing there.

(LEC, 59–60)

By now the reader of Ammons is familiar with his encounters
with brooks (*A Coast of Trees*) and waterfalls ("Cascadilla Falls").
The first half of his poem is another such encounter. He traces
the movement of water spilling over ledges, just as these lines
spill over, one into the other, the tauts and twists of syntax imitat-
ing the unpredictable movement of water as it crashes down
ledges. The wind and the falls influence the spills, and all this
is recorded by his ever-attentive eye.

Midway through the poem Ammons stands back to ask a series
of questions about what he sees and records. He wonders
whether the elements are indifferent to him, whether his address
to them is an abuse of their majesty, and whether he has defiled
them for his own purposes, the making of a poem. Helen Vendler
has pointed out these are questions no modern nature poet after
Wordsworth can avoid. The essential question, as she phrases it,
is: "Is nature hospitable of itself to meaning (by its rhythms and
its orders, its catastrophes and its variety) or are our symbolic
uses of it truly abuses, a foisting of our sentiment onto an inert
and indifferent scenery?"[32] At stake for Ammons is almost the
entire corpus of his poetry; by his own admission he has plun-
dered nature for his own purposes, often attributing to natural
images his own feelings and states of mind. In an intensely self-
conscious way he is concerned with the excessive use of the

pathetic fallacy. He is afraid that language and the forms of his poems may not have been true to natural forms and "speech"; elsewhere he acknowledges that the motion of a poem may at least imitate the motion of reality.

> Though words and things exist in different realms, the motion of the poem imitates the motion of reality, mirrors the motion of things. Perhaps that is as close as we can get to a correspondence between this system of language we have invented and use and the system of reality that is so profound.[33]

In "Meeting Place" he worries that he has wrenched "reality" for his own purposes: "to destinations of my own / forming." The acute self-awareness of "Meeting Place" is not entirely new for Ammons—in a poem entitled "Plunder," appearing toward the end of Collected Poems 1951–1971, he fears: "I have appropriated the windy twittering of aspen leaves / into language, stealing something from reality like a / silverness" (CP, 318). The poem ends with his own admission of guilt—"my mind's indicted by all I've taken." The poet as thief is again Ammons's concern in "Meeting Place." Has he diminished perception by encoding it, and has the form of his record been untrue? Yet as Vendler chides, "no poem is made a poem by asking questions about poiesis and the pathetic fallacy, of course."[34] Ammons is neither paralyzed by his questions and self-accusations nor stymied in posing solutions. Nature is indifferent to his intentions, unaffected by the practice of his craft. Once this is given, he nevertheless continues to find ways to merge the self with the world, "leaning" into the swerves of wind, water, and falls. At the crucial moment of intersection, when the outward eye and nature's spheres meet, "instruction" commences, "recognition" looms.

> I know
> instruction is underway, an
> answering is calling me, bidding me rise, or is
>
> giving me figures visible to summon
> the deep-lying fathers from myself,
> the spirits, feelings howling, appearing there.

Ammons is an interpreter of all that he sees—the ancestral waters awaken ancestral stirrings within himself. The falls, as in "Cascadilla Falls," present him with visible figures—both scientific and metaphorical—enabling him to free the poetic stirrings so deep within himself. Vendler suggests that the "poetic fathers" born of the natural encounter are both Freudian "ancestral" figures and Christian ones—Adam and Eve. This may be so, and one could also posit Ammons's acknowledged poetic fathers— Whitman and Emerson. But Ammons himself, through appositional phrases, defines these "fathers" as "the spirits, feelings howling, appearing there." The spiritual and internal feelings howling within the poet's psyche are released by the encounter with landscape. He sees them in the falls, by a brook, along the shore of an inlet. Ammons discovers in the meeting place between eye and matter, mind and landscape, a dynamic intercourse between internal feelings and thoughts and outward visible signs that richly rewards him and his readers.

6

Ridges of Vision

> I am
> seeing: I am looking to make
> arrangements:
> > —A. R. Ammons, "The Ridge Farm"

In 1986 A. R. Ammons turned sixty years old. In the same year a major colloquium honoring his work was held at Salem College in Winston-Salem, North Carolina. *Pembroke Magazine*, a literary journal, devoted its entire issue (no. 18, 1986) to a critical response to Ammons's poetry, an event that had not occurred since *Diacritics* did something similar nearly thirteen years before.[1] A year later, in 1987, Ammons published *Sumerian Vistas*, an important collection of new poems, and three years after that he came out with *The Really Short Poems of A. R. Ammons*. These two volumes, the former with two long poems, and the latter a compendium of tiny lyrics, suggest his enduring creative drive and his prolificness.

Ammons, of course, has always been interested in expanding "vistas," and *Sumerian Vistas* is no exception. The Sumerian association dates back to Ammons's first poetic stirrings in *Ommateum*. Helen Vendler points out that there are several lyrics in that first volume "in which he adopted, as a refuge from acute temporal anxiety, the persona of a prophet who had come to ancient Sumer."[2] In this latest volume, however, Ammons more readily assumes his own poetic identity.

Although the volume's title might suggest a mythic encounter with an ancient civilization, many of the poems are rooted in the contemporary landscape of upstate New York. "The Ridge Farm," for example, a major long poem collected here, is situated on a ridge not far from Ammons's home in Ithaca. Alice Fulton, in her review of the book in *Poetry*, suggests that Ammons invokes Sumeria in the title as a metaphor of inception.[3] The volume's title also suggests a duration of time dating back thousands of years. Throughout *Sumerian Vistas* he will return to this concept of duration, redefining it for the reader so as to widen scope.

The initial poem in *Sumerian Vistas*, "The Ridge Farm," was first published in *The Hudson Review* in 1983. In it Ammons expresses many of his previous concerns: poetic form as motion, perception as aesthetic, and nature as refuge. This is not surprising, given that "The Ridge Farm" strikes a reflective and retrospective chord. In section 29, for example, Ammons wakes from a nap "in a room I have worked / so many hours and years / in, made long poems & / dinky ones in."

Throughout this long poem, which is divided into 51 sections, the poet speaks with the assurance of a man who has wrestled long and hard with questions of poetic form and perception and has worked through to resolutions that suit him well. Ironically, "resolution" for Ammons is best defined as an openness to dissolution, flux, or "chaos" in the post-modern creative sense, a re-solving more than a resolving. In "The Ridge Farm" Ammons attempts to re-solve the poetic, aesthetic, and perceptual problems he has mulled over before in his speculative long poems. In doing so he manages not to parody or dully echo earlier poems, but to renew himself and his readers through vigorous, imaginative language and creative poetic strategies.

This long, discursive poem incorporates the array of Ammons's poetic voices: droll humorist, poet-scientist, metaformalist, and philosopher. It jumps from recording changes in local weather and meditations on poetic form to phenomenological and ultimately spiritual concerns in the same breezy, yet not flippant manner of many of his earlier long poems, most especially *Tape for the Turn of the Year*, *Sphere*, and "Hibernaculum."

The multiple connotations suggested by the poem's title, "The Ridge Farm," introduce at the poem's outset the multiplicity of connections, or likings, Ammons conveys in the poem. Ostensibly, the ridge farm is the destination of a hike Ammons describes in section 32 of the poem. Ammons, his wife, Phyllis, and two of their friends, Jerry and Fran, set out "to see the high farm out by Mecklenberg." Ammons describes the climb with a twist of humor, his good-naturedness aroused by the obvious pleasure he takes in the walk:

> the brook runs way up and
> on the way is the low pond but further
> up, the larger high pond and then
> there are a couple of fields of
> ascension and then the old woods of
> the ridge, precipitous in climb, not
> available to hassling lumbermen:
> along the ridge is a long march
> you don't have to sweat once you're
> there

(SV, 26)

The "fields of ascension" are not just the literal fields providing a geographic interlude between woods and ponds. These "fields" are the visual and spiritual reward for making the ascent to the ridge, a trek beyond the limited and narrower constrictions of sea level. Ammons injects through his punning a touch of humor, a reminder that playfulness with language is another way of heightening and altering perspective. The phrase "precipitous in climb" suggests another language device of particular importance in this volume, his using of nominative verbals or verbal nominatives—words that can be verbs or nouns, depending on how they are projected into a line. Just what is the word "climb" in Ammons's phrase? It would seem to be a noun, but it exists in a halfway state. It is both a *thing* done and a *process* in motion. Such verbal nominatives, with their dual function, can be read in at least two ways and are a language analogue for ambiguous figure drawings used by visual optometrists to suggest multiple perspectives of a single image.

Ammons also sounds a chord of disdain in these lines toward those who would cut and burn, "hassling lumbermen" who represent the forces of progress and technology that he has lambasted before in his ecologically minded, longer poems "Extremes and Moderations" and "Hibernaculum." In order to discover the auditory and visual nourishment he needs, Ammons ascends to the ridge's vista, hikes its trail, and arrives at an old farmhouse, which in its imperfection serves as an emblem of much that he admires. He hears a cock crow and calls it "a sound I've been as hungry / for as the lean throats of cockerels." The animals on this farm—shabby sheep, a number of cocks, and a single dog—suggest that the farm's owner is neither a corporate nor a gentleman farmer, but more akin with the poor, rural farmers of Ammons's North Carolina boyhood. The poet spies "an apple tree a hundred / years old looking better in spring /

leaf than the house a hundred years / old." Then, in a moment revealing of his distrust of late-twentieth-century civilization and in particular its penchant for overdevelopment, the poet comments: "it's got so the only place you / can appreciate won't appreciate." As we have seen before, value, in his often topsy-turvy world, is seen in the lowly, the neglected, the unpopulated, the unappreciated—the small wildflower beside a boulder, the run-down farm at the ridge's edge. Unlike real estate, one can set no price on the sounds of a lark, or in this case a cock, or on the silence Ammons hears at the ridge farm: "silence was ineluctable: I heard it / & heard it." The unavoidable sound of silence, he says at the section's end, "deepens down and picks up ground / boulders and deepens down to springwater." It is a transformative silence, one that penetrates to the depth of his own being and the natural world he knows so well.

The poem's title then, insomuch as it takes its name from a place, is named for this ramshackle farm, with all its sights and sounds and silences in section 32. The word "ridge," however, figures prominently elsewhere in the poem, and *ridge farm* is its central metaphor. "Ridge Farm": the title itself is turned static, "recalcitrant," nounlike, by the placement of the definite article "The Ridge Farm." But without the definite article, we are left with two words (ridge farm) that hover between verb and noun, between flow and thing. The verb/nouns are both suggestive: to ridge is to create lines that rise between furrows; and to farm is to create furrows and plant seeds in those furrows. The title becomes a condensed version of much that Ammons says about poetry—that it is concretized activity, that it is formed flow. The poem is finally the ridging and the farming of experience and thought (which are themselves flows of energy and by nature formless).

The ridge, with its rolls and uneven terrain, its physical dura-bility and stability, and its height, provides the vista this poet's imagination needs. Alice Fulton, in her review of the poem, writes, "a ridge, after all, is a *line* where two upward sloping surfaces meet."[4] Ammons, the surveyor, records the ridge and its terrain from many different perspectives. His poetic lines emerge from the same confluence of forces that produce the ridge he hikes along. The irregular lines of his poems are but the visual manifestation of the convergence of different forces, the physical manifestation of all kinds of flow.

As we track the irregularity of his lines and stanzas, our experi-ence as readers mirrors his experience of following the ridge: it

is a steady line that wanders, a single line with rolls and uneven-
ness, a line that makes traveling at great heights easy, once we get
there as long as we follow its wavering course. Thus his poems
themselves "ridge," in the active verbal sense.

In section 13, he writes "I like the ridge, its rolls my fixed
ocean." In the same section, he notes "I like the ridge . . . it
regularizes my mind though it has / nothing to do with me intentionally." Amidst all the flux of perception, shape, and form embodied in the poem's configuration and perception, the ridge
stands as a metaphoric "anchor," "its rolls" his fixed ocean. The
ridge, Ammons writes:

> was a line
> in the minds of hundreds of generations
> of cold Indians: and it was there
> approximately then what it is now
> five hundred years ago when the white
> man was a whisper on the continent

(SV, 10)

His shift to a historical and geological perspective suggests that
the ridge provides a natural landmark, a signpost or reminder
that puts into perspective the comings and goings of generations
and natural forces. It provides a "measure" against which the
poet gauges his own mortality and that of his readers. It is what
he comes up against, the measure of his own limited days against
the longer spans of geological time the ridge has endured. Curiously, Ammons says of the ridge, "it regularizes my mind though
it has / nothing to do with me intentionally." Although "regular"
can mean "customary," Ammons's conversion of the noun to the
verb form transforms the meaning to something more profound.
"To regularize" is to make orderly, or symmetrical, and it is this
effect of the ridge on Ammons's consciousness that compels him
to return to it, as a place to which and from which the poet's eye
can freely saunter.

Whether one stands atop the ridge and scans the lower-lying
areas, or whether one stands at a distant point on the earth beneath the ridge to look up at it, or whether one walks along the
ridge, as Ammons does to reach the Mecklenberg farm, one's
perspective is altered, enlarged by the encounter between self
and the ridge's landscape. That the ridge is suggestive of both
stability and change, irregularity (of shape) and regularity (of
duration), is not inconsistent with Ammons's vision, whose
mind and imagination are stirred by dynamic tensions.

He concludes this meditation on the significances of the ridge
with the lines:

> the ridge,
> showless, summary beyond the trappings
> of coming and going, provides a
> measure, almost too much measure,
> that nearly blinds away the present's
> fragile joys from more durable woes
>
> (SV, 10)

Ironically, Ammons ends this section with a rhythmical and
semantic emphasis on the verb "blinds." The poet, never willing
to rest on too easy a summation, suggests that the ridge can also
blind our vision, if we are not careful, from seeing the fine veil
between whatever joys the present offers and "more durable
woes."

The poem "The Ridge Farm," like the trek up the ridge and
across it, transverses a good deal of aesthetic "ground." Ammons,
often at his best when self-reflexive, pauses at significant moments during the poem to reflect on poetic voice and poetic form.
When the poem is not turned inward on itself, it casts its net on
the external world, sharing with the reader the poet's perceptions
of the relative world, with its natural joys and sorrows and its
own quirky events.

"The Ridge Farm" begins with an observation of cedar trees,
their branches hung with snow and battered by wind. The
grackles, the blackbirds of winter, try to find a place on the wag-
ging branches. The poem's second section, like the first, offers a
casual yet sharply defined perception of landscape and weather
and a touch of Ammons's wry humor.

> last night, the wind clunked
> the icy heads of shrubs
> against the house—
> a long night of chunk-money spilling
>
> (SV, 3)

At the outset he resists any attempt at abstraction, surrendering
language in the service of his ever-active visual perception. Yet
the poet knows such observations alone will not sustain a long
poem, and in "The Ridge Farm," as in his other longer poems,
he quickly darts back and forth between sections of visual surveying and consideration of more abstract configurations. Early

in this poem he examines the concept of poetic voice, often defined as the distinctive tone of a poet's work. It is against this
definition of voice, with its emphasis on individual uniqueness,
that he poses a more vexing and radical definition. Ammons,
who has spent a good deal of his working life as a teacher of
creative writing at Cornell University, something he often comments about in a self-deprecating and occasionally even self-
ridiculing manner, begins section 3 with recalling how a poet,
presumably a student, handed him a poem. The poet complained
that the poem did not express his "true voice," and to the student's surprise Ammons replied "good." Ammons then comments on the incident and reflects on his own radical conception
of voice:

> he wants to write by the voice, to
> separate out the distinctive
> in himself, a distinctive, and write to it:
> that is not the way, the way
> is to say what you have to say
> and let the voice find itself
> assimilated from the many tones and sources, its
> predominant and subsidiary motions
> not cut away from the gatherings:
>
>   (SV, 4)

This seemingly pedagogical anecdote suggests much more than
a way to handle an aspiring poet's concern about discovering
voice. The issue at stake here is central to Ammons's poetic vision. He has consciously renounced conventional understandings of poetic voice, which exhort poets to cull from their
individual selves a distinctive, "personal" manner of expression.
Ammons, the subverter of convention, the trickster, says that this
is not the way. Rather, the way is to "let the voice find itself /
assimilated from the many tones and sources." His attitude here
is similar to that expressed in the earlier poem "Poetics," where
he talks of the need to be "available" to natural shapes. The
aspiring poet is not encouraged to write to a contrived sense of
voice, but rather to let the voice develop naturally. Discovering
poetic voice for Ammons paradoxically requires a de-emphasis
of individuality and a re-emphasis on assimilating the many
tones and sources of the self and the larger world. The word
"assimilation" has a very specific biological meaning that describes "the process by which nourishment is changed into living tissue." Ammons himself often engages in a kind of

"constructive metabolism," in which he takes in nourishment through the senses and transforms the "material" into poetic language and shape. Ammons is capable of expressing many "tones" and "sources" evidenced in a variety of poetic voices. Yet he would have the reader believe that these are formed out of an engagement with the world rather than an attempt to "separate out the distinctive in himself."

Clearly, Ammons's concept of voice is not shared by many poets of his own generation and the one that immediately preceded him. When asked in a 1986 interview to respond to a description of his work ("he is neither polemical, esoteric, alienated nor even suicidal"), Ammons reveals quite a lot about his own taste in poetry. "I think there are two types of poets," he says. He describes John Berryman and Robert Lowell as representatives of one type, who "try to get into as troubled a state as possible out of which to write great poems."[5] He describes them as hacking at their selves "in such a way as to get the greatest conflict and density and brutality and energy and tension and whatever else concentrated and focused in the poem."[6] They have each developed their own distinct poetic voices, yet at great personal liability.

"Apart from this poet who is constantly trying to intensify," Ammons comments, "there is the poet who is himself in such an anxious state that he turns to the poem not to create an even more intense verbal environment, but to do just the contrary; to ease that pressure."[7] Ammons, who disdains confessional poetry, is defining an alternative way, in which the poet discovers and writes out of the natural energies in the world rather than "working himself up." The pressure, he says, must not be lost. The channels of poetic voice and method, however, and ultimately the content of the poems themselves, will sound far different. "I experience myself as turning to poetry as a way to ease my anxiety rather than to penetrate a flamboyant atmosphere that's going to convince somebody else that I'm a person with deep feeling," he says in a follow-up question in the same interview.[8]

Ammons also takes up the question of poetic form in "The Ridge Farm," especially as it relates to his own longer poems. He begins section 28 by considering "overloading" the poetic line:

> it doesn't matter to me if issues
> overload a line:
> or if real poetry shrugs shucking
> bugs of small intentions

off the shoulders of its purer
streams—

(SV, 21)

Like the limbs of the cedar hung with snow in the very first
section of "The Ridge Farm," the poetic line itself can accommodate "heavy" significance. In order for Ammons to include the
"suasions" of his own participatory mind in its encounter with
the natural and its meditation on poetic process, the poet invents
and reinvents both the poetic line and stanza to bear the weight.
In Ammons's own vernacular he is willing to "overload" the line,
to pack it full with "events," if necessary. As he said in his earlier
poem *Sphere*, he is tired of poems that resemble "painted gourds
on a shelf," decorated and lacquered and stripped of their original nature. As Stephen Cushman has written in his fine essay
on the "metaformalism" of A. R. Ammons, "the flight from form
is constant and the refuge in form temporary."[9]

In these lines from "The Ridge Farm," Ammons confesses his
disregard for fixed measure, not much of a surprise given his
career-long commitment to breaking away from conventional
form. He suggests here that "real" poetry is vigorous, meditative,
and unencumbered, unafraid to dispense with the "bugs of small
intentions" in favor of discussing larger, more substantive concerns. The implication is that tightly structured stanzas and
rhythmical lines will do just fine for more limited concerns, but
the issues Ammons returns to—ecology, the polarity of form and
formlessness, process as a mode of discovery—need a "roomier,"
more open prosody.

Like *Sphere* and "Hibernaculum," "The Ridge Farm" employs
numbered sections as a loose organizing principle. The numerals
serve in some way to signal transition. In all three of these
poems, however, Ammons does not rigidly limit his thought
within the confines of a single section, but in a regular irregularity spills language and perceptions over from one section to the
next. Thus, a principle of order never becomes fixed or arbitrary,
which is consistent with the poet's vision. Whereas Ammons
has embraced some kind of typographical stanzaic regularity in
the tercets he used to compose "Hibernaculum" and *Sphere*, he
rejects even that as a design principle in "The Ridge Farm," with
its highly irregular lines and blocks of text resembling the irregu-
larities of topology on a ridge.

Ammons, as he enters the latter stages of a fine poetic career,
retains his playfulness and his subversiveness in order to cele-

brate the provisional nature of reality. For Ammons to rest on a single definition of poetic form would be self-contradictory. Poetic form, like reality itself, is slippery, subject to moments of stasis but quickly disrupted by movement and chaos. It is the provisional itself, including the not so sharp distinction between subjective and objective realities, that compels Ammons to experiment with form and to reflect on that experiment. In turn, we discover him exposing the inherent polarities of his and our natures: unity and diversity, form and formlessness, stability and flux.

He writes, for example, in section 34:

> don't think we don't
> know one breaks
> form open because he fears
> its bearing in on him
>
> . . . .
> and one hugs form because
> he fears dissolution, openness,
> we know, we know:
> one needs stanzas to take
> sharp interest in and
> one interests the stanza
> down the road to the wilderness:
>
> (SV, 28)

The first four lines of this section echo the youthful iconoclastic poet. What are we to make, however, of the seeming embrace of form, of the "stanza" itself as an organizing principle in the latter half of this group of lines? Ammons does in fact "fear dissolution" as a threat to poetic form, which, when carried to an extreme in his own work, results in The Snow Poems. Moreover, as we have seen in Sphere, "Essay on Poetics," "Hibernaculum," and "Extremes and Moderations," Ammons embraces stanzaic regularity in otherwise highly irregular poems. In one sense, his regularly shaped stanzas serve as a way to bind the chaos in the longer poems, a creative chaos that the poet sees in nature and that he seizes upon as a method of liberating himself to reflect on the wide range of his interests. He dares to contradict himself, and herein lies the tension between form and formlessness that is reflected not only in the varying shapes of his poems, but also in the oscillations of his inquiring mind.

In earlier poems Ammons wavers between the Unseen and the Seen, and again in these lines from "The Ridge Farm" he articulates a principle of poetic vision. He is unwilling to pin himself down to a limited field of perception, either formally or visually, and prefers the freedom and latitude and ultimately the poetic tension derived from a dialectical engagement with form and the world. He subverts even his own assertions about form in order to prove the provisional nature of consciousness and the shapes it designs.

Later in "The Ridge Farm" he makes a frontal assault on the couplet, the quatrain, and the sonnet, boxes of poetic shape and line.

> my business is to make
> room for the truth, to bust the couplet,
> warp the quatrain, explode the sonnet,
> tear down the curvatures of the lengthy:
>
> (SV, 30)

To form the flow is to write a poem; to overform the flow is to write a sonnet or a conventional poem, to kill the flow. But to "ridge" the flow is to allow for irregularity, a line that emerges from the dual slopes of experience, a line that tracks the meeting of fluency and recalcitrance, definition and indefinition. So Ammons's poems are the turning of the flow into lines, into "The Ridge Farm," a farm that is not only on a ridge, but that also cultivates ridges, that grows ridges like other farms grow wheat: there are wheat farms and there are ridge farms. Ammons's farm grows ridges, and ridges are what he cultivates.

In the book *Space, Time & Medicine*, author Larry Dossey describes the work of the physicist David Bohm, who proposes an entire new language, called the "rheomode," to be consistent with physics' understanding of reality.[10] The term is derived from the Greek word meaning "to flow." This new language would give primacy to verbs instead of nouns, which would reduce the emphasis on subject-and-object dualism. Dossey recalls Buckminster Fuller's dictum: "I seem to be a verb!"—which in Fuller's mind conveyed a truer relationship with the world. Ammons, who is anxious to let as much "flow" into his long poems as possible, effectively uses disruptive verbs in this attack on form, an iconoclastic gesture not inconsistent with his own creation of regularly irregular tercets and quatrains in some of his earlier long poems. Unlike the traditional couplet, quatrain, and sonnet, Ammons's "containers" are always constructed to accommodate maximum "swoosh" and "flow" of the universe. They flow over from one to the other and seem to defy their very uniformity of shape. In this sense, Ammons's stanzas can be seen as temporary "holdings" for the more ongoing motion of the poem. They are like the physical world itself, where apparently even the most fixed forms are, on the subatomic level, process and flow.

Ammons declares in section 30, "I am / seeing: I am looking to make / arrangements." This is a neat summation of one of his major poetic strategies. The "arrangements" he is *looking* to make are of course the lines of his poems, arranged on the page in a variety of shapes and forms. It is curious that one explanation of the etymology of the word "arrange," from the Old French *arangier*, means to put in a line, whereas another explanation traces the root back to the Frankish root *hring*, meaning ring or circle. Ammons, who elsewhere in "The Ridge Farm" says that "life is roundabout / and roundabout," must try nevertheless to subsume perception within the linearity of poetry. Rather than chaff at the seemingly irreconcilable difference between circles and lines, Ammons instead celebrates the polarity.

In his talk to the International Poetry Forum in 1967, entitled "A Poem Is a Walk," Ammons articulated his faith in poetry as a means of bridging duality.

> Once every five hundred years or so, a summary statement about poetry comes along that we can't imagine ourselves living without. The greatest statement in our language is Coleridge's in the *Biographia*. It serves my purpose to quote only a fragment from the central statement: that the imagination—and I think, poetry—"reveals itself in the balance or reconciliation of opposite or discordant qualities." This suggests to me that description, logic, and hypothesis, reaching toward higher and higher levels of generality, come finally to an antithesis logic can't bridge. But poetry, the imagination, can create a vehicle, at once concrete and universal, one and many, similar and diverse, that is capable of bridging the duality and of bringing us the experience of a "real" world that is also a reconciled, a unified, real world.[11]

That vehicle, of course, is the poem, an expression of words that in Ammons's mind is capable of reconciling opposites: roundness and linearity, or as in "The Ridge Farm" "recalcitrance" and "fluency." "A work of art," he says, "creates a world of both one and many, a world of definition and indefinition."[12] Ammons believes that the poem alone can reconcile paradoxes and is by its very nature "inaccessible to the methods of logical exposition."[13] It is the poem alone that can reveal that the separate particles of creation are connected to all other particles in the universe. It is the poem, at once "concrete and universal," that can reveal the unity of matter from the level of the electron to the stars and galaxies. The apparent conflict between circles and lines derives from a limited dualistic vision and is replaced by a more radical unifying vision that sees them both as manifestations of the same underlying quantum field.

Even poems, which Ammons freely admits are language constructs, struggle to render the realities of perception. He continues in section 30 to say:

> I said the
>
> words as truly as I could
> say them, according to
> themselves: the words
>
> are not responsible: they
> are not the truth: they
> caught the swerve, they
>
> revealed the glint:
> .   .   .   .
> I speak to show not
> the substance but
> the curvature of the going

(SV, 24–25)

Ammons, an admirer of Lao-tse, knows the awful secret that Lao-tse writes of in the *Tao Te Ching*, and which Ammons uses as an epigraph in the reprinted version of his Pittsburgh talk: "Nothing that can be said in words is worth saying."[14] For Lao-tse, the ineffable Silence that lies at the heart of things cannot be evoked through language or meaning, and for Ammons, the poet of the late twentieth century, words are also incapable of conveying the "true" nature of reality, which is not "substance," but rather "field." Even the curvature of space-time is a manifestation of the gravitational field. What we once thought of as "solid" and "fixed" is indeed permeable and fluid. In the Newtonian world there were particles, but today particles are seen as levels of excitation of abstract underlying fields. Ammons knows that what can be told is not the entire story, that at best he can evoke the flux, not the substance. His medium, poetic language, must go with the "flow" of the fields. However, because they are quantum fields, words cannot ever "catch" them, any more than the physicists' measurements can. It is through the curvature of the eye that this new "vision" is perceived by the viewer, and the poet, the seer, uses language as a vehicle that at best can "catch" the "swerve," evoke the "curvature," but never arrest it completely. Still, this act has its value, and Ammons affirms this through his own "recalcitrance" manifest in his on-going reinvention of form and language.

When Ammons looks for consolation and redemption, as he did in "Easter Morning" after confronting in a North Carolina graveyard the gravity of the death of many of his loved ones, he most always looks to the "swerve" of the natural world. It is a healing experience for him. It "cultures" him in a way that more artificial "cultures" cannot. This sentiment is epitomized toward the end of "The Ridge Farm" in section 46.

> culture, hardened to shellac's empty
> usage, defines in definitions
> hoaxdoms of remove from the true life
> which
> is smaller, leaner than a brook, no
> louder, variable as, to the true rain:
> the true life feels about its small
> shoulders the traces and burdens of
> death and turns for relief to berries,
> bushes bent in abundance,
> to dives into fell pockets of streams,
> to musings on the clean forward edging
> of the moon, to the eye of the other,
> consolation, what there is, in the small
> humbling touch
>
> (SV, 38)

"Culture" for Ammons is not only the pop culture, which competes for our attention and bombards perception with contrived images, but also human culture, which he distrusts as deceitful. Covered by a thin veneer of "shellac," "culture" in Ammons's usage represents the superficial. It is a mere hoax, a deceit that tricks us away "from the true life" to be found in "bushes bent in abundance," "fell pockets of streams," the "forward edging / of the moon," and the private, intimate encounters with other human beings. When "the burdens of / death" impinge upon our shoulders, as they do upon Ammons's in "Easter Morning," he resorts to taking a walk, which he described as "the externalization of an interior seeking."[15] When the goal of such seeking is consolation, the walk provides the possibility for discovering the proper stimuli, the serendipitous "arrangements" of the natural world perceived through the "curvature" of the eye that reawaken in us "majesty and integrity." That is why Ammons says in the final section of "The Ridge Farm":

> I like nature poetry
> where the brooks are never dammed up or
> damned to hauling dishwater or
> scorched out of their bottoms by acids:
> the deep en-leafing has now come and
> the real brook in certain bends dwells, its
> stone collections dry-capped, shale shelves
> in shade, leaves and falls murmuring
> each to the other—and yesterday I
> looked upbrook from the highway and
> there flew down midbend a catbird to
> the skinny dip, found a secure
> underwater brookstone and began, in a
> dawnlike conclave of tranquility, to
> ruffle and flutter, dipping into and
> breaking the reflective surfaces with
> mishmashes of tinkling circlets.

> (SV, 41)

Ammons's return to the brook at the end of "The Ridge Farm" is reminiscent of previous encounters near water, to which he returns for music and movement. He is careful, however, to distinguish the "real brooks" from others, those that "culture" spoils by pollution. He watches closely the flight of a catbird as it finds a place on an "underwater brookstone" and begins to disturb the tranquil surface of the brook with "mishmashes of trinkling circlets." The final image evokes Ammons's visual aesthetic, which informs not only "The Ridge Farm" but many of his greatest poems, including but certainly not limited to "Easter Morning," "Corsons Inlet," and *Sphere*. The bird "disturbs" the mirrorlike surface of the brook, and the "mishmash" that emerges is "trinkling circlets." These circlets will fan out and reach the margins of the brook, reminding us that small, local disturbances may have broad, often unseen impact, an important message of this poem as well as of Ammons's other long poems. Moreover, the disruption, or "breaking," of tranquility yields flux, in this case "trinkling circlets," which offer aesthetic consolation to the seer by virtue of their shape and movement. These "ridges" of vision excite Ammons, for they break the stillness and promise the hope of new creations and redemptive forms.

"The Ridge Farm" is followed by "Tombstones," a sequence of numbered lyrics, which together compose a meditation on mortality. Like Walt Whitman in his final years, the aging Ammons returns to the subject of death, this time in the form of an encounter with death's markers, the very slabs of stone that have inscribed upon them the names of the deceased. We have seen Ammons in the graveyard before in his poem "Easter Morning."

In that earlier poem, the graves and their markers are of Ammons's next of kin. The tone of the earlier cemetery poem, and its locale, is much different than that of in "Tombstones." Whereas the former poem is very much rooted in a specific place, the latter poem seems to be devoid of defined geographical locale. The tombstones in *Sumerian Vistas* could be anywhere. The power of "Easter Morning" is derived from the depth of feeling Ammons conveys through his encounter with the grave of his little brother, and the poet's transcendence of death derives from the strength of his faith in a natural world that resurrects him on Easter morning. Ammons's deeply personal, heartfelt pain expressed in "Easter Morning" is refreshing and uncharacteristic, and this is replaced by a cooler, more contemplative, poetic strategy in "Tombstones."

"Tombstones" is not entirely devoid of compassionate moments, however, and for at least one Ammons reader it represents one of his greatest poetic achievements. Ashley Brown, in his review of *Sumerian Vistas* in *World Literature Today*, writes of Ammons: "His best typical poetry is a sequence of *meditations*, and a new group of twenty-nine short lyrics called 'Tombstones' is one of his finest achievements."[16] Brown is correct in calling this sequence meditative, but for the reader who felt "Easter Morning" was one of Ammons's greatest poetic moments in what is proving to be another long and startling phase of his career after the writing of *Sphere*, "Tombstones" may seem too detached, ultimately too wry in its approach to human mortality.

One of this poem's subjects is inscription, the writing of the names of the dead upon stone. Ashley Brown suggests that the letters etched on tombstones are reminiscent of early Sumerian cuneiform characters preserved on rocks and clay tablets. Such inscriptions are gestures to provide permanence to that which is mortal, and this tension between inscription and the ravages of time, the mortal and the immortal,, provides the catalyst, the frictional incentive that stirs Ammons's imagination. The chiseling into stone of the names of the deceased is a positive action, one that seems to preserve them against the desultory attacks of wind and rain. In one of the more touching moments of the poem, Ammons recognizes the irony of inscribing memory upon mute, seemingly inert stone. He says in section 2:

> it breaks the heart
> that stone holds
> what time let go
>
> but the stones are
> the time left
> that the names can be in

(SV, 45)

Much of the rest of the poem is a series of meditations on the significances of inscription and memory. In the process, Ammons celebrates the power of consciousness and perception as transformative, as ways of altering conventional notions of stability. This is the poem's deeper secret, that apparent moments of and attempts at fixation, such as the inscription of names on tombstones, and ultimately death itself, are mere fictions. Just as poetry itself fails in its attempt to arrest reality, in large measure because as Ammons has suggested one cannot fully represent the curvature of time and space within the confines of linearity, so too does life and death escape the attempt to inscribe it in a fixed manner. Poems, like tombstones, are attempts to preserve experience, but experience itself is ultimately too varied, too multidimensional, to be arrested in time.

There is a dramatic difference between casting poems as a ridge and a ridging, and casting them as "tombstones." Ridges track a wavering line that balances two forces; tombstones use words to memorialize an absence. The kinds of inscriptions in these poems are not so much an attempt to fix "life and death" in words as an attempt to mark the absence of something by turning it to stone. If opposing slopes of force produce ridges, the collapsing of opposing forces (which would be death) produces tombstones. Ridges rise out of the conflict (and tensions) of life; tombstones rise out of the silence (and stasis) of death. Ammons knows that stasis is not possible in nature, however, so the imagination turns even tombstones into sites of activity (just as nature never treats a tombstone as eternal).

"Tombstones" is composed of a series of numbered lyrics, many of which offer alternative ways of seeing. Ammons begins his assault on rocklike stability by suggesting in section 4 of his poem that tombstones contain much more than meets the eye. As he knows from quantum mechanics, reality is "layered," not superficial, and beneath the apparently fixed rocklike surface of matter is the swirl of protons and electrons. He describes the stone as having "levels of existence / in existence."

Although Ammons provides the conventional explanation in section 6 for why we use stones to memorialize the dead—

> we put a stone there
>
> . . . .
> weighty enough
> to hold time down,
> a memorial, often without
> recoverable recollection,
> a deed to a million
> facts, all missing
>
> (SV, 46)

—he also knows the futility of attempting to "hold time down," which by its nature is ongoing, ineluctable, elusive. Moreover, the dynamics of a life cannot be encapsulated by an engraving. Life is multiple, varied, "a deed / to a million / facts," all missing from such an artifact. The paradox of "Tombstones" is that time cannot be held down no matter how hard we try, that memory and consciousness rather than mere inscriptions on rock preserve the dead for us, and that "radiant vision" is the perceptive mode by which we gain perspective on life and death.

In sections 12 and 13 the poet imagines different scenes. In the first of these, one of many paired lyrics in the poem, "a mockingbird sings to a whole / graveyard: the turbulence, / polishing the gravestones, / melts the names." The bird's song and vibrant sound, and their imagined impact on time and space, alter the scene and transform the markers of death. The names of the deceased are melted, one of the many moments in which the temporariness of inscription is evoked by the ongoingness of time and nature.

Ammons moves on to still another perspective on the gravestones. In section 13 he describes the onslaught of wind and rain, leaves and puddles, on the slabs of stone. In contrast to section 12, where the bird's song "melts the names," in section 13 "among the swirling / motions, the stone's slow swirl / keeps the name." In this section all the power of the elements cannot erase that which is etched in stone, whereas in the preceding section the mere song of a bird makes the inscriptions "disappear." By reading these two lyrics as a pair, one realizes that we have entered the realm of the poet's imagination, that these gravestones, unlike those in "Easter Morning," are not "real," but rather the poet's fictive creation.

Consciousness, then, both the poet's and our own, is transformative. It is the survivor who carries the memory of the dead, who has the power both to transform the past and to make it endure. In this sense, we are all "tombstones," all markers and containers of previous lives that have shaped our own and that have left the scene. This is the central truth Ammons celebrates near the midpoint of this lyrical sequence. In section 16, he writes:

> stones, names in them, are
> just stones: when the stone
> brushes mind, memory
> changes the stone clear through
>
> (SV, 50)

Without their brushing up against human consciousness, the tombstones remain dull and inert. The survivor, like the poet, has the power to transform "reality." The survivor's encounter with the tombstone of a dead friend or relative can be seen as a metaphor for the poet's encounter with the world. Both situations offer the potential for imaginative exchange, for transmuting the mute into something vocal and palpable. We speak out our memories of the dead, just as the poet speaks out and records his or her encounter with the world.

Ammons also alters "reality" by offering imagined perspectives culled from his intimacy with modern science. While scientific allusions are sprinkled throughout "Tombstones," clearly one of the most arresting passages is section 18.

> stones, as if forms of intelligence,
> stir: concentrate light
> still and you have them:
>
> still, other durances exceed stones'—
> a pulse in one of earth's orbits
> beats once in four hundred thousand years:

in certain orders of time
stones blow by like the wind:
starlight pricks them like bubbles

                                                (SV, 50)

While decaying monuments and tombstones are a long-standing
trope in Western poetry, Ammons approaches them from a more
scientific perspective. As he does in Sphere, the poet slips into
an astronomical perspective to call into question our own notions of "reality" and "fixity." "Stillness," as Ammons knows, is
a relative term. The stone, he said earlier, has layered "levels of
existence," and within it are many "times in time." Slabs of stone
seem fixed, stationary, immobile to the naked eye; nevertheless,
modern physics has shown that matter, even cemetery tombstones, is not inert and fixed, but rather "as if forms of intelligence / stir." There is not fixity on the subatomic level, where
particles ("the time of protons and electrons") exhibit curious
"fieldlike" behavior, appearing everywhere in their orbit at once.
   In contrast to "other durances," the subatomic "activity" of a
stone seems fleeting. Larry Dossey points out in his book Space,
Time & Medicine that as a result of Einstein's theory of relativity,
"reality" could be ordered differently for different observers, or
as Ammons attests, differently for the same observer.[17] In this
case, Ammons calls into question the fixed notion of stone by
comparing it to "a pulse in one of earth's orbits" that "beats once
in every four hundred thousand years." Ammons, clearly playing
on the word "still," knows that still one can find other durances
more still than that of stone. The orbit of the earth has various
cycles—the precession of the equinoxes is one of them. Ammons
alludes to a pulse in one of earth's orbits that has a periodicity
of 400,000 years. Now that's durability, he seems to be saying.
The different orders of time Ammons invokes are the different
time scales that govern different levels of existence. The orbit of
the sun around the galactic center may take many millions of
years. The life cycle of the universe is on the order of 60 billion
years. The vibrational period of a nuclear particle may be a billionth of a billionth of a second. Ammons conveys the truth that
each level of life has its characteristic scale of distance, time,
and energy.
   He continues his attack on conventional notions of "reality"
in section 19, where he boldly declares, "there is no nature."
Instead, he asserts that what we think of as stones and brooks
are "pools of energy cooled into place." Nature, then, can be seen

as the remnant pools of energy that have coalesced in time and
space after the Big Bang. The phrase may also be an allusion
to the fact that when particles bind together the energy seems
coalesced. Since this is a poem in which alternative perspectives
are constantly generated, Ammons does not rest with this description of matter, but proposes yet another way of looking at
"things." "They are starlight pressed / to store" he says. Ammons
here reveals the truth that Chet Raymo writes of in his chapter
on "Stardust" in *The Soul of the Night:* "Every atom of the earth,
excepting the hydrogen and some of the helium, was made in
the hot core of a star or in the energetic convulsions that accom-
pany the end of a star's life."[18] For Ammons, it is important to
share this perspective with the reader, that indeed much of the
world around us is composed of stardust. He will state this more
boldly in section 24, where he writes "ninety percent / of the
universe is dead stars."

Ammons proposes yet a third way of "seeing" things in section
19, suggesting that "objective reality" is simply "speeding light
held still." Light, however, can never be "at rest" (it has zero
rest mass)—we simply do not see the dynamism underlying the
apparent "stillness." In proposing these three perspectives, Ammons demonstrates how his knowledge of science is used as a
generative tool in his quest to widen scope.

Curiously, even as he celebrates the transformative knowledge
of astronomy and physics, and long after he has shown in this
poem and elsewhere how the power of imagination can reinvent
the universe, Ammons focuses on the image of the eye. It is, after
all, through the eye that Ammons encounters the world. For all
his serious play in using science to propose radical perspectives,
Ammons remains primarily a poet whose favorite metaphor is a
walk, and whose career-long occupation has been to record his
observations. Even his scientific understandings must be assimilated through vision. The poet reads, absorbs, and then assimilates the data. He feels compelled toward the end of this
sequence of meditations once again to express his awe for that
marvelous organ, the eye.

> the light in an eye
> transfigured in
> frames of feeling—
>
> how is this small well,
> so shallow and
> deep, so magical

and plain able to
center all
the circumferences—

the eye itself
vision's vision
and visionary sway

(SV, 52)

Ammons has paid homage to the mechanism of the eye before. In his December 31 entry in *Tape for the Turn of the Year*, he expresses wonder about the subcellular mechanism in the eye that converts radiant energy into electrical signals to the brain. He has always been fascinated by this process. In the first tercet here he once again alludes to it and suggests that such light is the source of not only how we see the world, but also how we feel about it. Thus, the eye, which structurally is a very small "well"—and, as Ammons points out, anatomically rather "shallow"—is also "deep," the vehicle by which the world is absorbed into the recesses of the brain and heart.

As the poet testifies here, the eye's capability is magical, not only in its mechanical function and structure, but most assuredly in its ability "to / center all / the circumferences." The eye then is the organ of vision, "vision's vision," and the anatomical center for the necessary assimilation of the world's circumferences, its manifest and manifold expressions. Ammons, who is biologically attuned to the world, enables epistemology, poetics, and anatomy all to coalesce in this section's concluding tercet. In this contemplative poem, ostensibly about death, he registers the truth that knowledge is a function of vision, that vision is the poet's aesthetic approach to composing the world, and that the eye itself, like the world it drinks in, literally "sways" in its constant oscillations.

In "Tombstones" Ammons ultimately confesses the futility of attempting to arrest time. The final sections of this poem build to this conclusion, which for Ammons, as we have seen is cause not for despair but rather for celebration. To fix things permanently is to entrap them, and one of the enduring truths of his work is that the unfixing of apparently stable configurations is liberating. This was the messsage of "Corsons Inlet," and, in its own peculiar way, of "Tombstones." It is tempting to suggest that from the birth of Ammons's poetic career in *Ommateum* to its seeming twilight in "Tombstones," he has remained steadfast in this vision.

He ends "Tombstones" with the image of inscriptions rising off the tombstones like balloons.

> in so many hundred years,
> the names
>
> will be light enough
> and as if balloons
> will rise out of stone

(SV, 55)

The final image then is one of transcendence and is consistent with the tone and thematic emphasis of what has come before. The names themselves, letters inscribed upon stone, apparently fixed and concrete, are imagined to be light enough to "rise out of stone." Once again, as at the end of "Easter Morning," Ammons discovers a mode of resurrection, of bringing to life that which has died. It is a marvelous image, one also suggestive of Whitman's death poems, in which he envisions the soul's release from the body as liberating. Here, the letters are released from the stone tablets in an equally suggestive transcendence.

"Tombstones" is not an elegy, however, but rather a philosophical poem on the meaning of time. It frustrates the reader's expectations by continually posing through its "curious science" different perspectives on time and "events." This strategy may prove irritating for the reader who is unwilling to submit to Ammons's seemingly detached, ironic, coolly intellectual approach to the significance of death. In "Tombstones," no one seems to have actually died. However, within the context of Ammons's long career, both the tone and the poet's stance toward his subject seem consistent and offer further testimony not only to his cleverness, but to his unique and compelling encounter with "reality."

It is hard to know what motivated the writing of "Tombstones." One can speculate that Ammons may have felt the need to confront death in his work. Or, given the philosophical bent of his own mind, he may have discovered that the subjects of mortality, inscription, and time provided sufficient grist for his own curious imagination. Whatever the reasons, Ammons's central strategy of relying upon science, vision, and imagination coalesces to form a powerful statement. Its truth is not simple, however; it rarely is in Ammons's poems. In "Tombstones" he seems to be urging the reader toward a new picture of the world, one described by Dossey in *Space, Time & Medicine* as "a tapestry in which sense impressions, consciousness, time, space, and light are the threads, combining in a delicately entangled way to form what we perceive as 'event.'"[19]

The third major "event" in *Sumerian Vistas* is a collection of over fifty lyrics that compose the final section of the book ("Motions' Holdings"). Many of these lyrics first appeared in the special *Pembroke Magazine* issue. Others appeared in various poetry magazines throughout the early 1980s. Together, they form a tapestry, presenting in sharp relief many of Ammons's voices and concerns.

Here we find shorter lyrics that give themselves up to direct observation: "20 January," "Frost's Foretellings," "Early Indications," "Upper Limits," and "Working Out." "Working Out," whose punning title is typical of the wit and charm in many of these lyrics, presents Ammons's sense impressions of an electrical storm. The combustions of energy in the sky, working themselves out ("celestial tensions") as recorded in the poem, are mirrored by the workings-out of smaller grounded phenomena. The Japanese beetles shined "bronze-green" on the newly grown elm leaves "through the blue-bronze highlightings." The poem, through its open tercets, presents a working-out itself of the larger and smaller circulations of energy that fascinate Ammons.

We also discover in "Motions' Holdings" several of Ammons's natural-landscape dialogue poems. "Scaling Desire," "Dominion," and "Subsidiary Roles" all present a poetic voice engaged in "conversation" respectively and respectfully with the wind, a river, and a brook. In the first of these, the persona imagines an encounter in which the wind asks the speaker to sit down by a boulder in the middle of the desert for a year. At the end of that time the wind will show him something really interesting. The poet knows, however, that "interest" is relative and a matter of "scale."

In "Dominion" the speaker barks commands at a "glittery river," only to have it ignore him. He tells the river to rise, but it refuses. Next he commands it to stop, but again it fails to comply. By the poem's end the poet realizes he needs to change his tone. Nature can be oblivious to human desire, independent of us in its own "dominion." "Don't turn back," he tells the river, "and it eased on / by, / majestic in the sweetest / command." Ammons reenacts a small but important lesson. One must first gauge, or scale, the "dominion" of rivers, where flux is a law of

nature, before addressing them. One cannot coerce rivers to be-
have otherwise. We may try to usurp power from nature, but
fail. Ultimately, the river, representative of all natural "things,"
maintains its autonomy. The best humanity can do is to recognize this and adjust our commands to coincide with nature's
ways. When our speech becomes attuned to the natural facts and
forces, then there can be harmony; otherwise, as the poet reveals
here, nature will not comply.

Along with these natural encounters, Ammons continues his
meditation on death in this group of lyrics. In "Chiseled Clouds"
he recalls a cemetery, the "skinny old / slabs" leaning in different
directions, memorials to fallen aunts and uncles and other family. As in "Easter Morning," he looks up, this time at a group of
silver clouds, "cathedrals" that fill the afternoon sky, and imagines their housing all those who have been lost from the "light's
returning." It is a slender, finely wrought poem, clear and much
more direct than "Tombstones." "Chiseled Clouds" presents yet
another perspective on time and provides evidence that when
he chooses, Ammons can be unabashedly direct and lucid. In
"Backcasting" Ammons imagines his own death, with gravel
spilling through him and light finding him transparent. He uses
both of these imagined eventualities to heighten his experience
of the here and now. It's all right to "mess around," he says, given
the forthcoming gravity of death. For Ammons "messing around"
is the high-minded play of his own poems.

Perhaps the most interesting of these "death" lyrics is "Telling
Moves," a poem in which the poet alludes to his own aging and
his unwillingness to accept the grave. Ammons describes the
"telling moves" of three natural "events": a hawk swooping before a dust storm, the gold of a willow tree changing to green and
the floating away of its twigs on gusts of wind, and the meeting of
fall with freezing winter. In each instance, he observes nature
meeting the crisis of change ("pain") presentably well. The aging
poet feels differently about his own moves, however. He contrasts
himself to what he observes around him: "but I'm / not getting
things right," he says at one point, perhaps a hint of his own
sense of aging, or a moment of creative doubt. He concludes the
poem with his reluctance to give in to transformation gracefully:

> hawk and willow, the stilt-right
> arrivals of the old:

the grave, I cannot accept it,
there is no way to give it up.

(SV, 116)

While the hawk and willow seem to rise above ("stilt-right")
circumstance and meet change head-on and with grace, the poet
himself cannot accept death. "Grave" and "gravity" are from the
same root, meaning "heaviness." Graves are the places of ultimate
gravity (in both senses—seriousness and pull-toward-earthness),
the final "downer," the place of down-ness. There is no way to
give it "up"! Unlike at the end of "Tombstones," here the poet
cannot pull transcendence out of it, to give gravity lightness, to
give graveness lightness. The final "it" in the poem is purposefully ambiguous; it refers to the grave, but also to Ammons's
reluctance to give up life, sense perception, and the lifelong giving "up" of himself to poetry.

"Motions' Holdings" has many other fine lyrics, including
"Power Plays," a short love poem in which Ammons discovers
"splendor" not in the "drifts of stars" but rather in the bone of
another's arm; in "Information Density," a poem dedicated to
Kenneth Burke, the poet contrasts "generalization" ("the wider
forms of disposition") with "concretion," the "pull and haul" of
the particular; and in "Tertiaries" he reflects on the body of his
poetry, calling it "heaps of verbal glitterment." In this cryptic
twelve-line poem, Ammons suggests that those who are sated
and "well-founded" in themselves may have no need for his
work, whereas those for whom "reality" is perishing may discover abundance in Ammons's shards of inscription.

The two poems "Eidos" and "Motion's Holdings" work well
together as a pair and serve to frame the entire volume of *Sumerian Vistas*. In the first of these the poet watches the dance of
old flies.

On those late March afternoons
when a flurry nearly rain
eases over and the few big

flakes, old flies, stall,
lift, dive, sweep in a slow
loose-knotted breeze, I watch

the lineations of the dance, air's
least-holding script, whose
figures carve on my retina

motions the mind mulls over
and subdues to
intelligible reticula, informing shapes.

(SV, 102)

As Ammons watches the configuration of flies on a spring afternoon in "Eidos," he transcribes the flies' radiant energy into electrical energy. The poem, casual, open-ended, unstopped except
for the final closure, sweeps along from one stanza to the next,
mirroring the breezy movement of the aerial performers. This
"script of the air" entertains Ammons, and he records in his
poem the registering of the event in consciousness. The poem's
title, "Eidos," is Greek for "form" or "shape" and became the
English word "eidolon," which connotes both specter and an
image of the ideal. The lineations of the dance are specterlike,
transient, and derive whatever substance they may have from the
mind. The retina, the innermost coat of the back part of the
eyeball, is the mechanism by which the performance is appreci-
ated. After all, the images formed on the retina are carried to the
brain by the optic nerves. Thus, the patterns the flies make, the
"intelligible reticula," are cognized through a subtle, dynamic
process in which shape and motion are "carved" on the retina
and then sent to the brain for interpretation.

Ammons's choice of "carve" and "mulls over" to describe the
process of vision seems apt. Moreover, the poem and these verbs
seem to suggest much of what is happening in Sumerian Vistas.
Ammons, ever keen to explore new vantage points, moves from
the ridge in "Ridge Farm" to the imagined cemetery's tombstones
in the poem by that title, to his more familiar natural encounters
in "Motions' Holdings." In each section, however, he seems eager
to explore and register how the "carvings" or "ridges" of the
world around him, sometimes mere transparencies, at other
times substantial and deep impressions, register in consciousness. In "Tombstones" he reveals the irony that the "carvings"
on the stones are less permanent than we might think. In this
short poem entitled "Eidos," the sensory impression—the flies'
shapes—are interpreted as "intelligible reticula" by the mind. It
is the mind that gives vision its meaning, an idea consistently
upheld in Sumerian Vistas.

"Motions' Holdings," the title of the concluding section of
Sumerian Vistas, is also the title of one of the section's most
interesting poems. Its paradoxical suggestiveness, evoking both
movement and stasis, flux and arrested time, is reminiscent of

the subtitle of *Sphere*, which is "the form of a motion." Form, Ammons knows, is often a temporary "holding" of motion.

By calling this large group of individual lyrics "Motions' Holdings," Ammons seems to be suggesting that the poems themselves are configurations that not only convey shape but also "hold" motion and meaning. The poem "Eidos," for example, is a "holding" of the flies' motions, just as the image of them on the retina is a "holding" of their perception. The joy and terror of being alive, at least as Ammons experiences the world, is to recognize that all of motion's holdings are temporary, and on more than one occasion Ammons has referred to the provisional nature of even his own poems. The eponymous poem "Motion's Holdings" evokes several images of motion fixed in a holding pattern, only to have that symmetry broken and released.

> The filled out gourd rots, the
> ridge rises in a wave
> height cracks into peaks, the peaks
>
> wear down to low undoings whose undertowing
> throws other waves up: the branch
> of honeysuckle leaves arcs outward
>
> into its becoming motion but,
> completion's precision done, gives
> over riddling free to other
>
> motions: boulders, their green and white
> moss-molds, high-held in moist
> hill woods, stir, hum with
>
> stall and spill, take in and give
> off heat, adjust nearby to
> geomagnetic fields, tip liquid with
>
> change should a trunk or rock loosen
> to let rollers roll, or they loll
> inwardly with earth's lie
>
> in space, oxidize at their surfaces
> exchanges with fungal thread and rain:
> things are slowed motion that,
>
> slowed too far, falls lose, freeing debris:
> but in the ongoing warps, the butterfly
> amaryllis crowds its bowl with bulbs.

(SV, 113–14)

The images are illustrative examples of how motion or growth achieves "completion," a kind of "holding," and how "completion's precision done," chaos, change, a movement of displacement, arrives to disturb and alter the arrested motion. In this way, the universe remains a constant dance of energy in which "objects" are merely temporary stays of light and energy. The gourd ripened on the vine now rots, and its pattern of expansion and contraction imitates the universe.

In the poem's first tercet Ammons also give his clearest definition of a ridge—a wave made substantial ("the / ridge rises in a wave"). In "Motion's Holdings" Ammons acknowledges that such embodiments, or ridges, are often temporary. The conversion of forces that creates ridges can undo them. An ocean wave rises until its ridge "cracks into peaks," the motions and forces of which are submerged beneath the water and "throw other waves up." The cyclical pattern of motion is evoked here, with creation and destruction alternating roles in the formation of ever new waves. Ammons suggests that creation may in fact depend upon destruction, and destruction upon creation. In chaos theory, a cyclical steady state, pushed just a hair over the limit of stability, breaks down into chaotic motion, from which a new, sometimes more complex and intelligent, steady state can emerge. The "becoming motion" of the honeysuckle branch arcing outward is attractive in its "becoming-ness," yet the poet knows this completion will give way to other motions. The holding of the arc is temporary, to be replaced by other forms. The moss molds on boulders, seeming holdings of shape and form, are ripe with change. They receive and give off heat, adjust to geomagnetic fields, and "oxidize exchanges with fungal thread and rain." In them coalesce the forces of motion and holding.

As in the earlier poem "Clarity," Ammons here arrives at the truth of a subtle kind of metamorphosis lurking within and behind all form. Just as the rockslide in the former poem reveals shambles of knowledge, so too in "Motion's Holdings" does change invoke discovery. The "ongoing warps" of change seem to contain within them the birth of ever new form, just as the flowering amaryllis, the poem's final image, "crowds its bowl with bulbs." Its going to seed is inherent in its flowering, and its rebirth is inherent in its death.

Three years after the publication of *Sumerian Vistas* (1987), Ammons came out with *The Really Short Poems of A. R. Ammons*, a collection of brief lyrics, most of which are less than twelve lines in length, with many as short as three or four lines. Such a gesture, after the publication of *Sumerian Vistas* with its two long poems, is characteristic of Ammons, who often in the past has followed the writing and publication of longer poems with shorter, crisper ones.

He has always felt comfortable with the shorter poem, and about thirty of the lyrics in this latest volume are culled from the earlier *Collected Poems 1951–1971*. Twenty come from *Highgate Road* (1977), a privately printed, limited edition of thirty-six copies. Many of the others were first printed in *Pembroke Magazine*. Thus *The Really Short Poems of A. R. Ammons* represents four decades of poetic productivity. When asked in a 1986 interview to comment on his favorite poems, Ammons refused to cite titles or draw up a list. He did say, however, that "the ones I feel comfortable with are the smaller, more concrete, sort of delightful poems. They're sort of like friends."[20]

These short poems are "really" short in the sense of dealing directly with "reality" in the concrete way Ammons describes. Their concern is the real, so they are "really" short. Ammons's inclusion of the adjective "really" is in itself a friendly gesture, a kind of reassurance to the reader that these poems are indeed short and therefore not time-consuming. Moreover, the poet's use of the modifier seems to distinguish these *really* short lyrics from the other shorter poems (not *really* short) that compose most of his work. The volume is, as one reviewer writes, "perfect for those who claim [they have] no time for poetry."

As a group, these poems not only serve as a foil to Ammons's longer, more complex poems, but they also make, as a collection of small, lyrical moments, a statement about the significance of the tiny, the humble, the overlooked. The stillness that lies at the heart of many of these short poems, coupled with their brevity, suggests Asian influence. One thinks of haiku, although Ammons shuns the strict formal limitations of the Japanese format. Yet the clarity, the sharply observed detail, the expansiveness and perceptive surprise evident in these poems is reminiscent of the best haikus.

The first poem of this volume, "Weathering," is just two lines and establishes the playful, witty, and perceptive tone of much that follows.

> A day without rain is like
> a day without sunshine
>
> (RSP, 1)

As someone who has lived in the Pacific Northwest for more
than five years now, I can appreciate the wry humor and intelligence that informs this poem. In Seattle, from October to March,
one expects rain, even looks forward to it, and a day without rain
can be as disappointing to some as a day without sunshine is to
others. Ammons subverts the conventional notion of weather by
giving rain as privileged a position in the landscape as sunshine.
This subversion of hierarchy, this turning expectation upside
down, informs much of the lyrical playfulness of this volume.
Ammons achieves this in "Weathering" through the preposi-
tional selection of "without," which casts the poem into its radical light. If he had written "a day *with* rain is like a day without
sunshine," he would have made more logical sense but less interesting poetry. Through the deft maneuver of adding "out" to
"with" and repeating "without," Ammons turns logic on its head
and invites the reader into an engaging kind of meditation.

The poem "Weathering" also establishes a motif of observation
in this collection of short poems, for many of them are "weatherings," that is, observations on how weather affects natural phenomena. The poet who is enamored of change, "the transient
beauty of natural things," as he himself has called it, sees weather
much as he did in *The Snow Poems,* as an instrument of change,
a creative and regenerative force, both in the landscape and in
his own vision. The surprise is that after four decades of poetic
"weatherings," neither the poet nor his reader grows tired of this
mode. In "Release" Ammons traces the loosening of rain after a
long pent-up muggy day.

> After a long
> muggy
> hanging
> day
> the raindrops
> started so
> sparse
> the bumblebee flew
> between
> them home.

(RSP, 2)

The form of the slender poem, with one word hanging on three
of the first four lines as if suspended in time, evokes the suspen-
sion of movement before the drops start to fall. Even once they
are released, they fall so sparsely that all movement appears

slowed down, the space between the drops wide enough for a bumblebee to fly home between them. The kinesthetics of form thus mirror the kinesthetics of weather and natural movement, and the poem entertains through its visual and formal slow-motion effect. Just as the release of rain after a muggy day provides relief, so too do Ammons's "weatherings" provide a refreshing perspective. Several of the other weather poems in this collection, including "After Yesterday," "Settlement," and "Soaker," work by suggesting a release from limitation, a widening of scope.

In another major group of lyrics in this volume, Ammons plays his role as naturalist. He observes in "Hype" the imitation of a pollen fly to the "sounding" of a bee. In "Triplet" he observes the way iris leaves, "three-in-one," cut broadside in the sun and release the iris bloom. In "Clarifications," one of several poems in which birds and trees figure, crows land on spruce boughs during a heavy snowfall, only to "chisel the neighborhood / sharp with their cries." The blackness of the crows stands in sharp contrast to the whiteness of the snowstorm. Their sharp cries ring through the neighborhood's silence, "clarifying" the landscape, providing sharp distinction in an otherwise blurry world. In "The Mark," one of the most striking lyrics in the entire volume, Ammons once again seems concerned with his own mortality.

> I hope I'm
> not right
> where frost
> strikes the
> butterfly:
> in the back
> between
> the wings.

> (RSP, 144)

The violence in this poem is all the more terrifying because of its swiftness and destructiveness. The image of the hit, or "mark," between the butterfly's wings is suggestive of the angel of death, which comes suddenly, sometimes without forewarning. The physical form, susceptible to change, is struck down violently. The poet's response is naturally self-protective. Moreover, Ammons's fear of being struck from behind suggests his terror of the social world, where one is vulnerable to attack without forewarning. This is echoed in another of the poems in this volume,

"Success Story," where Ammons once again reveals his uneasy relationship with "the world" by declaring "I never got on good / with the world."

Despite these moments of contraction, the poet seems intent in *The Really Short Poems of A. R. Ammons* to continue his quest to widen scope. This enables him to evoke large spans of time as a measure against which the human life span seems short. Despite its relatively short duration, its obvious frailty, and its tenuous relationship with others, the self for Ammons both remains a discriminating assimilator of natural forces and is itself worthy of celebration.

In "Glacials" Ammons suggests the relatively short duration of a human life span as the poet speculates on the boulders in a geological rock garden which have frozen in them "a hundred million years or more."

> In the geological rock garden
> split boulders
> lie about as kinds and ages,
>
> a hundred million years or more in
> many frozen solid:
> dusty thaws flow
>
> steam-loose from the surfaces and
> wind on the way
> at last, the wind mixing
>
> old and current time
> in mixings beginning and
> ended, time unbegun, unended.
>
> (RSP, 22)

The rock garden, a different type of "cemetery," provides a place where "historians" and "glacialists" can view the relics of natural history. These boulders are another example of motion's holdings. They are broken bits and pieces of glaciers. A glacier, after all, is a river of ice, a motion's holding, frozen yet moving, slowly making a gradual descent until it reaches a point where the temperature is high enough to melt the ice as fast as it descends. "Dusty thaws flow / steam-loose from the surfaces" and the boulders wind their way down. These boulders are the "tombstones" of nature, with their own unique inscriptions, their own discourse and genre ("kind"). In the past they may have formed a mountain ridge, or been lodged upon declivities between mountains. In the present these split boulders evoke still another ridge of vision, for the sides of a boulder slope upward to create a ridge at the top. They themselves represent an intersection of natural forces. Ammons, who has climbed many "ridges of vision," sees in these boulders another printout of duration ("a hundred million years or more in / many frozen solid"). All the material the glaciers carry through the ages gets mixed together and we see it now. The boulders in the rock garden embody both old and current time, "time unbegun, unended." Ammons has thus created yet another perspective from which to broaden our own sense of vision and duration.

Another kind of duration Ammons contemplates in *The Really Short Poems of A. R. Ammons* is his ongoing relationship with the reader of his poems. Although he admits to an uneasy relationship with the world, Ammons seems to reserve a special place for his readers. In his poem "Salute," whose title echoes Whitman's poem "Salut Au Monde!" the poet salutes his reader much as Whitman did in the final four lines of his poem, which he added in the 1860 version.[21] The differences between Ammons's ten-line poem, with its narrow lines and understatement, and Whitman's world vision sung in his sprawling verse ("within me latitude widens, longitude lengthens") over thirteen long sections are vast. Whitman salutes myriad nationalities in his poem, and Ammons his single reader. Whitman's imagination takes him across the steppes of Asia; in Ammons's poem landscape is simply a "clearing." Whitman claims the nationality of the nations of the world ("I am a real Parisian"; "I am of London"; "I am of Madrid"); Ammons shuns such identification. Yet the spirit of saluting the reader, and in such a salute wishing him or her good will ("happiness"), is similar in Ammons's poem, albeit a gesture that is more toned down and less physical than that of his nineteenth-century forebear. "Salute" is not only a statement of greeting, but also a statement of parting, Ammons's legacy to his readers.

> May happiness
> pursue you,
>
> catch you
> often, and,
>
> should it
> lose you,

                    be waiting
                    ahead, making

                    a clearing
                    for you.

(RSP, 108)

This poem is a kind of blessing—Ammons's wish for the well-being of his reader. The poet who thinks of his own shorter poems as "friendly" has enacted that friendship in this poem. His wish for his reader is simple, to be caught in the web or net of happiness. Yet Ammons, who knows well the provisional nature of emotional states, plans for the contingency that such a "holding" pattern may be lost. Just as natural things reach completion only to be disturbed, so too is this true of our states of being. He plans for this contingency, however, by wishing that "happiness" carve out a "clearing" for "you" in the future. "Happiness" is another kind of duration, a continuance in time, which, though interrupted, the poet hopes will continue by forging a "clearing," a place where scope is widened. Unlike clear-cutting, which can strip even ridges of their trees, the motions of happiness are gentle, the clearing it makes a visual and emotional brilliance.

Brilliance, after all, is one of the discoveries Ammons's poems make, whether the poet is out walking beside an inlet or exploring the shards of rock from a mountain slide. In "Juice" he uplifts the seemingly unbeautiful, bestowing radiance upon that which is not ordinarily so.

                    I'm stuck with the infinity thing
                    again this morning: a skinny
                    inexpressible syrup, finer than light,
                    everywhere present: the cobweb becoming
                    visible with dust and the tumblelint
                    stalled in the corner seem worthy.

(RSP, 123)

In this lighthearted "sticky" poem Ammons exposes the serious truth that an underlying radiance permeates and bestows sanctity upon all things, great and small. This too is a Whitmanian gesture, democratic and subversive. It is the visionary enacted in the real, the *really* large embodied in the *really* small, the infinite in the finite. The length of this short, six-line poem belies its wide scope. The poet, caught up momentarily in this "inexpressible syrup," sugary and sweet, transcendental and "finer than light," squeezes the "juice" out of the concrete and real, only to discover that it is spirit.

"Juice" echoes Ammons's earlier and more fully realized "The City Limits," a poem admired greatly by his wife, Phyllis. In that earlier poem, which appeared toward the end of *Collected Poems 1951–1971*, Ammons begins by establishing a thesis:

> When you consider the radiance, that it does not withhold
> itself but pours its abundance without selection into every
> nook and cranny not overhung or hidden
>
> (CP, 320)

The final five tercets of the poem provide evidence for Ammons's radical idea. He discovers such radiance in "the glow-blue / bodies and gold-skeined wings of flies swarming the dumped / guts of a natural slaughter or the coil of shit," and in so doing uncovers and uplifts the seemingly repugnant. This is not only poetic strategy, but also a visionary enactment, a literal encounter with the radiance even in the most gross ("dumb, beautiful ministers") aspects of manifest life.[22] In "The City Limits" Ammons traces the implications of such a discovery to the heart, which expands from such encounters, its fear replaced by praise. The double-edged meaning of the title "The City Limits" suggests in one sense (which reads "limits" as a transitive verb) that such vision is limited by the city. However, Ammons converts the myopic vision of the city into a more all-encompassing vision, spiritual and positive, that is enacted at the city limits (a noun), the dumping ground for refuse and therefore a suitable testing ground for radical vision. In "Juice," a much shorter version of and a companion poem to the earlier "The City Limits," Ammons discovers the radiance once again, "a skinny / inexpressible syrup" that is present everywhere, including in cobwebs and tumblelint.

The very short "Small Song" seems like an appropriate poem to end a discussion of *The Really Short Poems of A. R. Ammons*. After all, this is a volume of "small songs." Moreover, the modesty of length (only four lines) bespeaks the humility of his vision, a humility finally that Ammons himself ascribes to, even though he is aware of prideful feelings of ownership and importance that threaten the humility of "Small Song."

The reeds give
way to the

wind and give
the wind away

(RSP, 54)

Most of the poems in this volume are punctuated with a period.
"Small Song," like "Poem," is not, and in both there is a giving
away of something, a release that a period should not and cannot
enclose. Ammons wisely shuns closure in these two poems,
where natural elements are given away. The reeds, ostensibly
victims of the wind, are in Ammons's universe of perception
representative of the flexible, willing not only to bend but to
embrace and then to surrender and give back. This pattern of
bending—motion that results in holding—and then unfolding
back upright into motion, represents in Ammons's mind the radical "event," the configuring and reconfiguring of shape by natural forces.

The reeds, rather than being victimized by the wind, endure
the wind by virtue of their nonresistance. Instead of seeing them
as weak and trampled upon, the poet sees them as strong, em-
boldened enough to give the mighty wind away. In this sense
their gesture is "political" ("passive-nonresistance"). They fend
off the powerful by not subscribing to it, by resisting an entangle-
ment with power, by refusing to be enmeshed in the terms of
power. Of course, such a gesture may seem politically dangerous,
for the seizure of power is always seductive. Yet Ammons is
deeply suspicious of power; his sympathy is with the small, the
neglected, the overlooked.

The reeds embody a Taoistic stance, releasing rather than
grasping, giving way rather than possessing. The unassertive
character of the reeds should not be misconstrued as passivity.
Ironically, their assimilation of the wind, much like the poet
who makes himself "available" to form, is a distinctive type of
triumph, a victory for flexibility over rigidity, for giving away
rather than consuming, for a widening of scope rather than a
limiting of vision.

In *The Really Short Poems* Ammons has once again demonstrated the expansiveness of his vision, wishing his readers
"happiness," discovering radiance in unlikely places, and dem-
onstrating the naturalness of his vision in encounters with birds,
reeds, brooks, and trees. I doubt, however, as one reviewer sug-

gested, that this volume will be spotted frequently at subway stops and luncheonettes. Although the poems in this volume can be read quickly, between bites of a sandwich or stops on the subway, they invite, like much of Ammons's work, reflection and re-reading. For Ammons, like his visionary forebears, would have us remake our minds, learn to look anew, and through our looking redeem not only the world, but one another and ourselves.

Epilogue: A Note on Ammons's *Garbage*

As this book was being prepared for publication, I learned from A. R. Ammons that although his poetic output has been slowed since his 1990 heart surgery, he continues to revise "old, stubborn poems."[1] One of these, *Garbage*, written in 1989, is described by Ammons as "my last poem."[2] Published by W. W. Norton in the summer of 1993, *Garbage* may indeed prove to be Ammons's last major long poem.[3]

I am interested in exploring briefly how *Garbage* manifests the poet's career-long preoccupation with "widening scope." This is accomplished in *Garbage* through its form, its meditations, and most acutely through the poet's expansive vision. Doubtless, future readers and critics will find other elaborations of scope to trace.

Garbage is reminiscent of Ammons's longer poems *Sphere* and "Extremes and Moderations," which employ numbered sections between groupings of tercets, quatrains, and couplets (this last type of grouping employed in *Garbage*). In all, *Garbage* has eighteen sections, each of which runs several pages. Ammons's creation of a large, sprawling poem after the publication of *The Really Short Poems of A. R. Ammons* is further evidence of his unwillingness to be caged into a single mode.

The rays of the poet's attention, both outward through vision and inward through thought, compose the major segments of this poem. *Garbage* provides Ammons with the amplitude to record the loops and turns of his own vision and mind. For those willing to take the ride out to the "dump," sparkles of glass and hidden joys lurk here.

Ammons's vision for the form of his poem is revealed in section 7, where he describes a visit to the library for a computer search on the term "garbage."

> I punched
>
> out Garbage at the library and four titles
> swept the screen, only one, Garbage Feed,

seeming worth going on to; and that was about
feeding swine right: so I punched Garbage Disposal

and the screen came blank—nothing! all those
titles, row on row, of western goodies, mostly

worse than junk, but not a word on Disposal: I
should have looked, I suppose, under Waste Disposal

but, who cares, I already got the point: I
know garbage is being "disposed" of—but what

I wanted I had gotten, a clear space and pure
freedom to dump whatever

Frustrated by his inability to call up a title related to his subject, the speaker discovers what he had really wanted all along, "a clear space and pure / freedom to dump whatever." The long poem has always provided Ammons with the space and freedom to with "dump" whatever he likes into it. *Garbage* is no exception and is likely to be criticized for what Spiegelman has identified as two characteristic flaws in Ammons's work, "the dullness of prosaicism and the airiness of abstraction."[4] *Garbage* suffers from both, with the poet erecting unabashedly his own "ziggurats" of thought and word-play. Others may object to the occasional bawdy joke that finds its way into the poem. But these are risks the poet is willing to take to have the freedom and space his vision demands. He insists on inventing a form that enables him to "dispose" of both the clutter in his life and its meditative re-collections. He even invites humorous comparison between the poem's title and its content, referring to his work as "straw bags full of fleas the dogs / won't sleep on."

Its mission is to declare "the perfect / scientific and materialistic notion of the / spindle of energy." Just as a spindle serves as an axis for larger revolving parts, so too do the eighteen different sections of *Garbage* serve as "spindles" for Ammons's ongoing quest to track and record the "rocklike" and "mystical refinements" of energy. The couplets that compose each section serve as smaller "spindles" upon which the threads of Ammons's reflections are spun. The two-line stanzas create merely the illusion of confinement, however, for this pattern of stanzaic regularity in *Garbage* is designed to allow for maximum "spill" and "flow" between and through each pairing of lines.

At the beginning of the second section of the poem, Ammons

declares that "garbage has to be the poem of our time." He then invokes a mock ritual in which garbage is collected and piled high in mounds of disposal along Florida's flatlands. What to do with "waste"—organic and inorganic, medical and radioactive—poses a major environmental dilemma, and this underlying motif testifies to the largeness of Ammons's concerns. He evokes the hazards of burning garbage which "shut us / in as into a lidded kettle." The poet laments the effects of "toxic waste, poison air, beach goo" and anticipates the global crises which bring nations together at "internationalist gettings-together" like the Earth Summit held in Rio in 1992.

Garbage, however, is much more than an environmentalist's outcry. It is, like most of Ammons's other long poems, philosophical and meditative. He takes up, among other subjects, the wisdom and frailty of old age, the "finality" of death, and the languages of animals, especially whales and birds. As the poem moves from topic to topic, the poet intersperses accounts of excursions. A memorable one is a ride to the farmers' market by Lake Cayuga in New York, where he discovers an array of "sweet pleasures."

The poetry of widening scope in Ammons's poem Garbage includes the latter phase of the poet's own life cycle. He declares early in the poem: "since SS's enough money (I hope) to live / from now on in elegance and simplicity." He jokes, in a folksy voice that he returns to again and again, that Social Security can help pay for soy beans. Yet old age is not merely a time for "rehearsing the sweetnesses / of leisure," but also a time when "we tie into the / lives of those we love." In section 2 of Garbage, Ammons shares poignant reminders of his own aging:

> I can't believe
> I'm merely an old person: whose mother is dead,
>
> whose father is gone and many of whose
> friends and associates have wended away to the
>
> ground, which is only heavy wind, or to ashes,
> a lighter breeze

Just as the heap of garbage at the city's limits is "the gateway to beginning, here the portal / of renewing change," so too is old age a kind of gateway—not only to impending death, but to spiritual renewal. He describes the driver of a bulldozer who stares into the fire of a heap of garbage burning up as seeing "eternity, the burning edge of beginning and ending."

Ammons has not lost his sense of wonder, although it is tempered now by the infirmities of age. The poet's fascination with time, especially "durances" that expand individual consciousness, is evident in section 7, where he asks:

>   have
> you stopped to think what existence is, to be here
>
> now where so much has been or is yet to come and
> where isness itself is just the name of a segment
>
> of flow: stop, think: millennia jiggle in your eyes
> at night, the twinklers, eye and star:

Individual "isness" is just another of "motion's holdings." Our existence provides a vista on vast stretches of time. The eye, a "jiggler" itself, on a clear night sees stars (those "twinklers") and through them back to the origins of creation. For Ammons, "to pay attention is to behold the / wonder."

Ever aware of the destructive forces in the self and in the natural world, the poet seeks out life-affirming possibility. He acknowledges in *Garbage* that "in the grief of failure, loss, error do we / discern the savage afflictions that turn us around." The poet has lived through his own bouts of personal grief and poor health. What endures, however, is a cosmic vision. Nowhere is this more apparent than in these lines from section 2 of *Garbage*, a fitting passage to conclude with because it evokes Ammons's pursuit of widening scope and poetic vigor into his mid-sixties.

>   nature, not
>
> we, gave rise to us: we are not, though, though
> natural, divorced from higher, finer configurations:
>
> tissues and holograms of energy circulate in
> us and seek and find representations of themselves
>
> outside us, so that we can participate in
> celebrations high and know reaches of feeling
>
> and sight and thought that penetrate (really
> penetrate) far, far beyond these our wet cells,

> right on up past our stories, the planets, moons,
> and other bodies locally to the other end of
>
> the pole where matter's forms diffuse and
> energy loses all means to express itself except
>
> as spirit

"Participate," "celebrate," "penetrate"—the sound echoes of these key verbs in this passage link one to the other, much as these lines call attention to the linkage between the self and the cosmos. This is borne out by Ammons's own version of history, which starts with the fact that essential elements that constitute the natural world circulate in us. Biology and astronomy converge on the same startling truth as quantum physics: the "membrane" between the observer and the observed is permeable. This is the participatory vision Ammons celebrates, a "scope" that enables him to redeem the lowly and to transcend "far beyond these our wet cells"—through "reaches of feeling / and sight and thought"—past planets and moons until energy becomes so diffused it becomes "spirit." Ammons's reality at the end of the twentieth century is penetrating *and* transcendental. He fills up his poem *Garbage* with such discoveries, and in so doing creates his own radical solution to the problem of waste in our lives.

Notes

Preface

1. A. R. Ammons, *Collected Poems 1951–1971* (New York: W. W. Norton, 1972), 151. Future references to lines from this text will be indicated by the abbreviation CP followed by the page number. Quotations from A. R. Ammons's other works are cited in the text using the following abbreviations; when lines are sufficiently located by sections of longer poems, no citation appears. *Tape for the Turn of the Year* (T), *Corsons Inlet* (CI), *Sphere* (S), *Diversifications* (D), *The Snow Poems* (SP), *A Coast of Trees* (CT), *Worldly Hopes* (WH), *Lake Effect Country* (LEC), *Sumerian Vistas* (SV), and *The Really Short Poems of A. R. Ammons* (RSP).

2. "Lofty Instruments Discover Traces of Ancient Peoples," *The New York Times*, 10 March 1992.

Chapter 1. Introduction: The Poet and the Scientist

1. Cynthia Haythe, "An Interview with A. R. Ammons," *Contemporary Literature* 21:2 (Spring 1980): 182.

2. Wendell Berry, "Antennae to Knowledge," *The Nation* 198 (23 March 1964): 304–6.

3. *Diacritics* 3 (Winter 1973).

4. *Pembroke Magazine* 18 (1986).

5. Harold Bloom, ed., *A. R. Ammons* (New York: Chelsea House, 1986). The essays collected in this volume date from 1969 through 1985, prior to the publication of *Sumerian Vistas* and *The Really Short Poems of A. R. Ammons*. Most of the essays collected in this volume were written and published in the 1970s. The volume is an excellent critical introduction to Ammons, including several fine early essays by Bloom, Howard, Vendler, and Waggoner.

6. James S. Hans, *The Value(s) of Literature* (Albany: State University of New York Press, 1990), 119–56. Also Willard Spiegelman, *The Didactic Muse* (Princeton: Princeton University Press, 1989), 110–46.

7. John Elder, *Imagining the Earth: Poetry and the Vision of Nature* (Urbana and Chicago: University of Illinois Press, 1985), 136–50.

8. Elder, *Imagining the Earth*, 136–37.

9. Elder, *Imagining the Earth*, 146.

10. A. R. Ammons, "Numbers," *Diacritics* 3 (Winter 1973): 2.

11. Jim Stahl, "Interview with A. R. Ammons," *Pembroke Magazine* 18 (1986): 82.

12. Ibid.

13. Richard Howard, *Alone with America: Essays on the Art of Poetry in the United States Since 1950* (New York: Atheneum, 1969), 1–17.

14. Alan Holder, *A. R. Ammons* (Boston: Twayne Publishers, 1978), 36.

15. Philip Henry Fried, "Three Essays on the Poetry of A. R. Ammons" (Ph.D. dissertation, State University of New York at Stony Brook, 1978).

16. Miriam Marty Clark, "The Gene, the Computer, and Information Processing in A. R. Ammons," *Twentieth Century Literature* 38:1 (Spring 1990): 1–9.

17. Spiegelman, *The Didactic Muse*, 111.

18. Elder, *Imagining the Earth*, 210.

19. Arthur Seiderman and Steven Schneider, *The Athletic Eye* (New York: Hearst Books, 1983).

20. Hyatt Waggoner, *The Heel of Elohim: Science and Values in Modern American Poetry* (Norman: University of Oklahoma Press, 1950), 108.

21. Hyatt Waggoner, "Science and the Poetry of Robinson Jeffers," *American Literature* 10 (November 1938): 280. Waggoner refers to several poems where this sentiment is expressed by Jeffers.

22. Waggoner, "Science and Poetry of Jeffers," 280.

23. Walt Whitman, *Leaves of Grass*, ed. Harold W. Blodgett and Sculley Bradley (New York: New York University Press, 1965), 261. Future references to poems from this volume will be indicated by the abbreviation LOG.

24. Stephenson, "Interview with A. R. Ammons," 200.

25. Albert Einstein, *Ideas and Opinions* (New York: Dell, 1973), 22.

26. Elder, *Imagining the Earth*, 166.

27. Ibid.

28. Elder, *Imagining the Earth*, 162.

29. Alfred North Whitehead, *Science and the Modern World* (New York: The Free Press, 1967), 156.

30. Whitehead, *Science and the Modern World*, 3.

31. Whitehead, *Science and the Modern World*, 13.

32. Stillman Drake, *Discoveries and Opinions of Galileo* (New York: Doubleday Anchor Books, 1957), 47.

33. Drake, *Opinions of Galileo*, 182.

34. Whitehead, *Science and the Modern World*, 15.

35. Ibid.

36. Fritjof Capra, *The Tao of Physics* (Berkeley: Shambhala Publications, 1975), 67.

37. Capra, *The Tao of Physics*, 68.

38. Capra, *The Tao of Physics*, 136.

39. Capra, *The Tao of Physics*, 138.

Chapter 2. "Curious" Science: Ammons and His Forebears

1. A. R. Ammons, "A Poem Is a Walk," *Epoch* 18: 1 (Fall 1968): 116.

2. Cynthia Haythe, "Interview with Ammons," 173.

3. David I. Grossvogel, "Interview/A. R. Ammons," *Diacritics* 3 (Winter 1973): 50–51.

4. Haythe, "Interview with Ammons," 186.

5. Ammons's claim in his interview with Cynthia Haythe not to have read Emerson before Bloom started to speak of their connection seems odd. Ammons states in the much earlier Grossvogel interview (*Diacritics* 3) that early in his career Emerson led him to Asian sources. This suggests that he did read Emer-

son before Bloom ever started to write about Ammons. This contradictory testimony is further evidence of Ammons wanting to avoid appearing too consciously Emersonian.

Bloom's first article on Ammons, "A. R. Ammons: When You Consider the Radiance," appeared in *The Ringers in the Tower: Studies in the Romantic Tradition* (Chicago: University of Chicago Press, 1971), 257–89. Bloom makes much of Ammons's connection to Emerson, particularly each poet's attraction to transcendence. Many of Ammons's poems are read in the context of quotations from Emerson's essays. This article was the first of five Bloom published in the early and mid-1970s that significantly enhanced Ammons's reputation.

6. Hyatt Waggoner, "The Poetry of A. R. Ammons: Some Notes and Reflections," *Salmagundi* 22/23 (Spring–Summer 1973): 286.

7. Harold Bloom, "Dark and Radiant Peripheries: Mark Strand and A. R. Ammons," *Southern Review* 8 (January 1972): 134, 142.

8. Harold Bloom, "The New Transcendentalism: The Visionary Strain in Merwin, Ashberry, and Ammons," *Chicago Review* 24 (Winter 1973): 36. According to Bloom, "Ammons expounds a 'science' that now seems curious, but Emerson called it 'true science.'"

9. Harold Bloom, "When You Consider the Radiance," 257–89.

10. Patricia A. Parker, "Configurations of Shape and Flow," *Diacritics* 3 (Winter 1973): 27.

11. Janet Elizabeth DeRosa, "Occurrences of Promise and Terror: The Poetry of A. R. Ammons" (Ph.D. dissertation, Brown University, 1978), 220.

12. Ralph Waldo Emerson, "The Poet," in *Ralph Waldo Emerson: Essays and Journals*, ed. Lewis Mumford (New York: Doubleday, 1968), 253.

13. Ralph Waldo Emerson, "Country Life," in *The Heart of Emerson's Essays*, ed. Bliss Perry (Boston: Houghton Mifflin, 1933), 295.

14. Sherman Paul, *Emerson's Angle of Vision* (Cambridge: Harvard University Press, 1965), 208–20. Paul notes that Emerson "was chiefly a scientist of the mind."

15. Emerson, "The American Scholar," "The Poet," in *Essays and Journals*, 33, 256.

16. Paul, *Angle of Vision*, 15.

17. Emerson, "Nature," in *The Complete Essays and Other Writings of Ralph Waldo Emerson*, ed. Brooks Atkinson (New York: Random House, 1940), 16.

18. Leo Marx, *The Machine in the Garden* (New York: Oxford University Press, 1967), 233. Marx notes that, "the prudent, sensible Understanding may be trained in Schools and cities," whereas "the far-ranging visionary Reason requires wild or rural scenes for its proper nurture." Ammons also prefers the country to the city, where the eye has more latitude to discover relationships.

19. Emerson, "Nature," *The Complete Essays*, 16.

20. Emerson, "The American Scholar," *Essays and Journals*, 34.

21. Emerson, "Thoreau," *Essays and Journals*, 612.

22. Edward Waldo Emerson and Waldo Emerson Forbes, eds., *Journals of Ralph Waldo Emerson*, Vol. 5 (Boston and New York: Houghton Mifflin, 1911), 252.

23. Grossvogel, "Interview/A. R. Ammons," 47.

24. Holder, *Ammons*, 39.

25. Ibid.

26. Ralph Waldo Emerson, "Astronomy," in *Young Emerson Speaks*, ed. Arthur Cushman McGiffert, Jr. (Boston: Houghton Mifflin, 1938), 174.

27. Holder, *Ammons*, 39.

28. Ibid.

29. Paul, *Angle of Vision*, 83.

30. Emerson, "Astronomy," *Young Emerson Speaks*, 171.

31. Harry Hayden Clark, "Emerson and Science," *Philological Quarterly* 10 (July 1931): 237.

32. Emerson, "Nature," *The Complete Essays*, 5.

33. Emerson, "Astronomy," *Young Emerson Speaks*, 175.

34. Emerson, "Astronomy," *Young Emerson Speaks*, 172.

35. Henry David Thoreau, *Excursions* (New York: Corinth Books, 1962), 42.

36. Nancy Kober, "Ammons: Poetry Is a Matter of Survival," *Cornell Daily Sun*, 27 April 1973, 12.

37. Henry David Thoreau, *Walden* (New York: New American Library, 1960), 17.

38. Haythe, "An Interview with A. R. Ammons," 184–85.

39. Kober, "Matter of Survival," 12.

40. Emerson, "Nature," *The Complete Essays*, 6.

41. Thoreau, *Walden*, 155.

42. Thoreau, *Walden*, 156.

43. Herbert H. Gilchrist, *Anne Gilchrist: Her Life and Writings* (London, 1887), 237.

44. Haythe, "An Interview with A. R. Ammons," 186–87.

45. Thoreau, *Walden*, 17.

46. Thoreau, *Walden*, 208–10.

47. Emerson, "Thoreau," *Essays and Journals*, 606.

48. Ibid.

49. William Ellery Channing, *Thoreau: The Poet-Naturalist* (New York: Biblo and Tannen, 1966), 39.

50. Channing, *Thoreau: The Poet-Naturalist*, 66.

51. Emerson, "Thoreau," *Essays and Journals*, 606.

52. Bradford Turrey and Francis Allen, eds., *The Journal of Henry David Thoreau*, Vol. 2 (Salt Lake City: Peregrine Smith Books, 1984), 18.

53. Turrey and Allen, *Journal of Thoreau*, Vol. 2, 15.

54. Perry Miller, "Thoreau in the Context of International Romanticism," *The New England Quarterly* (June 1961): 150.

55. Turrey and Allen, *Journal of Thoreau*, Vol. 3, 23.

56. Thoreau, *Walden*, 221.

57. Thoreau, *Walden*, 200, 205.

58. Turrey and Allen, vol. 2, 68.

59. Henry David Thoreau, *A Week on the Concord and Merrimack Rivers* (New York: Scribner's, 1921), 17.

60. Thoreau, "The Succession of Forest Trees," *Excursions*, 137.

61. Thoreau, *Walden*, 192.

62. Thoreau, *Walden*, 194.

63. Emerson, "The Poet," *Essays and Journals*, 256.

64. Thoreau, *Walden*, 194.

65. Carl Bode, ed., *The Selected Journals of Henry David Thoreau* (New York: New American Library, 1967), 175.

66. *The American Heritage Dictionary*, (New College Edition, 1980), 1363.

67. A. R. Ammons, "Note of Intent," *Chelsea* 20/21 (May 1967): 4.

68. Bloom, *Ringers in the Tower*, 270. Bloom writes that "the Ammonsian literalness, allied to a similar destructive impulse in Wordsworth and Thoreau,

attempts to summon outward continuities to shield the poet from his mind's own force." Robert Bly has also criticized Ammons for too often drawing on bare facts. Bloom cites Bly's parody of Ammons, which prints a passage from *The Mushroom Hunter's Field Guide*, under the title "A. R. Ammons Discusses the Lacaria Trullisata."

69. A. R. Ammons, *Collected Poems 1951–1971* (New York: W. W. Norton, 1972), 314. Ammons quotes this line in his poem from the following source, cited in the text of the poem. Robert C. Miller, *The Sea* (New York: Random House, 1966), 165.

70. Ammons, *Collected Poems*, 314; Miller, *The Sea*, 165.

71. Ammons, *Collected Poems*, 314. Ammons quotes this paragraph in his poem from the following source, cited in the text of the poem. Paul B. Weisz and Melvin S. Fuller, *The Science of Botany* (New York: McGraw-Hill, Inc., 1962), 48.

72. F. O. Matthiessen, *American Renaissance* (London: Oxford University Press, 1941), 51.

73. Turrey and Allen, *Journal of Thoreau*, Vol. 3, 26.

74. *The Complete Writings of Walt Whitman*, ed. literary executors, Camden Edition, 10 vols. (New York and London: G. P. Putnam's Sons, 1902), Vol. 5, 12.

75. Joseph Beaver, *Walt Whitman—Poet of Science* (New York: King's Crown Press, 1951).

76. Fried, "Three Essays on Ammons." The first of Fried's three essays focuses on evolutionary and ecological science in Ammons's work.

77. Fried, "Three Essays on Ammons," 6.

78. Walt Whitman, "Preface 1855—Leaves of Grass, First Edition," *Walt Whitman: Leaves of Grass*, ed. Harold W. Blodgett and Sculley Bradley (New York: New York University Press, 1965), 720.

79. Walt Whitman, *The Complete Writings*, Vol. 10, 10.

80. Harold Aspiz, *Walt Whitman and the Body Beautiful* (Urbana and Chicago: University of Illinois Press, 1980), 37.

81. Walt Whitman, "Democratic Vistas," *The Portable Walt Whitman*, ed. Mark Van Doren (New York: Penguin, 1945), 328.

82. Walt Whitman, *An American Primer*, ed. Horace Traubel (Boston: Small, Maynard, and Company, 1904), 4.

83. Matthiessen, *American Renaissance*, 51.

84. Beaver, *Walt Whitman—Poet of Science*, 43.

85. Walt Whitman, "Leaves of Grass and Two Rivulets," *LOG*, 754.

86. Ibid.

87. Ibid.

88. Hope Werness, "Whitman and Van Gogh: Starry Nights and Other Similarities," *Walt Whitman Quarterly Review* 2:4 (Spring 1985): 39.

89. William Wordsworth, "Preface to Lyrical Ballads," *The Prose Works of William Wordsworth*, ed. W. J. B. Owen and Jane Worthington Smyser, Vol. 1 (Oxford: Clarendon Press, 1974), 141.

90. Ammons, "Note of Intent," 3–4.

Chapter 3. Flex Your Eyes: Ammons's "Visual Calisthenics"

1. Emerson, "Nature," *Complete Essays*, 42.

2. Hyatt H. Waggoner, *American Visionary Poetry* (Baton Rouge and Lon-

don: Louisiana State University Press, 1982), 6. In American poetry, Waggoner lists Whitman, Hart Crane, William Carlos Williams, Theodore Roethke, A. R. Ammons, and David Waggoner as poets whose "visionary" poems derive from visual encounters with the world. He excludes Emily Dickinson for being too "cerebral," Wallace Stevens for being too "philosophical," and T. S. Eliot for being too "religious."

3. Waggoner, *American Visionary Poetry*, 2.

4. Waggoner, *American Visionary Poetry*, 3.

5. Richard Kavner, O.D., and Lorraine Dusky, *Total Vision* (New York: A & W Publishers, 1978), 15.

6. Kavner and Dusky, *Total Vision*, 1.

7. Kavner and Dusky, *Total Vision*, 31.

8. Kavner and Dusky, *Total Vision*, 22.

9. Emerson, "The Poet," *The Complete Essays*, 329.

10. Grossvogel, "Interview/A. R. Ammons," 48.

11. Waggoner's essay on Ammons in *American Visionary Poetry* fails to develop the analogy between the poet and the vision therapist. In his preface Waggoner acknowledges that "the essays were never intended as an exhaustive or definitive treatment of visionary poetry." My chapter 3, on vision and Ammons, goes beyond Waggoner by probing in more detail Ammons's visual poetics and by reading the poems in the light of behavioral optometry.

12. A. R. Ammons, "Event: Corrective: Cure," interview with *Poetry Miscellany*, reprinted by Richard Jackson, in *Acts of Mind* (Tuscaloosa: University of Alabama Press, 1983), 33.

13. Ammons, "Walk," 116.

14. John T. Gage, *In the Arresting Eye* (Baton Rouge and London: Louisiana State University Press, 1981), 21. Pound, Hulme, and other early Imagists sought to record phenomena "objectively," without moralizing or engaging in abstractions that interfered with "direct observation." They were influenced in this by Ernest Fenollosa's essay "The Chinese Written Character as a Medium for Poetry." Gage writes that, "the Oriental poet was assumed to have no moral stance toward the things he observed; he did not editorialize."

15. Gage, *Arresting Eye*, 79–82.

16. "An instant of time" is a crucial phrase in Pound's famous definition of the poetic image: "An 'Image' is that which presents an intellectual and emotional complex in an instant of time." About this Gage says, "The definition repeats the Hulme/Bergson principle that art must free us from the limitations of time, and to free us from time is to stop it 'in an instant'" (p. 14). The Imagists' compulsion to "escape time" is in contrast to Ammons's concept of the poem as motion, as a way into "events" that are dynamic.

17. In his poem "Essay on Poetics," Ammons expresses concern that language as a medium "suppresses reality." Despite its artificiality, he writes that "language must not violate . . . the concrete" (CP, 298). Gage, in his discussion of the Imagists, sees language as a discursive medium preventing the Imagist poet from presenting objects "directly," no matter how much they thought this was what they were doing.

18. Gage, *Arresting Eye*, 20. The Imagists admired Fenollosa's "ideogram" because it came "as close as language could come to *things* in themselves." Although the embodiment of things in language was the goal of Imagism, Gage's study demonstrates that the Imagists could not escape the rhetorical nature of language.

19. David Kalstone, "Ammons' Radiant Toys," *Diacritics* 3 (Winter 1973): 19.

20. Kavner and Dusky, *Total Vision*, 49.

21. Kavner and Dusky, *Total Vision*, 43.

22. Emerson, "Trifles," in *Young Emerson Speaks*, ed. Arthur Cushman McGiffert, Jr. (Boston: Houghton Mifflin, 1938), 48.

23. Kavner and Dusky, *Total Vision*, 160–61.

24. Grossvogel, "Interview/A. R. Ammons," 50.

25. Paul, *Angle of Vision*, 82.

26. *Journals of Ralph Waldo Emerson*, Vol. 5, 310–11.

27. Grossvogel, "Interview/A. R. Ammons," 51.

28. The distinction between "hard" and "soft" eyes is made by George Leonard in his book *The Ultimate Athlete* (New York: Viking Press, 1975). Leonard explains that in *aikido*, a Japanese art of self-defense, "you don't have time to see everything in sharp focus, but you must see movement and relationship clearly." Seiderman and Schneider, in *The Athletic Eye*, also discuss the distinction as it relates to peripheral vision.

29. Harold Bloom, "A. R. Ammons: The Breaking of the Vessels," *Salmagundi* 31/32 (Fall 1975–Winter 1976): 193.

30. Ammons's rejection of Unity is curious. It is based upon a fear that experience of an Absolute will diminish the world of vision. The last third of this chapter examines this fear and locates it within the context of Ammons's work as a "vision therapist."

31. Ammons, "Walk," 116.

32. A. R. Ammons, Foreword to *Ommateum* (Philadelphia: Dorrance, 1955). Although the foreword to this early book is unsigned, it has been attributed by Holder and other critics to the poet.

33. Edwin Folsom, review of *American Visionary Poetry*, by Hyatt Waggoner, *Walt Whitman Quarterly Review* 2 (Summer 1984): 44–46.

34. Paul Zweig, "The Raw and the Cooked," *Partisan Review* 4 (1974): 610.

35. DeRosa, "Promise and Terror," 66.

36. Grossvogel, "Interview/A. R. Ammons," 51.

37. Arthur Waley, *The Way and Its Power* (London: George Allen and Unwin Ltd., 1934), 51.

38. Waley, *Way and Power*, 54.

39. Elder, *Imagining The Earth*, 196.

40. Bode, *Selected Journals*, 11.

41. Waley, *Way and Power*, 146, 149.

42. Emerson, "Self-Reliance," *The Complete Essays*, 155.

43. Capra, *The Tao of Physics*, 189.

44. The parallels between the unified field as described by modern physics and an underlying Unity as described by Eastern religious texts have been discussed by many in recent years. Capra's book *The Tao of Physics* is still the most popular discussion of parallels between Eastern thought and modern physics. Peter Matthiessen, in *The Snow Leopard* (New York: Viking Press, 1978), writes, "The Progress of the sciences towards theories of fundamental unity, cosmic symmetry (as in the unified field theory)—how do such theories differ, in the end, from that unity which Plato called "unspeakable" and "undescribable," the holistic knowledge shared by so many peoples of the earth" (p. 62).

45. Waley, *Way and Power*, 56. The "unassertive" is a virtue in Taoist thought.

Opposed to it is aggressiveness. Ammons distinguishes a way of looking that
is unassertive as opposed to aggressive.

46. Capra, *The Tao of Physics*, 35.

47. Ibid.

48. Several of Ammons's later poems take up his ambivalences about Transcendence. The most prominent of these is "He Held Radical Light," where the
seer fights against his own will to transcend. The compensation derived from
"heightened" unity experiences is also questioned in "Loft," "Levitation,"
"Concerning the Exclusions of the Object," "Moment," and "Zone."

49. Capra, *The Tao of Physics*, 29.

50. *The Thirteen Principal Upanishads*, trans. Robert Ernest Hume (London: Oxford University Press, 1921), 335.

51. Howard, *Alone with America*, 2.

52. Bloom, "A. R. Ammons: The Breaking of the Vessels," 191.

53. Waggoner, *American Visionary Poetry*, 145.

54. Robert Morgan, "The Compound Vision of A. R. Ammons' Early Poems,"
Epoch 22:3 (1973): 346.

55. Bloom, "A. R. Ammons: The Breaking of the Vessels," 191.

56. In his frequent journeys to Asia, Snyder learned meditative techniques
for transcending. Snyder, like Ammons, is a walker, and "he merges East and
West by bringing his Oriental insight to bear on the wilderness beneath pres-
ent-day America." See Edwin Folsom's article "Gary Snyder's Descent to Turtle
Island: Searching for Fossil Love," in *Western American Literature* 15 (Summer
1980): 106.

57. Matthiessen, *The Snow Leopard*, 27. Matthiessen calls walking around
"without gainful destination—*gnaskor*, or 'going around places,' as pilgrimages
are described in Tibet." Ammons's casual style of walking is reminiscent of
such pilgrimages. His essay "A Poem Is a Walk" extolls the virtues of walking
to stimulate creativity.

58. DeRosa, "Promise and Terror," 111–18.

59. Kavner and Dusky, *Total Vision*, 43.

60. DeRosa, "Promise and Terror," 275. DeRosa notes that "many of Ammons's shorter lyrics recall haiku in their conciseness, their economy of words,
and the way they concern themselves with simple, trivial, usually overlooked
material of everyday life; with things which, however insignificant on the surface, are nonetheless precious treasures and inexhaustible riches to anyone
who has learned not only to look but to see."

Chapter 4. Ammons's Telescopic and Microscopic Vision

1. Loren Eiseley, *The Immense Journey* (New York: Random House, 1946),
161.

2. Robert Frost, *The Complete Poems* (New York: Holt, Rinehart, and Winston, 1964), 264–66.

3. Frost, *The Complete Poems*, 221.

4. Hyatt H. Waggoner, "Science and Poetry of Jeffers," *American Literature*
10 (November 1938): 280.

5. Robinson Jeffers, *Thurso's Landing* (New York: Liveright Publishers, Inc.,
1932), 135–36.

6. Chet Raymo, *The Soul of the Night* (Englewood Cliffs, N.J.: Prentice-Hall,
1985), 38.

7. Raymo, *The Soul of the Night*, 39.

8. Ibid.

9. Robinson Jeffers, *Give Your Heart to the Hawks* (New York: Random House, 1933), 73–74.

10. Walt Whitman, *Walt Whitman's Leaves of Grass*, ed. Malcolm Cowley (New York: Viking Press, 1959), 48. This quotation appearing in the first edition of *Leaves of Grass* was later changed by Whitman to read "Walt Whitman, a kosmos, of Manhattan the son."

11. Holder, *Ammons*, 37.

12. Geoffrey H. Hartman, "Collected Poems 1951–1971," review of *Collected Poems 1951–1971*, by A. R. Ammons, *The New York Times Book Review*, 19 November 1972, 40.

13. Bloom, "Breaking of the Vessels," 193.

14. Holder, *Ammons*, 172–74.

15. DeRosa, "Promise and Terror"; Fried, "Three Essays on Ammons."

16. Cary Wolfe, "Symbol Plural: The Later Long Poems of A. R. Ammons," *Contemporary Literature* 30:1 (Spring 1989): 78–94; Gerald Bullis, "In the Open: A. R. Ammons' Longer Poems," *Pembroke Magazine* 18 (1986): 28–53.

17. Raymo, *The Soul of the Night*, 24.

18. Walt Whitman, *Leaves of Grass*, Norton Critical Edition, ed. Sculley Bradley and Harold Blodgett (New York: W. W. Norton & Co., 1973), 88.

19. In the late 1960s and early 1970s A. R. Ammons, along with Gary Snyder, Allen Ginsberg, Wendell Berry, and W. S. Merwin, among other contemporary American poets, expressed in their work grave concern about ecology and the fate of the American landscape. Ginsberg and Snyder, especially, were politically active in the ecology movement of the time.

20. Carl Sagan, *The Cosmic Connection* (New York: Doubleday, 1973), viii.

21. Sagan, *The Cosmic Connection*, 60.

22. Ibid. Sagan notes that "what was striking was the number of works in the *Catalog* that related to a scientific cosmic perspective. The title of *The Whole Earth Catalog* derives from its founder's urge to see a photograph of our planet as a whole. The Fall 1970 issue expanded this perspective, showing a photograph of the whole Milky Way Galaxy."

23. Sagan, *The Cosmic Connection*, viii.

24. For a detailed account of Galileo's controversies with the church, see Stillman Drake's *Discoveries and Opinions of Galileo* (New York: Doubleday, 1957).

25. Robert Jastrow and Malcolm H. Thompson, *Astronomy: Fundamentals and Frontiers* (New York: John Wiley and Sons, 1972), 208.

26. Jastrow and Thompson, *Astronomy*, 245.

27. Ibid.

28. Jastrow and Thompson, *Astronomy*, 246.

29. DeRosa, "Promise and Terror," 204.

30. DeRosa, "Promise and Terror," 199.

31. Ammons, "Walk," 119.

32. Stahl, "Interview with A. R. Ammons," 81.

33. See Capra's *Tao of Physics*. Capra explores the parallels between modern physics and Eastern mysticism. He is particularly fascinated with scientific corroboration of Eastern concepts, particularly the "unity of all things."

34. Calvin Bedient, "Wanted: an original relation to the universe," review of

Sphere: The Form of a Motion, by A. R. Ammons, *New York Times Book Review*, 22 December 1974, 2–3.

35. Beaver, *Whitman—Poet of Science*, 7.
36. Waggoner, *American Visionary Poetry*, 58.
37. Elder, *Imagining the Earth*, 136.
38. Elder, *Imagining the Earth*, 138.
39. Elder, *Imagining the Earth*, 137.
40. Bedient, "Wanted," 2.
41. Elder, *Imagining the Earth*, 198.
42. Elder, *Imagining the Earth*, 193.
43. John Pfeiffer, *The Cell* (New York: Time-Life Books, 1972), 8.
44. Paul B. Weisz and Melvin S. Fuller, *The Science of Botany* (New York: McGraw-Hill, 1962), 48.
45. Bedient, "Wanted," 2.
46. Weisz and Fuller, *The Science of Botany*, 48.

Chapter 5. Persistences

1. The following volumes of Ammons's poetry were published between 1975 and 1987: *Diversifications, The Snow Poems, Highgate Road* (limited edition), *The Selected Poems: 1951–1977, Selected Longer Poems, A Coast of Trees, Worldly Hopes,* and *Lake Effect Country.* In 1986 he published an expanded edition of *The Selected Poems.*
2. *The Bhagavad-Gita,* trans. Maharishi Mahesh Yogi (Middlesex, England: Penguin Books, 1969), 81.
3. DeRosa, "Promise and Terror," 246–47.
4. DeRosa, "Promise and Terror," 246.
5. In *Collected Poems 1951–1971,* there are many moments of good humor. Perhaps the most famous example is "Guitar Recitativos" (p. 219), a jazzy love poem that illustrates Ammons at his playful best. Also, a series of six poems in *Collected Poems,* beginning with "Alternatives" (p. 222) and moving through "Emplacement" (p. 225), reflects the fun-loving side of Ammons's nature.
6. Sagan, *The Cosmic Connection,* 3.
7. Grossvogel, "Interview/Ammons," 52.
8. Ibid.
9. Michael McFee, "A. R. Ammons and *The Snow Poems* Reconsidered," *Chicago Review* 33:1 (Summer 1981): 32–38.
10. McFee, "Ammons and *Snow Poems,*" 37.
11. McFee, "Ammons and *Snow Poems,*" 33.
12. Waggoner, *American Visionary Poetry,* 172.
13. DeRosa, "Promise and Terror," 264.
14. Ammons, "Event: Corrective: Cure," 37.
15. Peter Stitt, in his review of *The Snow Poems* for the *Georgia Review* 32 (Winter 1978), is the most strident on this point. He writes: "One has to wonder why this book was issued. It may be that the publisher wanted to cash in on Ammons' current high popularity. But where was the poet's editor, whom one would expect to try to protect both poet and publisher from one another and themselves" (p. 940).
16. DeRosa, "Promise and Terror," 263.
17. DeRosa, "Promise and Terror," 264.

18. Ibid.

19. Matthiessen, *The Snow Leopard*, 27.

20. Hayden Carruth, "Reader Participation Invited," review of *The Snow Poems* by A. R. Ammons, *New York Times Book Review*, 25 September 1977, 30.

21. DeRosa, "Promise and Terror," 263.

22. Waggoner, *American Visionary Poetry*, 172.

23. Helen Vendler, "Reason, Shape, and Wisdom," review of *A Coast of Trees*, by A. R. Ammons, *The New Republic*, 25 April 1981, 28–32.

24. Vendler, "Reason, Shape, and Wisdom," 31.

25. Elder, *Imagining the Earth*, 138.

26. Lloyd Motz and Anneta Duveen, *Essentials of Astronomy* (New York: Columbia University Press, 1977), 440.

27. David Lehman, "Where Motion and Shape Coincide," *Parnassus* 9 (Fall 1981): 73–89.

28. Wendell Berry, *A Continuous Harmony* (New York: Harcourt Brace Jovanovich, 1975), 4.

29. Helen Vendler, "Spheres and Ragged Edges," *Poetry* 36 (Winter 1983): 30.

30. William Carlos Williams, *The Selected Poems* (New York: New Directions, 1969), 54.

31. Whitman, *LOG*, ed. Bradley and Blodgett, 252.

32. Vendler, "Spheres and Ragged Edges," 26.

33. Ammons, "Event: Corrective: Cure," 35.

34. Vendler, "Spheres and Ragged Edges," 28.

Chapter 6. Ridges of Vision

1. *Pembroke Magazine*, 18 (1986).

2. Helen Vendler, "Veracity Unshaken," *The New Yorker*, 15 February 1988, 100.

3. Alice Fulton, "Main Things," *Poetry* (January 1988): 362.

4. Fulton, "Main Things," 363.

5. Stahl, "Interview with A. R. Ammons," 79.

6. Ibid.

7. Stahl, "Interview with A. R. Ammons," 79–80.

8. Stahl, "Interview with A. R. Ammons," 80.

9. Stephen B. Cushman, "Stanzas, Organic Myth, and the Metaformalism of A. R. Ammons," *American Literature* 59:4 (December 1987): 513–27.

10. Larry Dossey, *Space, Time & Medicine* (Boulder, Shambhala, 1982), 204.

11. Ammons, "Walk," 114.

12. Ammons, "Walk," 115.

13. Ibid.

14. Ammons, "Walk," 114.

15. Ammons, "Walk," 116.

16. Ashley Brown, review of *Sumerian Vistas*, by A. R. Ammons, *World Literature Today* (Spring 1988): 283.

17. Dossey, *Space, Time & Medicine*, 234.

18. Raymo, *The Soul of the Night*, 84.

19. Dossey, *Space, Time & Medicine*, 31.

20. Stahl, "An Interview with A. R. Ammons," 79.

21. Whitman, *LOG*, Norton Critical Edition, 137–48.

22. Whitman uses the phrase "dumb, beautiful ministers" toward the end of "Crossing Brooklyn Ferry" to refer to the "appearances" that "continue to envelop the soul." *LOG*, Norton Critical Edition, 165.

Epilogue: A Note on Ammons's *Garbage*

1. A. R. Ammons, letter to author, 14 August 1992.
2. A. R. Ammons, letter to author, 8 September 1992.
3. Ammons, *Garbage* (New York: W. W. Norton, 1993).
4. Spiegelman, *The Didactic Muse*, 144.

Select Bibliography

Allen, Gay Wilson. *The Solitary Singer: A Critical Biography of Walt Whitman.* New York: Macmillan, 1955.

Ammons, A. R. *A Coast of Trees.* New York: W. W. Norton, 1981.

———. "A Poem Is a Walk." *Epoch* 18 (Fall 1968): 114–19.

———. *Briefings: Poems Small and Easy.* New York: W. W. Norton, 1971.

———. *Collected Poems 1951–1971.* New York: W. W. Norton, 1972.

———. *Corsons Inlet: A Book of Poems.* Ithaca: Cornell University Press, 1965.

———. *Diversifications: Poems.* New York: W. W. Norton, 1975.

———. *Expressions of Sea Level.* Columbus: Ohio State University Press, 1964.

———. *Garbage.* New York: W. W. Norton, 1993.

———. *Lake Effect Country.* New York: W. W. Norton, 1983.

———. *Northfield Poems.* Ithaca: Cornell University Press, 1966.

———. "Note of Intent." *Chelsea* 20/21 (May 1967), 3–4.

———. "Numbers." *Diacritics* 3 (Winter 1973): 2.

———. *Ommateum: With Doxology.* Philadelphia: Dorrance, 1955.

———. *The Really Short Poems of A. R. Ammons.* New York: W. W. Norton, 1990.

———. *The Selected Poems, 1951–1977.* New York: W. W. Norton, 1977.

———. *The Selected Poems.* Expanded Edition. New York: W. W. Norton, 1986.

———. *The Snow Poems.* New York: W. W. Norton, 1977.

———. *Sphere: The Form of a Motion.* New York: W. W. Norton, 1974.

———. *Sumerian Vistas.* New York: W. W. Norton, 1987.

———. *Tape for the Turn of the Year.* Ithaca: Cornell University Press, 1965.

———. *Uplands: New Poems.* New York: W. W. Norton, 1970.

———. *Worldly Hopes.* New York: W. W. Norton, 1982.

Aspiz, Harold. *Walt Whitman and the Body Beautiful.* Urbana and Chicago: University of Illinois Press, 1980.

Beaver, Joseph. *Walt Whitman—Poet of Science.* New York: King's Crown Press, 1951.

Bedient, Calvin. "Wanted: An Original Relation to the Universe." Review of *Sphere,* by A. R. Ammons. *The New York Times Book Review,* 22 December 1974, 2–3.

Berry, Wendell, *A Continuous Harmony.* New York: Harcourt Brace Jovanovich, 1975.

———. "Antennae to Knowledge," *The Nation* 198, 23 March 1964:, 304–6.

Bloom, Harold. "A. R. Ammons: The Breaking of the Vessels." *Salmagundi* 31/32 (Fall 1975–Winter 1976): 185–203.

————. "Dark and Radiant Peripheries: Mark Strand and A. R. Ammons." *Southern Review* 8 (January 1972): 133–50.

————. "Emerson and Ammons: A Coda." *Diacritics* 3 (Winter 1973): 45–47.

————. ed. *A. R. Ammons.* New York: Chelsea House, 1986.

————. "The New Transcendentalism: The Visionary Strain in Merwin, Ashberry, and Ammons." *Chicago Review* 24 (Winter 1973): 25–43.

————. "A. R. Ammons: When You Consider the Radiance." In *The Ringers in the Tower: Studies in Romantic Tradition,* 257–89. Chicago: University of Chicago Press, 1971.

Bode, Carl, ed. *Selected Journals of Henry David Thoreau.* New York: New American Library, 1967.

Brown, Ashley. Review of *Sumerian Vistas,* by A. R. Ammons. *World Literature Today* (Spring 1988): 283.

Bullis, Gerald. "In the Open: A. R. Ammons' Longer Poems." *Pembroke Magazine* 18 (1986): 28–53.

Capra, Fritjof. *The Tao of Physics.* Berkeley: Shambhala, 1975.

Carruth, Hayden. "Reader Participation Invited." Review of *The Snow Poems,* by A. R. Ammons. *The New York Times Book Review,* 25 September 1977, 30.

Channing, William Ellery. *Thoreau: The Poet-Naturalist.* New York: Biblo and Tannen, 1966.

Clark, Harry Hayden. "Emerson and Science." *Philological Quarterly* 10 (July 1931): 237.

Clark, Miriam Marty. "The Gene, the Computer, and Information Processing in A. R. Ammons." *Twentieth Century Literature* 38:1 (Spring 1990): 1–9.

Clausen, Christopher. *The Place of Poetry.* Lexington: University Press of Kentucky, 1981.

Cushman, Stephen B. "Stanzas, Organic Myth, and the Metaformalism of A. R. Ammons." *American Literature* 59:4 (December 1987): 513–27.

Davie, Donald. "Cards of Identity." *The New York Review of Books* 22 (6 March 1975), 10–11.

Degani, Meir H. *Astronomy Made Simple.* Doubleday, 1955.

DeRosa, Janet Elizabeth. "Occurrences of Promise and Terror: The Poetry of A. R. Ammons." Ph.D. dissertation, Brown University, 1978.

Dossey, Larry. *Space, Time & Medicine.* Boulder: Shambhala, 1982.

Drake, Stillman. *Discoveries and Opinions of Galileo.* New York: Doubleday, 1957.

Einstein, Albert. *Ideas and Opinions.* New York: Dell, 1973.

Eiseley, Loren. *The Immense Journey.* New York: Random House, 1946.

Elder, John. *Imagining the Earth: Poetry and the Vision of Nature.* Urbana and Chicago: University of Illinois Press, 1985.

Emerson, Ralph Waldo. "The American Scholar," "The Poet," and "Thoreau." In *Ralph Waldo Emerson: Essays and Journals.* Edited by Lewis Mumford. New York: Doubleday, 1968.

————. "Astronomy" and "Trifles." In *Young Emerson Speaks.* Edited by Arthur Cushman McGiffert, Jr. Boston: Houghton Mifflin, 1938.

————. *The Complete Essays and Other Writings of Ralph Waldo Emerson.* Edited by Brooks Atkinson. New York: Random House, 1940.

————. "Country Life." In *The Heart of Emerson's Essays*. Edited by Bliss Perry. Boston: Houghton Mifflin, 1933.

————. *Journals of Ralph Waldo Emerson*. Edited by Edward Waldo Emerson and Waldo Emerson Forbes. Boston and New York: Houghton Mifflin, 1911.

————. "Nature" and "Self Reliance." In *The Complete Essays and Other Writings of Ralph Waldo Emerson*. Edited by Brooks Atkinson. New York: Random House, 1940.

Folsom, Edwin. "American Visionary Poetry." Review of *American Visionary Poetry* by Hyatt Waggoner in *Walt Whitman Quarterly Review* 2 (Summer 1984): 44–46.

————. "Gary Snyder's Descent to Turtle Island: Searching for Fossil Love." *Western American Literature* 15 (Summer 1980): 103–21.

Fried, Philip Henry. "Three Essays on the Poetry of A. R. Ammons." Ph.D. dissertation, State University of New York at Stony Brook, 1978.

Friedman, Herbert. *Amazing Universe*. Washington, D.C.: National Geographic Society, 1975.

Frost, Robert. *The Complete Poems*. New York: Holt, Rinehart, and Winston, 1964.

Fulton, Alice. "Main Things." *Poetry* (January 1988): 362.

Gage, John T. *In the Arresting Eye*. Baton Rouge and London: Louisiana State University Press, 1981.

Gilchrist, Herbert H. *Anne Gilchrist: Her Life and Writings*. London, 1887.

Grossvogel, David I. "Interview/A. R. Ammons." *Diacritics* 3 (Winter 1973): 47–54.

Hans, James S. *The Value(s) of Literature*. Albany: State University of New York Press, 1990.

Hartman, Geoffrey H. "Collected Poems *1951–1971*." Review of *Collected Poems 1951–1971*, by A. R. Ammons. *The New York Times Book Review*, 19 November 1972, 39–40.

Haythe, Cynthia. "An Interview with A. R. Ammons." *Contemporary Literature* 21 (Spring 1980): 173–90.

Holder, Alan. *A. R. Ammons*. Boston: Twayne Publishers, 1978.

Howard, Richard. "A. R. Ammons: 'The Spent Seer Consigns Order to the Vehicle of Change.'" In *Alone with America: Essays on the Art of Poetry in the United States Since 1950*, 1–17. New York: Atheneum, 1969.

Hume, Robert Ernest, trans. *The Thirteen Principal Upanishads*. London: Oxford University Press, 1921.

Jackson, Richard. *Acts of Mind*. Tuscaloosa: University of Alabama Press, 1983.

Jastrow, Robert, and Malcolm H. Thompson. *Astronomy: Fundamentals and Frontiers*. New York: John Wiley and Sons, 1972.

Jeffers, Robinson. *Give Your Heart to the Hawks*. New York: Random House, 1933.

————. *Thurso's Landing*. New York: Liveright Publishers, Inc., 1932.

Kalstone, David. "Ammons' Radiant Toys." *Diacritics* 3 (Winter 1973): 13–20.

Kavner, Richard, O.D., and Lorraine Dusky. *Total Vision*. New York: A & W Publishers, 1978.

Kober, Nancy. "Ammons: Poetry Is a Matter of Survival." *Cornell Daily Sun,* 27 April 1973, 12–13.

Lehman, David. "Where Motion and Shape Coincide." *Parnassus* 9 (Fall 1981): 73–89.

Leonard, George. *The Ultimate Athlete.* New York: Viking Press, 1975.

Liebowitz, Herschel. *Visual Perception.* New York: Macmillan, 1965.

Maharishi Mahesh Yogi, trans. *The Bhagavad-Gita.* Middlesex, England: Penguin Books, 1969.

Marx, Leo. *The Machine in the Garden.* New York: Oxford University Press, 1967.

Matthiessen, F. O. *American Renaissance.* London: Oxford University Press, 1941.

Matthiessen, Peter. *The Snow Leopard.* New York: Viking Press, 1978.

McFee, Michael. "A. R. Ammons and *The Snow Poems* Reconsidered." *Chicago Review* 33:1 (Summer 1981): 32 – 38.

McKenzie, A. E. E. *The Major Achievement of Science,* Vol. 1. Cambridge: Cambridge University Press, 1960.

Miller, Perry. "Thoreau in the Context of International Romanticism." *The New England Quarterly* (June 1961): 147–59.

Morgan, Robert. "The Compound Vision of A. R. Ammons' Early Poems." *Epoch* 22:3 (1973): 343–63.

Motz, Lloyd, and Anneta Duveen. *Essentials of Astronomy.* New York: Columbia University Press, 1977.

Muller, Robert. *The Sea.* New York: Random House, 1966.

Nordenskiold, Erik. *The History of Biology.* St. Claire Shores, Mich.: Scholarly Press, Inc., 1977.

Ornstein, Robert N. *The Psychology of Consciousness.* New York: Viking Press, 1977.

Orr, Linda. "The Cosmic Backyard of A. R. Ammons." *Diacritics* 3 (Winter 1973): 3–12.

Parker, Patricia A. "Configurations of Shape and Flow." *Diacritics* 3 (Winter 1973): 25–33.

Paul, Sherman. *Emerson's Angle of Vision.* Cambridge: Harvard University Press, 1965.

Perry, Bliss, ed. *The Heart of Emerson's Essays.* Boston: Houghton Mifflin, 1933.

Pfeiffer, John. *The Cell.* New York: Time-Life Books, 1972.

Raymo, Chet. *The Soul of the Night.* Englewood Cliffs, N.J.: Prentice-Hall, 1985.

Ross, Nancy. *The World of Zen.* New York: Random House, 1960.

Roszak, Theodore. *Where the Wasteland Ends.* Garden City, N.Y.: Doubleday, 1972.

Sagan, Carl. *The Cosmic Connection.* New York: Doubleday, 1973.

Seiderman, Arthur, and Steven Schneider. *The Athletic Eye.* New York: Hearst Books, 1983.

Shapley, Harlow. *Beyond the Observatory.* New York: Charles Scribner's Sons, 1967.

Spiegelman, Willard. *The Didactic Muse*. Princeton: Princeton University Press, 1989.

Stahl, Jim. "Interview with A. R. Ammons." *Pembroke Magazine* 18 (1986): 77–85.

Stephenson, Shelby. "Special Issue: The Work of A. R. Ammons." *Pembroke Magazine* 18 (1986).

Stitt, Peter. Review of *The Snow Poems*, by A. R. Ammons. *Georgia Review* 32 (Winter 1978): 940.

Thomas, Lewis. *The Lives of a Cell*: Notes of a Biology Watcher. New York: Viking Press, 1974.

Thoreau, Henry David. *Excursions*. New York: Corinth Books, 1962.

———. *Walden*. New York: New American Library, 1960.

———. *A Week on the Concord and Merrimack Rivers*. New York: Scribner's, 1921.

Turrey, Bradford, and Francis Allen, eds. *The Journal of Henry David Thoreau*. Salt Lake City: Peregrine Smith Books, 1984.

Vendler, Helen. "Reason, Shape, and Wisdom." Review of *A Coast of Trees*, by A. R. Ammons. *The New Republic*, 25 April 1981, 28–32.

———. "Spheres and Ragged Edges." *Poetry* 36 (Winter 1983): 30.

———. "Veracity Unshaken." *The New Yorker*, 15 February 1988, 100.

Waggoner, Hyatt H. *American Visionary Poetry*. Baton Rouge and London: Louisiana State University Press, 1982.

———. *The Heel of Elohim: Science and Values in Modern American Poetry*. Norman: University of Oklahoma Press, 1950.

———. "The Poetry of A. R. Ammons: Some Notes and Reflections." *Salmagundi* 22/23 (Spring–Summer 1973): 285–94.

———. "Science and the Poetry of Robinson Jeffers." *American Literature* 10 (November 1938): 257–88.

Waley, Arthur. *The Way and Its Power*. London: George Allen and Unwin Ltd., 1934.

Weisz, Paul B., and Melvin S. Fuller. *The Science of Botany*. New York: McGraw-Hill, 1962.

Werness, Hope. "Whitman and Van Gogh: Starry Nights and Other Similarities." *Walt Whitman Quarterly Review* 2:4 (Spring 1985): 35–41.

Whitehead, Alfred North. *Science and the Modern World*. New York: The Free Press, 1967.

Whitman, Walt. *An American Primer*. Edited by Horace Traubel. Boston: Small, Maynard, and Co., 1904.

———. *The Complete Writings of Walt Whitman*. Edited by literary executors. Camden Edition. 10 vols. New York and London: G. P. Putnam's Sons, 1902.

———. "Democratic Vistas." *The Portable Walt Whitman*. Edited by Mark Van Doren. New York: Penguin, 1945.

———. *Leaves of Grass*. Edited by Harold W. Blodgett and Sculley Bradley. New York: New York University Press, 1965.

———. *Leaves of Grass*. Norton Critical Edition. Edited by Sculley Bradley and Harold Blodgett. New York: W. W. Norton & Co., 1973.

————. "Leaves of Grass and Two Rivulets." *Leaves of Grass.* Edited by Harold W. Blodgett and Sculley Bradley. New York: New York University Press, 1965.

————. "*Preface 1855—Leaves of Grass, First Edition.*" *Walt Whitman: Leaves of Grass.* Edited by Harold W. Blodgett and Sculley Bradley. New York: New York University Press, 1965.

————. *Walt Whitman's Leaves of Grass.* Edited by Malcolm Cowley. New York: Viking, 1959.

Williams, William Carlos. *The Selected Poems.* New York: New Directions, 1969.

Wolfe, Cary. "Symbol Plural: The Later Long Poems of A. R. Ammons." *Contemporary Literature* 30:1 (Spring 1989): 78–94.

Wordsworth, William. "*Preface to Lyrical Ballads.*" *The Prose Works of William Wordsworth.* Edited by W. J. B. Owen and Jane Worthington Smyser. Oxford: Clarendon Press, 1974.

Zweig, Paul. "The Raw and the Cooked." *Partisan Review* 4 (1974): 608–10.

Index